FIRE BELL
IN THE NIGHT

FIRE BELL
IN THE NIGHT

CONSTANCE ROBERTSON

THE BLAKISTON COMPANY
Philadelphia

Copyright, 1944, by
CONSTANCE ROBERTSON

PRINTED IN THE UNITED STATES OF AMERICA

To
Dickie, Rube *and* Edith
with thanks

ACKNOWLEDGMENT

ONLY OCCASIONALLY, I think, should a novel be burdened with the paraphernalia of a bibliography. It must be obvious that a great deal of reading and research go into the making of any book laid in another period. The titles of these books are of interest to scholars but not to the general reader unless the story deals with matter so controversial that proof of its validity must be instantly available. This story, I believe, requires no such proof, and I am thankfully laying aside the long list of volumes read before it could be written. If any reader is curious to see this list, I will supply it gladly.

Thanks for kind and generous help rendered cannot be so lightly forgotten. I am deeply indebted, as usual, to the resourcefulness and wide learning of Miss Edna L. Jacobsen, Head of the Research Division of the New York State Library. The many books she has lent me have been the very foundation of my necessary reading. To the Onondaga Historical Association and its able secretary, Major Harry C. Durston, must go my equal thanks for making available to me a wealth of local material without which I should have been lost. Through the courtesy of Major Durston, I was allowed to meet Mr. Richard N. Wright, 2nd, whose knowledge of Abolition activity in Syracuse was extremely useful. I also wish to thank particularly Dr. W. Freeman Galpin, of the Maxwell Graduate School of Syracuse University, who, as custodian of the Gerrit Smith Papers and as an authority upon all Syracuse local history, has been an invaluable adviser and critic. I owe thanks to Mr. Arthur Pound, State Historian, for lending me papers from the State Archives; to Dr. Harold O. Whitnall of Colgate University, for advice on the Underground Railroad; to Dr. Charles Worthen Spencer, Librarian Emeritus of Colgate University, for the help he always gives so generously. I am grateful to the Houghton Library of Harvard University and to the Syracuse Public Library for assistance during the time of my reading in their institutions. And lastly, I have no adequate way to thank my friends, Helen Dick Davis, Reuben Grady Davis and Edith Ellsworth Kinsley, for their interest, criticism and encouragement.

CONSTANCE ROBERTSON

(From a letter to John Holmes, on the Slavery Question)

MONTICELLO
April 22, 1820.

. . . But this momentous question, like a fire bell in the night, awakened and filled me with terror. I considered it at once as the knell of the Union. It is hushed, indeed, for the moment. But this is a reprieve only, not a final sentence. . . . The cession of that kind of property, for so it is misnamed, is a bagatelle which would not cost me a second thought, if, in that way, a general emancipation and expatriation could be effected, and gradually with due sacrifices, I think it might be. But, as it is, we have a wolf by the ears, and we can neither hold him, nor safely let him go. Justice is in one scale and self-preservation in the other. . . . I regret that I am now to die in the belief that the useless sacrifice of themselves by the generation of 1776 to acquire self-government and happiness to their country is to be thrown away by the unwise and unworthy passions of their sons, and that my only consolation is to be, that I live not to weep over it.

THOMAS JEFFERSON

CHAPTER ONE

On that night—and on every night, rain or shine, hot or cold, winter or summer or spring or autumn—a strange thing was happening. Along the shores of Lake Erie men were pushing out in boats, carrying dark passengers; beside the sand beaches of Lake Ontario men hid in clumps of bushes, awaiting the sound of oars and a soft whistle from across the water; on the Suspension Bridge—The Bridge, it was called, simply, as far south as the rice fields of Georgia and South Carolina—two men, perhaps, or a woman with three children, or an old woman alone, were hurrying to reach the northern shore of the river.

At the windows of darkened, remote farmhouses, hands were raised to knock softly. The windows would slide up, open a crack.

"Who's there?"

"A friend with friends."

Then, after a moment, footsteps would sound, the shed door would open, and a half dozen men would enter, treading softly.

In a hundred kitchens, lamps were lit at midnight, women would pull the shades and hurry from buttery to stove, warming up food. They would load the table and draw up the chairs, and a company of dark-skinned men would sit down—hesitating at first to sit with white folks—until hunger made them snatch at the good food, gulp down the fresh milk, tear at the leg of a chicken.

Along dark roads, late at night, horses were trotting, pulling covered wagons, three-seated Liberator wagons crowded with passengers, closed carriages, peddlers' carts, open lumber wagons filled with loads of straw that in turn covered other loads. Men with their hats pulled down over their eyes, and their coat collars turned up to hide their faces, drove rigs along at a fast clip. They must get to wherever they were going before daylight.

Next morning, in a barn thirty miles away, a quiet man in a wide-brimmed Quaker hat would harness his sleek team to the family carryall and drive it up to the front door. Out would come a party of ladies, all neatly dressed in gray with Quaker bonnets and veils over their faces. Demurely they would mount the horse block and step into the carriage. The driver would cluck to his team, the carriage would roll out of the drive and away through the streets of the village, as innocently as you please. The driver would nod and raise his whip to salute a friend, the ladies would bow, the strangers hanging around the post office or the village store would glance at them and then away.

Or, south of the Line, men might be cutting their way through swamps. They would come to a stream and creep along its banks until they found a skiff tied to a stump. Then they would turn, perhaps, and an owl would be heard to cry in the night, hooting softly under the leaves of the forest, until one by one, three men, two women, gaunt, frightened, stopping to listen when a twig snapped, when a dog howled, would glide through the shadows until they came to the boat. They would get into the boat and oars would move, carefully, silently, until the boat reached the northern bank of the river.

On railroad trains there were passengers huddled in seats they had not paid for. When they raised dark hands to pull their collars closer around their ears, the hands trembled. Conductors on the cars where they sat never looked at them; never asked for their tickets. If a noisy group of men—their hats cocked rakishly, perhaps; with handsome black mustaches, and wearing holsters at their belts—came into the cars, then the conductor would mutter a word to the passengers in the rear seat. "Slave catchers. Get to the last car." Or, perhaps, he would hurry them off at the next station.

On boats, paddling up the coast from Baltimore, from Philadelphia, from Charleston, black men were hiding, crouched in empty barrels, or down behind a pile of boxes, trying not to cough in the acrid stink of smoke, trying not to breathe when the inspectors came around, trying to look like a bale of cotton, down amongst the cargo.

Or perhaps, on this very night, a black man was lying in a box, pressing his hands and feet against the walls of the box to keep from sliding, from being battered as the box was moved; pressing his mouth against the tiny, bored holes in the side of the box to get air—more air—for his bursting lungs. If he could hold out, if he could bear the darkness and the bruising of his body and the choking in his lungs, he would be carried, tossed by porters into a wagon, jolted over the cobblestones in the street, carried along to a house. Then he would feel the box tilting again—now he was fairly standing on his head—as the box jolted up steps and he would hear a door close. At the last he would hear pounding; the wood beside his cheek would shiver, nails would screech as they came out, and finally the cover of the box would be opened. For a moment he would only want to breathe. Nothing else mattered; not the voices of his friends, not food, not water, not even the freedom he had been thinking about so hard in the darkness of the box. Only air. Then hands would touch him, faces bend over him, he would feel himself being lifted, carried—tenderly, this time—and the journey would be over.

In New York, in Vermont, in Ohio and Michigan and Illinois and Indiana, strange men came into the towns and villages. Tall, lean men wearing fine linen and nankeen pantaloons, and speaking in soft slurring accents; short heavy men, in rough clothes, with mud spattered on their riding boots; marshals with badges on their coats and new derringers in their belts. They would come in a posse, half a dozen of them, riding hard into the village just at dusk, reining short before the village lockup, leaping from their horses and running up the steps to see the head man.

Sometimes they did not stop in the village, but rode, hell for leather, out the sand road, galloping up Johnny-Cake Hill in a cloud of white dust, to stop at a farmhouse where their boots clattered across the kitchen porch. They would track mud and dirt over the scrubbed floors inside, pulling beds apart, pawing through closets, ransacking the attic, tumbling the woodpile in the cellar, mad as hornets if they did not find a black girl with a baby.

"She came this way," they would say, pounding on the kitchen table. "We have reliable information that she came to this farm tonight. If you're concealing her, it'll be the worse for you."

But the farmer and his wife knew nothing about any slave girl and her baby.

"Keep your damned cattle at home if you want them," the farmer would say, grinning.

And his wife would reprove him. "Now, Asahel," while the angry men stamped out of her disordered kitchen.

On the platform a tall figure in rusty black flung up his arms, and shadows cast by the naked gas jets in the hall flung up giant's arms behind him; a leaping black effigy that marked his words. The words came rushing and soaring, like a chant of a camp-meeting preacher. The voice was deep, rich, more melodious than a white man's voice ever sounds.

"What is life to me if I am to be a slave in Tennessee? My neighbors! I have lived with you many years, and you know me. My home is here, and my children were born here. And do you think I can be taken from you and my wife and children, and be a slave in Tennessee? Have the President and his Secretary sent this enactment up here to you to enforce on me in Syracuse? And will you obey him?"

Under cover of wild applause from the converted majority, a ground bass of talk ran from seat to seat, where men sat on wooden benches to watch the goings-on of the protest meeting. From the dark rear of the hall a few voices booed, a few feet stamped disapproval, but there was no quelling the outburst of enthusiasm. Thirteen men rose and swore to resist the local enactment of the Fugitive Slave Law to the limit of their powers.

The Reverend Mr. Raymond said, closing in a fine burst of Baptist oratory, "Shall a live man ever be taken out of our city by force of this law?" The crowd bellowed "No!" Mr. Raymond swayed in the storm. "I shall take the hunted man into my own house, and he shall not be torn away and I be left alive!"

A man pushed down the aisle between shouting men, and climbed the steps to the speakers' platform. He bowed briefly to the Chair, then with one hand raised for silence he turned to face the audience in Market Hall. "Fellow citizens!" His voice rose to top the sudden buzz of talk below him. "Fellow citizens of Syracuse!"

"It's young Palfrey," somebody said in a wondering tone, and the buzz carried his name through the crowded benches of the protest meeting. "Young Palfrey . . . Lawyer Palfrey . . . He's in with Burnet and Noxon and that crowd. What's he doing here?"

The kind of man who knew everything had an answer for that. "He's a worker for the party—Democrat, of course. Probably Major Burnet sent him up there to keep folks from joining the Abolitionists."

"He'll have his heart and hands full," someone leaned back to whisper. The young man on the stage was talking now. From the flaring gas jets raw yellow light painted his rather severe features, fell upon his hair in bands of light, made his eyes a blue glitter. His voice had none of the mellow persuasion of the earlier speaker's; it was clear, sharp, hard. His hands motioned briefly as he spoke.

"Let the Abolitionists—the Nigger Lovers—speak for themselves. Let them rave if they want to. Let them form their committees and swear to defy the law of their country. But the citizens of this city are too wise to join them in treason. Syracuse is not a city of hotheads, of rebels—" He made a wide gesture, and a murmur of assent, of denial, of uneasiness, rippled through the

[5]

room. "We are not all fools in this city. We know that slavery may be an evil—"

Someone shouted, "Hallelujah, Hallelujah!"

The young man's lips curled. "Is this a town meeting or a camp meeting?" he asked scornfully, and beat down the rising answer of the crowd with his voice. "Whether slavery is an evil or not is no business of ours. It was consented to by the founders of this republic. George Washington was a slaveowner. Jefferson said the slavery question was like a fire bell in the night. He said emancipation could come gradually, but if we went at it head first—the way some people want to do now," he said, glaring at them—"it would be the knell of the Union."

He was warming to his subject now, speaking quickly and with force. In his audience, the hotheads were burning under his strokes, longing to reply. The conservatives among them, the solid citizens, the merchants and shopkeepers, were beginning to lose the flush of fervor. Heads were seen to nod, beards wagged agreement.

Young Palfrey said, "Right here in New York State there are thousands of dollars owed by southern buyers to our own merchants. We buy their cotton and sell them our salt. Cotton's the foundation of our commercial life as well as theirs. Do you think we're likely to have good times up north—right here in Syracuse—if we band together to help the laborers of the South run away from their owners?" He leaned forward as he spoke, staring into the rows of faces before him. His words fell like hammers. "If you people of Syracuse let a lot of crazy fanatics run away with you, you'll have another panic now in 1850—as bad as the one in '37. But that won't be all. I'll tell you what you'll have," he said, biting the words off savagely. "You'll have civil war. You'll ruin the country. You'll ruin yourselves."

The answer to this speech was a shout that might have meant anything: agreement, defiance, anger, a threat or a promise. John Palfrey stood listening to its growing tumult for a moment, his face set like steel. Then, without bowing or making any response to the demonstration, he turned and walked rapidly from the stage. Mayor Hovey pounded the table unheeded while the crowd continued to roar.

Arriving at the back of the long room, Palfrey joined a group of older men, spoke a few words to them, and the whole party moved out of the hall and down the stairs. As they spoke, as they moved away, eyes followed them, hostile, friendly, merely curious.

An old man, tall, immensely broad, with a shock of curly hair, red and white like a roan horse, touched the arm of the young woman standing beside him.

"May as well go, Mahala," he said softly. "This is no place for us. We'd better skedaddle."

The girl said, "Yes," without turning her eyes from the spectacle on the platform. As she stood in the shadow, nothing could be seen of her except the shawled shape of her tall figure, nearly as tall as the man beside her, and as straight as a wand. After a moment she turned reluctantly and moved toward the door, walking beside her companion. A man who had been standing near by craned to stare after her.

"Cripus," he said to his friend. "That's a tall gal. Taller'n I be."

His friend followed his glance, saw the couple move under a light. He emitted a low whistle. "She's a good looker just the same," he said with relish. "Red hair. Fancy clothes, too. Now me, I always like a red-haired woman."

His friend hushed him sternly. After all, a meeting was going on.

After the protest meeting, every barroom and saloon in the city was crowded to the doors with excited men. At the Old Lib, the crowd was so great that certain of the regular customers were obliged to sit on the veranda and hear what they could through the windows.

"It's too bad," old Mr. Bobbin said, lowering his peg leg from the porch railing and stumping over to peek in through the window to the bar. "It's too bad to get folks all stirred up over this slavery business." He leaned forward to press his large red nose against the glass. His voice came back somewhat muffled. "They're getting real riled up, too. I shouldn't wonder if they'd commence fighting pretty soon. Jake Tyler and his boys are crowded right up to the bar. It don't take much to start a ruckus with them Salt Pointers."

Behind him on the narrow veranda, his crony Wilgus shook his head. "I dunno what anybody wants to fight *for*," he complained fretfully. "Jakie Tyler, of course. It don't take anything much to make *him* fight, because he likes to. But those other folks. A lot of 'em are respectable men. Folks that owns stores and mills. They got no call to take on so. Abolitionists, too, I shouldn't wonder. I thought those folks were all religious."

Mr. Bobbin said, "Jakie's yelling at 'em." Then he took time to answer his friend's objection. "These folks aren't the regular Abolitionists. Not the religious kind, anyways. These men just come from the big meeting they had in Market Hall. A lot of 'em ain't any more antislavery than you be. But this new law's got 'em all excited. And they don't like the way Jakie's talking. He's calling 'em Nigger Lovers," Mr. Bobbin reported after a moment's listening.

Wilgus shifted his ancient bones on the wooden chair. "Well, I don't see what call Jakie's got to push in. What's he care what people think about a law, one way or the other?"

"He's Burnet's man," Bobbin said loftily. "Major has the Salt Pointers right under his thumb. He tells 'em how to vote and what to do. I guess it's real useful sometimes." He broke off to chuckle. "Tonight, maybe he's told 'em to scare these new Abolitionists a mite."

"Do they act scared?" Wilgus wanted to know, stirring in anticipation. If there was really going to be a fight, he was willing to get up to see it.

Old Bobbin said, "No, I guess not," in a disappointed tone.

Then he began to shout at his friend. "Yes, they be, too. They're going to fight. Jakie's pushed young Sleight into the bar, and Sleight's swinging at him. It's starting—it's starting," he cried joyfully. "If we want to see it, we'd better get inside." He began to hobble as fast as he could go along the porch toward the door of the tavern. Groaning, lifting himself painfully from his chair, old Wilgus followed. A good fight wasn't anything to be missed. Recklessly they crowded through the door and into the barroom.

The bar parlor was filled with men. Men sitting around the scattered tables, leaning forward over their glasses to talk; men clustered in groups, standing to talk; men walking through the room together, talking. Men of all shapes and sizes, differing in every way except the single fact that they were all talking—at the tops of their lungs, it seemed—and all talking about the same thing. And from the sound of their raised voices, it seemed that they were all angry men. The voices were harsh, rasping, belligerent. They were talking about the meeting and the new law. Fists pounded on worn table tops, arms flashed upward in violent gestures. From the open doorway of the room beyond, more men were gathered around the playing tables. Cards and colored chips made a pretty show, but the players were too busy talking, even there, to pay attention to their play. Over the lights a reek of tobacco smoke hung like a pale-blue canopy. Lamps, in their hanging brackets, swung slightly, as though the violence in the room was making the very earth quake.

It took something to make that roomful of hatred call even a moment' truce. When the door opened and Mahala North stood under the flickering lights, a lull hushed the fury of voices, heads turned impatiently to see what was going on, surprise was painted on men's faces. From the back of the room a voice said admiringly, "Holy Tod. That's old North's girl," and a smothered laugh ran from chair to chair. Then the storm broke out again. Nothing, no woman on earth, could keep these men from shouting at each other tonight.

From her doorway, Mahala watched the faces turn toward her, then away, intent once more upon the subject that held them. Slowly she smiled, her eyes widening as the laughter took her, her lips curling at the corners, one eyebrow quirking upward in a queer little trick she had when she smiled. A woman in a yellow dress might be something, she was thinking; something to look at, something to think about—some other evening. But not tonight. Women think they are much of a muchness, but when men get to studying about something important, women don't matter. She moved forward into the room, pushing past the knots of talkers who barely turned their heads to look at her as she went. There was an old horsehair sofa behind a table in the corner, and from that place she would be able to watch, at least; to see what manner of men these were, who were so loud and angry; to hear what they said and learn which side they were taking. She squeezed past the table and settled herself in her corner.

Voices rose around her like a flood of water beating against rocks on the shore, separate words flew like spume through the noisy air, sentences, broken phrases, washed against her like small waves pursuing each other endlessly inland, and the wind that drove this storm of talk was the passion, the feeling, the furious beliefs and certainties, that were blowing across the whole country at that moment.

Here is an eddy, a little whirlwind, Mahala thought, watching the curtains blow in a wind of their own. Here the feeling is whirling around and around, blowing dust in everyone's eyes, blowing off our hats, blowing us down the streets. But later, she thought, watching a man's great lump of hairy fist bang on the table next to her, later, if the wind rises higher, it may pick up the houses and turn them upside down. It may pick up all these men as though they were twigs from the trees, or as though they were scarecrows stuffed with straw, and carry them away with it. Such a wind can do anything, she thought, watching the fist pound, seeing the furiously red face of the man who pounded. It can do anything at all.

"No one's talking about a war," the red-faced man was shouting. "No one thinks there's going to be a war. No one wants a war. But if the South's bound to keep slaves, and the North won't stand for it, we might as well split the Union right now, and let those that think alike run their own affairs."

A man behind him and out of Mahala's sight shouted back, "That's rank treason! You Garrisonites are as bad as Calhoun and the Nullifiers. You're going to break the country up just as bad as *he* wants to. And you can't none of you do it. This country's meant to stand together, and no bunch of hotheads—north or south—is going to break it up."

"That's right, Robelin—that's right—"

"Treason, God damn it—"

". . . break up everything over a bunch of niggers . . ."

A voice drawled contemptuously, "Why should we get all worked up about a lot of darkies a thousand miles away from us—"

Another voice cut in with violence, "That's just the point. Nobody but crazy Abolitionists are going to make a fuss about just niggers—but it's different from that now. It's this law. It's what we're asked to do. To keep their fences for 'em! To chase their livestock for 'em! What I say is, we're free men up here, if they ain't there. Who's to tell us we've got to catch the Southerners' slaves for 'em?"

There was such a roar at this, whether of agreement or of objection Mahala could not be certain, that the lamps swung in their cradles, and the knot of men around their table increased, pushing and crowding to hear what was said, and to make speeches of their own. From the barroom beyond, a commotion of some sort had begun; someone was shouting shrilly over the general din, and wood broke with a vicious snap. Mahala gathered her yellow skirts in her hands and prepared to rise. It won't amount to anything, she told herself. Father's big enough to handle them. But perhaps I'd better go.

Before she could rise, a man pushed through the crowd. He moved forward until he rested both palms on the table and leaned across it to speak directly to the red-faced man. His voice cut through the uproar like a honed knife. "It's men like you that are driving this country crazy," he said, and in the smoky light Mahala could see his eyes glitter like blue glass, hard and pure, as he glared at his opponent. His face, with its sharp, bony outline, was drawn with anger so that the skin seemed to be stretched tight over his high cheekbones; his lips curled back slightly from his white teeth as he spoke, and gave him the look of a creature that is about to attack. "You're the traitors! You're the ones that are tearing us all apart. If you have your way, you'll ruin the greatest country on earth. You'd rather stir up hatred than eat! Psalm-singers and troublemakers! Hypocrites, that's what you are!"

He lifted his hands from the table and straightened under the light, and as he moved, Mahala saw with surprise that this was the same young man who had addressed the meeting and caused such a commotion. As his face lost the drawn fury it had worn while he spoke, she was able to recognize the eyes, the wide brow, the look of fierce pride on the mouth. A curious sensation shook her. Here is the true enemy, she thought, watching him while the other man shouted his answer. Here is the real man for us to fight. The blusterers and zealots can be dealt with. This man means what he says. He thinks he is defending America. He believes that he is in the right. And he would die for it, just as I would die for what I believe. He will give us the real trouble.

As though to bear out her thought, at that moment the fight began. A chair sailed through the air, struck a man, fell to the ground. The man who was hit fell also, dropping down amongst the moving feet on the floor. He yelled. Someone else yelled. The disturbance in the barroom suddenly resolved itself into distinct blows, shouts. From the mere motion and excitement of heated talk, the drama became, in the twinkling of an eye, the scene of a fight. Knots of men began to struggle with each other indiscriminately, striking each other, wrestling, tussling. Men shouted and yelled; men groaned when they were hit. From the floor came an eerie screaming from the man who had fallen and was being ruthlessly trampled.

Because she was so tall, Mahala could see, over the heads of wildly struggling men, a hand raised, holding a bottle. Then it descended and a dreadful howl arose. Wood pounded upon wood and upon something softer. There was a great crash from the barroom; the bar had been ripped loose, or someone had demolished the cupboard of liquor bottles. A lamp fell or was put out, and the rest of the battle took place in a twilight where men groaned and struck and fell.

In her corner, Mahala barricaded herself behind her table and watched as well as she could. It was impossible to get away now. She could only hope to remain unnoticed and untouched. I wanted them to fight, she thought with a gleam of laughter. Now I've got my wish. It would serve me right to be hit, for saying such a foolish thing. Fighting, she thought, shrinking back as a man stumbled heavily against her protecting table, fighting is not the way. It accomplishes nothing. There are better ways of winning than this.

Even through this murk and confusion, she could make out something. From the barroom beyond, her father's voice was roaring like the Bull of Bashan. He would be fighting like seven men, and there would be broken heads to prove it. And in the room beside her, she could see the shape of the violent young man who had uttered the challenge, lawyer Palfrey, in the hottest part of the battle. He can fight as well as talk, Mahala thought, watching him, like a terrible shadow, move before her; wishing for the light so that she could see his face again, with its mask of bleak fury. He had seemed proud and cold when he spoke in the meeting, but in a fight he was dangerous. She saw his arm shoot out like a piston, and heard the sharp smack as it hit flesh. The man in front of him went down, and Palfrey's dark shape turned away to meet a new assailant.

He was not far away from Mahala's corner, but his back was toward her now, and she could not see what he was doing, except that he was a part of the melee. Then, as she watched, another shape, short and squat, came between her and Palfrey. Before she could do more than cry out from her corner, a thick arm rose, and a club in its hand fell upon the head of someone beyond him. Mahala could not see what happened next. The wide body of the man who had struck blotted out her vision of the fight. The fat man was very close now, and a heavy weight had fallen suddenly against the barrier behind which she stood. What has happened to Palfrey? she wondered, straining to see, through the moving darkness, that quick, lean figure leading the fight. Where is he? Has he gone down?

The fallen man rested for a moment against the table, unable to move farther. Now his antagonist came after him. Mahala heard a voice shouting. "I'm a traitor, am I? I'm crazy, am I? I'll show you whether I'm crazy!" His club rose and descended. There was a sickening thud of wood on flesh, a sharp snort of pain from the man hit, as the struggle began not more than an arm's length away from her. Unconsciously she leaned forward, and saw them moving in the dusk of the corner. The man who had fallen was still down, caught and pinned beneath the heavier body of his attacker. He did not speak or make any outcry. His assailant was making enough noise for two men, grunting and puffing and shouting. He seemed to say the same thing, over and over, "Traitor, am I? I'll traitor you. . . . I'll show you who's a traitor!"

Suddenly these almost incoherent grunts and mutterings began to make sense to Mahala, listening horrified in her corner. Traitor—who had been called a traitor? The fat, red-faced man, pounding his fist on the table. And who had called the name? It could only be Palfrey that was meant. He had been struck down from behind and was now fairly being killed before her eyes. Enemy he might be, but not that kind of enemy. This great hairy brute was certainly about to kill him; to batter his brains out at her feet. Mahala leaned forward over the upturned edge of her barrier and looked about wildly for some way to help. The fat man was astride his victim, who seemed to have given up. He was not fighting at all now. Perhaps he was unconscious or dead.

As the club flew upward for another blow, Mahala stretched out her arm and grasped it, snatched it from the fat man's upraised hand. He had never known there was anyone in that dark corner, she supposed. At any rate, he gasped with surprise and turned his head on its thick neck, peering up to see who had interfered. Mahala did not hesitate. As he struggled to his feet, she brought the club down, hard and true, upon his skull. He dropped without a sound.

With a great deal of trouble, because the room was still a dazing confusion of sound and movement, she managed slowly and painfully to creep around her barricade, push her own victim away from the motionless body of John Palfrey, and drag him, unconscious, to her safe refuge. Then she could only wait until the strife in the room began to abate; until her father's familiar roar began to dominate the shouting in the room; until slowly, one by one, the battered contestants began to fall away from each other, to gather themselves together into separate persons, to walk out of the room alone, or to be carried out if they were too far gone to walk. It was not until the room had nearly emptied, and someone thought to relight the lamp, that anyone saw her and the wreck she had salvaged.

It's too light, John Palfrey thought, opening his eyes and immediately shutting them again. Too light; bright, in his eyes, a lamp was shining, and it hurt. Pain, he continued to think, his thoughts swimming crazily. A pain in my head, in my shoulder, in my side. What happened? he thought dimly, the words coming into his mind all apart and forming themselves into sentences, straggling together and then slipping away again before he could more than glimpse them. What's happened to me? Why am I in pain? How am I hurt? And then, after a moment during which he could hear tiny, confused voices speaking at a great distance, suddenly his mind was as clear as a bell. He knew everything; where he was, what had happened, who had hit him. At once he tried to sit up. Someone said, so that he could hear it plainly, "He's coming round." A cloth dripping cold water touched his face; a hand pressed his shoulders back against the floor. The voice—a woman's, clear, soft, deep,—said, "Don't try to get up yet. You'd better rest awhile."

He'd never heard that voice before, nor any voice like it in his life. Curiosity made him open his eyes again and stare at the speaker. She was young, but not a girl exactly; perhaps about his own age—twenty-six or -seven, at a guess. Her features were modeled with the greatest economy and purity of line, broad white forehead, black brows, eyes of hot green shaded by long, straight lashes. The nose was narrow, high-bridged and aquiline; the mouth rather large, the lips curly, he thought to himself and felt pleased with the description. A curly mouth, curved richly, and the corners turning up a little. Now, in her concentration upon him, her lower lip was caught between fine white teeth. Perhaps because she had been working over him so desperately, her face was flushed, and her hair, as brightly red as copper wire, was disheveled, so that two heavy ropes of it had fallen down between her breasts.

The strange, plangent voice said, soothing him, "Don't try to get up yet. You've been hurt. Maybe you ought to have a doctor."

Palfrey knew at once that he didn't want a doctor. He was all right. The pain in his head was nothing, after all. He couldn't stay there any longer, sprawled on the floor, with this girl tending him. He pushed himself to a sitting position and looked around. A man's voice said in an unfamiliar accent, "He's all right, Haley. He isn't bad off."

Palfrey turned his head, which hurt him, and saw two men

sitting on broken chairs in the littered room. One of them was enormous, it seemed to him; twice as large as ordinary men. He was old, or at least his hair was partly white, above a face like the picture of God waking Adam he'd seen on the Sistine ceiling. The man's flowing beard was like God's, too, and the expression of peaceful benignity he wore. He was speaking now, and his made a third voice in the room. "It's all right, girl," he said in a gentle roar. "He won't die this time." His laugh rumbled deep in a chest like a barrel. "He'll just have something to remember the Nigger Lovers by."

The other man's voice belonged to a fellow lounging in a rickety chair. Palfrey looked at him and wanted immediately to be on his own feet. This fellow was certainly under thirty, dark, reckless-looking, with a lock of black hair ruffled over his brow, and black eyes gazing from a pale, angular face. There was something faintly rakish and devil-may-care about the man's whole getup, Palfrey thought; something that made you want to be on your guard, to be thinking, to be ready to move. This was no more than an instinct, certainly, because the dark man was sitting quiet in his chair, and his voice, when you heard it, was a soft, slow drawl, the way they talked down south. His languid speech, the perfectly relaxed posture of his body in the broken chair, the lazy amusement of his smile when he looked at the girl, gave not the slightest indication that he offered any danger. Still, John Palfrey wanted to get up, and did so. His head spun for a moment as he made the effort, but he was able to say, "I'm all right," and stood there looking at the three people who had rescued him.

On her knees, the red-haired girl began to gather up the basin of water, the linen napkins she had been using to nurse him. She had nothing further to say now; apparently her job was done. Palfrey had to thank her.

"I'm sorry to have been inconvenient. I don't remember exactly what happened at the last, but I have the impression that a man named Luckins came at me with a chair rung." He felt of his head, found a great lump behind one ear, and said, "He did a good job, if it was him. I've got a goose egg to remember him by."

The huge old man began to laugh again, as though he'd enjoyed the whole thing. "I suspicioned there'd be a fight tonight," he said comfortably. "Sit awhile, won't you? You might as well get your legs steady before you go out. There may be some more of Burnet's gang waiting for leftovers. You ain't in any shape yet for another go of it."

Palfrey said sharply, "Burnet? Why do you say his gang started this fight? The man who hit me was one of the Abolition crowd." He looked at the three persons in the room and said slowly, "I don't know how you feel about this business, but there's no reason to blame decent citizens for a row that was started by a lot of crazy fanatics." No one in the room spoke a word. Palfrey said harshly, "Maybe you folks sympathize with them."

It was the younger man who answered him. He rose, found the remains of a chair, brought it forward for John Palfrey to sit on. "You must pardon us, sir," he said politely. "You ought to rest. We're not interested in local fights unless they're forced upon us. This one we couldn't rightly avoid. We'd be interested to learn what it was all about."

Palfrey hesitated, eying them for a moment more, then sat down ungraciously enough. "I didn't mean to accuse you," he forced himself to say. "I gather that you're strangers in Syracuse. In that case, this fight doesn't really concern you. It's a pity it had to spoil your property." He couldn't help talking directly to the dark young man.

"Not mine," the young man said, bowing to his friend. "This tavern is the recent purchase of Mr. North, here. I'm only a visitor, but I thought he needed a little help in the emergency." He smiled, not at Palfrey this time, but at the girl. She had risen to her feet, and Palfrey saw with astonishment how tall she was; not more than a few inches below his own height; she was five feet ten, at least, he put it mentally, and was further surprised to observe that it didn't make her look awkward or ungainly. She stood now, perfectly straight, the china basin in her hands, the linen towels hanging on her arm.

She said, "This is our welcome to York State, Mr. Palfrey. A warm welcome." She looked at him in a way he couldn't read. "Do you always have a housewarming for newcomers in your town?"

You couldn't blame a woman for feeling that way, Palfrey thought. She'd have to be mad, with her house wrecked the first night. And it *was* wrecked, completely. Furniture smashed to smithereens, a window broken, lamps knocked about, liquor spilled over the floor. It would take a week's work and plenty of money to repair the damage. But was this girl the old man's wife?

Moses North answered that question. "My daughter isn't used to running a hotel," he remarked, as though this sort of brawl was the usual thing in a tavern. "She'll get used to it, after a while. She isn't frightened," he explained carefully to Palfrey. "Nothing alarms her. But she's surprised, for the moment. She'll get accustomed to eastern ways pretty soon."

Although the man's face didn't change by the movement of a muscle, Palfrey was aware that the Southerner was amused by this talk. Still, Palfrey couldn't resist defending his city to these strangers. "Syracuse isn't generally like this," he found himself saying with more heat than he had intended. "It's a good town; growing; a good lively place—and well-behaved most of the time. It's just the disturbance these radicals have stirred up." He looked at Mr. North sharply, but the old man showed no sign of special feeling. "Somehow, Syracuse has become a sort of center for these people. We've been having trouble lately. Everyone's excited. This new law seems to have upset everybody."

Palfrey hesitated, then went on. "That meeting this evening was a bad thing. A lot of men who ought to know better joined with the radicals." Anger rose in his mind as he thought about it. "We'll have trouble, if they go on this way. Worse trouble than a fight in a tavern. We'll ruin our business and upset everything

These people are crazy," he said in a bitter voice, and then shut his mouth hard. No reason to let off to these strangers. He had no idea how they might feel about all this Abolition business, but they certainly knew how he felt, now. For a moment Palfrey was sorry he'd said so much, then something obstinate in his make-up made him refuse that feeling. No; they might as well understand where he stood. If they were going to know him, they would know that he was fighting this Abolition movement with every bit of his power. They'd soon see, if his plans worked right.

But why did he assume that they were going to know him, Palfrey stopped his own thoughts to ask. Why should he, a man of good standing in the town, have dealings with a strange hotel-keeper and his family and friends? This was not the kind of hotel he was likely to frequent. He would not have come tonight, except that Noxon's crowd had suggested dropping in after the meeting, to see how the Salt Pointers were taking it. There was no reason for his stepping foot inside the Old Lib again for a year, or a dozen years. An obscure feeling in the back of his mind did not agree with such a conclusion. Oddly enough, this emotion seemed to indicate that he *was* coming to Old Lib again; that he *was* going to know more about Moses North and his strange red-haired daughter and his go-to-hell southern friend.

The Southerner's voice was curiously soft for a man. Not womanish in any way, not high or light, but breathed more softly than ordinary tones, somewhere between loud speech and a whisper, gentle, speaking with a hint of humor—or was it satire?—in its inflection. For no reason at all, Palfrey found himself thinking that such a voice might hold menace without raising its pitch or hurrying its utterance. It was saying now, "You can't reckon on how people are going to jump. There's no sense in it, on the outside. Down where I come from"—he waved his hand—"they couldn't possibly understand why anyone should get mad because they were asked to arrest a few niggers." Between narrowed lids he was watching Palfrey as he spoke. "They'd think any law-abiding man would be willing to return lost property and not fuss about it. They'll be mighty surprised," he said lazily, his eyes still on Palfrey's face, "they'll be taken aback, I expect, when they see what a ruction their little law's raising."

The woman's low voice broke into the conversation. "I thought Southerners understood everything," she said, and Palfrey was aware of the soft malice under her words, and of the fact that she was rallying and baiting the southern man, and that this one remark was really a part of another conversation altogether, an old conversation between those two, and an intimate one. There was an inexplicable resentment in his mind when he thought of this, and he turned to watch North's daughter as she spoke. Her face was pale again, now that she was rested, and the corners of her mouth were curved in a faint smile that held all the provocation in the world.

The Southerner met her look with his calm smiling. "Not everything," he said in his lazy voice. "In fact they often get fooled." But, once more, Palfrey thought that there was more behind his words than their surface meaning. The tall girl shrugged her shoulders and turned away, but not before Palfrey had seen that she was hiding laughter.

He wanted, foolishly enough, to make her look at him, talk to him, for a change. "Do you think any people understand everything, wherever they may live?" he asked her directly.

The girl turned to him and stood so that she was between the two men, her back squarely to the Southerner. "No, I don't think so," she said, and this time her tone was serious, her voice lower than ever. "People understand what they're made to understand, being the kind of people they are. They can't help it, and you can't change 'em. There are the kind of people who want things the way they are; the way they've always been. And even if those things have always been bad, they don't want anything touched to change them. And then there are the other people who can't help changing things. If anything's wrong, they've got to do something about it. And they can't help that, either. And the two kinds of people never do understand each other, and never will."

It was a curious speech, Palfrey thought, seeing excitement rise in her face and shine through as though a lamp had been lighted behind her eyes. She feels things, he thought, watching her. Then he began to wonder: Which kind of person is she? Which kind does she think I am? Which kind are these other men? But did it matter? These are strangers; people I may never see again. But I shall see this girl again, he said to himself strongly. I want to know more about her. However queer it is that I want to see a perfect stranger, and a girl whose father runs a low tavern, I shall see this girl again. I'm curious about her, he said to still the questioning in his mind. I'm only curious, because she is an odd person to find in a canal hotel. That's why I want to know more about her. I'll come back tomorrow to call and thank her, he decided while the talk flowed around him. I want to see her alone.

He got up and said rather stiffly, "I'll call later, if I may, and do myself the honor of thanking you for this assistance." No one said anything, and Palfrey stood staring straight at the tall girl in her draggled yellow gown. She stood quiet under his eyes, her hands raised to hold the heavy ropes of scarlet hair. He could not tell whether or not she wanted him to come back.

Behind her, the southern man said with gentle amusement, "I'm sure that Miss North will be pleased to have you call."

Palfrey turned rapidly and went out of the room and out of the Old Lib Tavern.

CHAPTER TWO

The meetings held in Syracuse that week were probably cut from the same pattern as hundreds of other meetings being held all over the country on those early October evenings. Protest meetings, they were; men and women gathering together to say in public that the new Fugitive Slave Law was wrong, an insult to their American freedom, an infringement upon their unalienable rights, a wickedness and a perpetual hissing, against which they were prepared to fight with all their powers as long as life was in them.

On the other side of the fence, there were an equal number of protest meetings, protesting, this time, against the first protest meetings. And in these secondary affairs, men shouted as loud, orated as passionately, felt as vigorously when they said that the law was no more than just; that it was, undeniably, a law of the land and should be kept by every decent citizen. They said that opposition to this law would shake the foundations of the Republic, would break the bonds of nation, would destroy trade, and bankrupt citizens. They said, at the tops of their lungs, that anyone who opposed the new law was no better than a common traitor, and should be dealt with as such. They, themselves, were prepared so to deal with any miserable Abolitionists who might dare to show their heads.

On the night after the meeting in Market Hall to protest against the iniquities of the Fugitive Slave Law, a second meeting was held, in the grand tradition, to protest against the protestors. This second meeting was in Mr. Malcom's new hall on

Salina Street, south of the Canal, and was well-attended and vociferous, although it was to be noted that the character of the audience was different in kind, if not in numbers, from the meeting the evening before. Major Burnet and Mr. Noxon were on the platform, surrounded by their cohorts, mostly lawyers and political personages. In the audience, a regiment of businessmen, millowners, storekeepers, hotelkeepers, sat together in the front rows, wagging their beards as the speakers made a point, looking solemn, weighty, like the practical men they were.

Behind them, toward the rear of the hall, fresh accents were to be heard, rich Irish brogues, occasionally German in the pure tongue, or broken English with a heavy guttural roll. And with them or behind them or beside them came the real American country twang, loud voices ripping out strange oaths, rough men jollying each other, not quite serious about the business in hand, perhaps, but willing to clap when one of their leaders had made a speech, ready for anything; looking around the crowded hall to see if anyone in this tony part of town wanted to start a row. These, for the most part, were the Salt Pointers, the boilers of salt or the makers of barrels to hold the salt. The boisterous, the untamed, the riotous North Enders, who were ready to break a head with the greatest of pleasure. Or, tonight, ready to cheer for Major Burnet and Mr. Noxon, who told them how to vote and made it worth their while to obey; ready to clap respectfully when young Palfrey, who was the Major's assistant, exhorted them about the new law.

Young Palfrey, they agreed, was a good man for the Major. He was smart, he was smoother than cat hair, he could talk the hind leg off a dog, if he was a'mind to. They'd actually seen him fight at the Old Lib, and he still carried a bruised eye—quite a neat shanty, they said to each other, grinning—to prove it. Now he was standing there on the platform, talking to them like sixty-bang about this Fugitive Slave Law. They did not understand all about the new law, but they did know a few things. They knew, first and most important, that the Major was for it, and that all good Democrats were for it. They knew that it was not directly their business except as it might—young Palfrey made this point carefully—affect their own wages.

"Do you want runaway niggers to come in here and take your jobs away from you? They'll come by the hundreds, and they'll offer to work for half the wages you're making—or quarter. They've never earned a cent in their lives. They can live on nothing, you might say, and so they'll underbid you and get your jobs. If there's nothing else to make a man decide to help the government carry out this law, his own job and his own wages ought to decide him. Are the Woolly Heads going to make salt in Syracuse?"

There was a great roar at this, cheering and stamping and yelling. No! the Salt Pointers shouted. No niggers were going to run them out of their jobs. Let the niggers stay in the South, where they were wanted. Let them keep out of the North—and let them stay away from Syracuse, or they'd be sorry for it. Hooray for the government! Hooray for the Fugitive Slave Law! Hooray for Major Burnet, the poor man's friend! Hooray for John Palfrey!

Someone yelled, "Where'd you get the shiner, Johnny?" and there was a great laugh. On the stage, Major Burnet leaned forward and spoke to Mr. Noxon. Both of them looked over toward John Palfrey, who was gracefully winding up his speech, and it was apparent that they were approving of him. This meeting, unlike the other, was entirely harmonious in feeling. Run the Abolitionists out of town; ride them on a rail; tar and feather them. That was the sense of the meeting. After Palfrey had ended his talk, the Major got up and said a little more.

"We're peaceful men," he said easily, looking back at the Salt Pointers and smiling, "all good citizens, who've got the best good of the community at heart. What we now propose is nothing violent. But the opposition has formed a regular group, with committees"— he smiled now, so that the whole audience knew what he thought of their committees—"with Vigilance Committees formed for the sole purpose of breaking the law and running stray niggers through the city. What we now propose is to form a little organization of our own to deal with such lawbreakers."

The audience liked this very much. The Major went on to elaborate his idea.

"This group will band together all the men of Syracuse who want to defend their country and their city from lawlessness."

The Salt Pointers clapped to the echo.

"This group," continued the Major, "is to preserve order, to assist the marshals of the United States when they're obliged to make an arrest. It will help to track down miscreants, whether they are runaway chattel slaves owned by honest southern planters, or the men who are even worse—the men who are actually stealing these valuable properties, since they are helping them to steal themselves out of the country!"

The notion of all this laudable activity caught on and spread like wildfire. Everyone wanted to belong, everyone wanted to see those Abolitionists stumped. Everyone began to talk about it; about what they were going to do; about what they knew of Abolitionists and their doings; about the reward that was offered to anyone giving evidence that secured a runaway slave. The Major had a hard time bringing the meeting under control again so that he could appoint his officers. He, naturally, was to head the movement. After him, his friend Mr. Noxon held a high office, and young Palfrey—they clapped like good ones when his name was put up—was given an important job. There were the usual committees to be appointed—no one saw anything funny now in appointing committees—and honorary offices to be doled out.

And at this point the question of a name for the new group came up. "A good rousing name," the Major said with enthusiasm. "Something that will show people we mean what we say." 'Law-Keepers' was too tame; 'Vigilantes' had already been appropriated by the Abolitionists. They were almost ready to agree on 'Minute Men,' which Palfrey had suggested, when a new figure rose in the audience and made another suggestion. A slim, dark man, a stranger, got up and said in a soft, southern voice that he thought the name 'Patriots' would be a fitting title for such a patriotic organization.

Everyone turned to look at this person. He met their gaze with perfect calmness, not in the least flustered by his sudden prominence, and even the Major was curious enough to question him a little. "We haven't the pleasure of knowing you, sir. Are you a newcomer to Syracuse? We're glad to have a convert to the right cause."

The new man bowed with a grace that was certainly foreign to Syracuse manners, and said in his sweetly slurring accent that he was a native of Virginia, sir. Merely a transient visitor in this fair city. But he was, he said modestly, impelled to make the suggestion because, knowing what he as a southern man and slaveowner knew of the evil these crazy fanatics were causing to decent people, he couldn't refrain from joining this new opposition group. And the name of Patriots, he said, warming a little as the crowd cheered this introduction, was the only name he felt could express the character of the enterprise.

After this, there was no question what name the group would choose. Patriots they were. The vote went with a bang. Everyone was pleased to bear so noble a name, and, after the meeting had broken up and everyone was milling around, talking to friends, discussing the meeting and slapping each other on the back, the Major made a point of seeking out this new fellow who had complimented them so eloquently, and thanking him for his suggestion.

The stranger made himself pleasant at once. "Yes," he said in his soft way, "I'm a Virginia man, myself. Just visiting Syracuse, but I admire to see the right spirit shown. I'd like to join your group, even though I'm not here all the time."

"Will you be coming to Syracuse occasionally, then?" the Major wanted to know. This fellow might be useful, if he knew something about the southern end of the business.

Mr. Ord—he had politely introduced himself: "Dallas Ord, sir.

At your service"—was happy to say that he would. "*Deo volente,* of course," he added, smiling charmingly. "You never know, of course, what the future may hold. But I have a little business that may bring me to this town from time to time."

Mr. Noxon pricked up his ears at this mention of business. What *was* Mr. Ord's business, if he might inquire?

Mr. Ord bowed again and said that he did a little salt business in Virginia—"Nothing to compare with your noble establishment here in Syracuse," he was careful to add. Merely a small affair, but he also jobbed in salt for various southern firms, and he might be buying some Syracuse salt, if the price was right.

Mr. Noxon commended this course earnestly, and invited Mr. Ord to visit him and the Solar Salt Works any time it was convenient.

Major Burnet, also, was gratified to have a stranger appreciate their manufactory. "We'll hope to see more of you at our Patriots' meeting next week," he said. "It would be inspiring if you were to tell us a little about the trouble you've had with escaped slaves down south. We're pretty far away from all that kind of thing. It would make folks feel more as if they were doing something important. We don't actually see many fugitives here in York State."

"What about this Underground Railroad I've been hearing about?" Ord asked. "Seems to me I've heard that this part of the state was one of their regular routes to Canada."

The Major frowned. "Well—I suppose it is," he admitted. "I haven't had much to do with it myself. But if they think we're going to let 'em run niggers through this town now, they're grandly mistaken." He looked at Ord keenly. "Where did you happen to hear about this town's being a station?"

Ord shrugged his shoulders in one of his foreign gestures. "I can't remember that, unfortunately. Someone spoke of it, I think. Perhaps it was on the cars coming up. It seems to me that they mentioned some other towns near here that were known to run slaves. It's very confused in my mind, I'm sorry to say," he confessed with his easy smile. "If I'd known I was going to have a hand in the fighting, I'd have listened closer. As it was, I merely wondered how it happened that good citizens put up with such a violation, if they knew all about it—knew who ran the slaves and where the headquarters were."

Before the Major could answer, Noxon said, "That's the trouble. We don't know much more than you do. We know who the rankest Abolitionists are, of course. Dr. May and this darky preacher, Loguen, and old Gerrit Smith, in Peterboro. But we've never caught any of them doing anything but talk about it. And if there's a station here, we don't know where it is. That's one of the things our boys will have to find out first of all."

The Major didn't exactly like this display of ignorance. "We won't have any trouble locating 'em," he said carelessly. "All we've got to do is watch the ringleaders. They'll lead us to the hideaway soon enough."

Mr. Ord agreed with him. "Yes. I should think that would be practical. What I admire," he said in his flattering way, "is to see this problem attacked by practical men, who go at it in a practical way. These fanatics may be all right in theory—they talk enough, God knows—but when it comes down to brass tacks, they don't know how to act."

The Major shook hands with him warmly. "It's a pleasure to know you, Mr. Ord," he said. "We'll hope to see you again when we have our next meeting."

Mr. Ord answered with equal cordiality. "If business permits—as it doesn't always," he said, shaking his head, "I'll be delighted to come. But if affairs prevent it next time, you may be sure that I'll be back as soon as possible. And meanwhile, I'll certainly be thinking of the Patriots."

They parted with most fraternal adieus.

As it had been after the first meeting, again talk began to run over the town before the Patriots' meeting was fairly dismissed. Men talked in groups on the corners of the ill-lighted streets; men talked in saloons and oyster shops and in groggeries behind the butchershops on Robbers' Row; men talked to their wives, drawing the curtains of their bedroom windows with a snap, closing all the doors and saying what they thought with great heat. Domestics talked in the dampness of back kitchens, whispering and giggling about it as though it was a joke; livery stable keepers talked to their customers, hitching old Betsy to the muddy Democrat wagon, lingering over the buckles so that they could get a fuller report of the doings. Even little ragamuffin boys on the street corners—the good and proper boys were at home and abed, of course, by this time of night—ran about shouting, "Patriots! I'm a Patriot!"

No one fought, this time, but everyone talked about what they had heard, and the stories grew and blossomed until, by the next morning, the stranger in town was said to be variously Daniel Webster, Mr. Fillmore himself, and a spy of the Abolitionists, trying to find out what the Patriots meant to do against them.

Mrs. Hovey, the Mayor's wife, was perhaps as alarmed about it as anyone, but for a peculiar reason. She wept, as she had been doing at frequent intervals ever since Mr. Hovey's spectacular appearance on the platform of an Abolition meeting. "You've ruined yourself, Mr. Hovey," she said, over and over, applying a handkerchief to her pink nose. "You've spoiled your career. You came right out in the middle of a nest of thieves and robbers, you might as well say, and admitted you were with 'em." Here she invariably burst into stormy sobs, and Mr. Hovey, who had a deep respect for his wife's nerves, made vain efforts to comfort her.

"They were some of the best people in town," he said, after all the other arguments were exhausted. "Some of the most important people. It will do me a lot of good if folks know I've taken a stand with 'em."

But after the Patriots' meeting Mrs. Hovey was really inconsolable. "Now see what you've done," she cried. "Major Burnet never even asked you to his meeting. You weren't asked to preside, or even to be on the platform. And Major Burnet's the most powerful man in town. And he's always liked you, up to now, and helped you. But you'll see," she prophesied darkly. "Your career is finished. You'll be run out of office, and the children and I will go to the Poor House, all because of a lot of niggers."

Hopelessly Mr. Hovey tried to assuage her grief, to explain that he could not have been expected to preside at both meetings; that a man had to take one side or the other. No; Mrs. Hovey was looking straight at the Poor House, and nothing would turn her gaze. Even Mr. Hovey, himself, had moments when he wondered whether he had been smart in taking such a radical step. In politics, a man had to be careful.

In his house on Foot Street—it was still difficult to remember that its new name was James Street, now—the Reverend Dr. May listened quietly to a report of the proceedings.

"They mean business, I guess," Mr. Wilkinson said thoughtfully, turning his handsome head to see how the others were looking at the matter. "Burnet wouldn't have had anything to do with it if it was just a flash in the pan. He ran the meeting, and he and Noxon appointed themselves the heads of the new society. According to what I'm told, they're planning to fight us, tooth and nail."

Dr. May was not alarmed. "We've had opposition before," he said mildly. "It won't be the first time." He smiled at the other men in the room. "Did they indicate what steps they are planning to take?"

Mr. Leavenworth grunted. "Nothing beyond stirring up the people to catch Negroes, and to help enforce this law," he said shortly.

Dr. Clary stirred in his chair. "Ord said they told him they didn't know where the station was, or who was running it—unless it was you," he added, grinning at May's amusement. "They think if they watch you and Loguen, they'll find out what they need to know."

[31]

Wilkinson asked in his sharp way, "What do we know about this man Ord? I'd like to be perfectly certain of him, if we're going to depend on him. He's a stranger to us, and he seems to be getting in with Burnet's crowd more than with ours."

Dr. May's silver head gleamed softly in the light. "We have Levi Coffin's word for him," he said, speaking more strongly than before. "If the Ohio people trust him, we can."

"What does Coffin say about him, exactly?" Leavenworth wanted to know. Coffin was a pillar, a tower of strength in the battle. And he was a shrewd judge of men; would have to be, to run as many fugitives through a hostile country as his record showed. They waited gravely for his opinion.

Dr. May read from a letter. "He doesn't altogether approve of him personally, I gather. He says, 'Ord is, I regret to say, a wicked man, daring and reckless in his actions. Yet he is faithful to the trust reposed in him, and benevolent to the poor.'"

"What does he mean by that?" Dr. Clary inquired. "If Levi Coffin thinks Ord's wicked and still uses him, he must have some good points. We've got to remember that Levi's a strict Quaker, and what he calls wicked mightn't shock us so much as it does him."

May looked at the doctor quizzically. "That's a fine speech to make to a minister of the gospel," he said with amusement. "Well, I'll read the rest of it. I confess that it didn't sound so terrible to me, although I don't believe in using force." He leafed through the pages of the letter. "Here it is: 'He seems to have no fear for his personal safety and is always ready to risk his life and liberty to rescue slaves—' That can't be the part. 'Ord always goes heavily armed and does not scruple to use his weapons whenever the occasion requires. He resorts to many stratagems, and is always ready to take money for his services, but if the fugitive has no money, he helps him all the same. He is equally ready to spend his own money, and would part with his last dollar to effect his object.'"

"That doesn't sound very bad," Clary said indulgently. "Of

course, I'm not a religious man, but I can't seem to hate him for being a little rough and tricky, if it's in a good cause."

Wilkinson looked dour. "We've got to be sure we aren't dealing with an adventurer," he said warningly. "We've all got too much at stake. Carrying a gun isn't necessarily a recommendation."

"He's heart and soul with the cause. That's why I trust him." Dr. May looked from man to man, fairly pleading with them now. "Any man who will risk his life for what he believes must have a true spirit. Even Levi Coffin admits that. This man Ord has brought more than a thousand slaves into freedom. He's a southern man, born a slaveowner. And yet he has turned his back upon his heritage and given his life to our work." He referred to the letter once more. "'Although I cannot sympathize or encourage Ord's mode of operation, yet I often take in the fugitives he aids to escape.'" May looked up. "That's a lot, coming from a man like Coffin. And he says at the last, 'With all his faults and misguided impulses and wicked ways, he is a brave man; he has never betrayed a trust imposed in him, and he is a true friend to the oppressed and suffering slave.'" The old man laid the letter down carefully, took off his spectacles and wiped his eyes with a linen handkerchief. "That's enough for me, too," he said gently.

Wilkinson shifted in his chair. "I guess you're right," he admitted. "I don't want to stand against Ord, if he's anxious to help us. We need help now, and maybe he's the man. But I like to make sure of the people I work with. We're adopting a new policy, taking strangers into positions of trust. The people at the hotel, now—"

Dr. Clary broke in at once. "We've got unimpeachable references for them," he said with some impatience. "We know their history in Ohio. We know what they've been through. They were arrested out there and warned to leave the state. We know what they're risking to work for us. And now, just when Burnet's beginning to take a hand against us, we've *got* to adopt a new policy, as you say. These Patriots may not know the stationmaster here, but they're going to be peeling their eyes good and sharp.

Our only chance is to set up a system they wouldn't think about. And these new people can do it."

Mr. Leavenworth cast the deciding ballot. "I agree with Clary. I think we're safe to go ahead with this new scheme. If it don't work, we can try something else. But we've got to get these slaves through Syracuse."

Since it was well after dark, the usual cronies had abandoned their post on the veranda of the Syracuse House, and adjourned next door, according to custom, to what the local wags called Tammany Hall. The little tobacco shop was crowded tonight with an audience that wanted to hear what the oracles had to say about the new organization.

Someone piped up with, "What do you think of this new business, Mr. Kirk?" and everyone crowded in to listen.

Mr. Kirk scooped up a handful of fine-cut from the barrel under the counter and filled his cheek. "It's a toss-up," he said judicially, working his jaws to get the quid into manageable shape. "First one side and then the other getting together and making a hullabaloo about this slavery business. Calling names, and saying how plumb awful the other fellows are, and how righteous they are, themselves. It's going to be worth watching," he said, grinning and spitting with beautiful accuracy at Mr. Palmer's Bennington cuspidor. "It's going to be a regular set-to." His fine Scotch r's burred in the respectful silence.

The pipsqueak who had dared to open the discussion asked another question. "Which side do you think will win, Mr. Kirk?"

This was a delicate matter. Feelings were on a hair trigger today, and some men didn't want to commit themselves. Mr. Kirk was a man of substance, with his brick kilns and his handsome block in the city, and moreover he was known as a stanch Democrat and a conservative. It seemed fairly safe to guess where he stood in a matter like this. Still, men stirred impatiently while he meditated his answer. It wouldn't be a good thing to make Mr. Kirk mad. Scotchmen were known to be peppery.

Mr. Kirk spat majestically and said, "It's a bad business. Stirring up strife never put a penny in anybody's pocket. These Abolition folks haven't got good sense—but who'd expect it of 'em? A lot of tub thumpers and daft preachers, who haven't enough know-how to run a grogshop. But I misdoubt if it'll do any good to oppose 'em. The Major's a smart man, but he may have bitten off more than he can chew this time. And it won't do business any good, while they're wrangling."

A rough voice in the crowd said, "We ought to call in the soldiers to settle this thing. It's a federal law that's being broken, and if local people can't stop it, the government ought to."

Another voice, hot with anger, answered him. "If they call in the militia, they'll find they've got a fight on their hands! Some of us are men enough to stand up to 'em! And to stand up to a federal law, too, if it tries to make decent men go against human nature."

At this point everybody joined in, shouting, pushing each other dangerously, so that Mr. Palmer, the proprietor of the shop, was obliged to take a hand. "You can argue all you like," he roared over the din of voices, "but you'll have to keep the peace if you're going to stay in my shop." He was a large man, and handy with his dukes. The shouting died down gradually, and the interminable argument went on.

The peddler's cart stopped, most weeks, at the back door of Mr. Gerrit Smith's big house in Peterboro. Hiley Purvee got down stiffly from his seat behind the two bony horses and stumped into the house. He was an odd stick, everyone said, but Mr. Smith had taken a liking to him; ordered things from him that he could have afforded to buy from the city. Sometimes, or so the story ran around the village, Mr. Smith would even ask the peddler to come into his study and talk to him awhile. It was like G'at Smith, they said proudly. He was everybody's friend, for all he had so much money and knew the bigwigs in Washington. He wasn't too stuck-up to pass the time of day with a peddler. Because of this condescension on Mr. Smith's part, Hiley was treated with greater indulgence than he might, otherwise, have received. A queer, moody man, everyone said; sometimes getting drunk and roistering all over the county, and other times as dumb as a beetle, without a good word for anyone, climbing into his rattletrap of a wagon and high-tailing it up the road as if Old Scratch was after him.

It wasn't a common thing for him to visit his friend Mr. Smith after dark, but on this evening he acted kind of queer and strung up, and Smith's cook thought it best to humor him. She was surprised when Gerrit Smith asked him into the study so late at night, but the great man was notional, sometimes. The visit didn't last long.

"They had their meeting," Hiley said, as soon as the study door closed. "Burnet's setting 'em on. Noxon and the crowd are with him. There was quite a considerable of excitement about it. I thought you'd want to know."

Gerrit Smith was looking away from Hiley, staring into the black mirrors of the windowpanes. His head, with its bush of graying beard and its mane of long hair, was leonine and majestic. His expression was grim, the mouth above the flowing beard was set in a line.

"I knew they'd do it," he said, and continued to stare at the darkened glass, as though he saw a picture there. Hiley Purvee stood without moving or speaking until the old man broke the silence. When Mr. Smith spoke, it was clear that he had come out of the clouds and was attending to the business at hand. "Don't pick up any passengers tonight, Hiley." It was an order. "I'm going to give these Patriots a little time, and see what they're intending before I make any plans. I doubt if they'll bother us much for a while, but I want to be sure. You'd better come in again next week."

Purvee said, "All right," and turned to walk out of the room.

"Tell the folks in Syracuse to look out," Gerrit Smith said, before the other man reached the door. "Burnet's going to watch everything they do."

Hiley's lanky figure was convulsed with laughter. "That's what Burnet's aiming at," he said, giggling like a schoolgirl. "He's planning to find out where the contraband is by watching Dr. May and Preacher Loguen." It seemed to him extraordinarily funny.

Smith didn't smile back at him. "Don't guess wrong about Burnet," he said. "He isn't a fool."

Hiley Purvee ducked his head without answering, and slipped out of the study.

"Was there another fight?" Mrs. Amidon Palfrey asked before her husband was fairly inside the door. "Did John get into another muss?"

Mr. Palfrey could afford to laugh at his wife's timidity. "You've got to stop worrying about that boy. He's twenty-seven years old, and he knows what he's doing. He can't have his mother fussing over him every time he turns around. He's got important work to do."

Mrs. Palfrey didn't care about that. "Did he *fight?*" she repeated, shaking her husband's arm. "*You* wouldn't care if he got his nose broken and his eyes blacked every night if you thought he was beating those Abolitionist fellows," she said in exasperation. "Now you tell me about it, right away. The next time, I'm going to go along with you and see with my own eyes. I 'most went crazy, waiting for you to get home."

Amidon Palfrey sat down in his particular chair and said comfortably, "Now, mother, be calm. John made a fine speech and there wasn't a blow struck. The Major knows better than to let a meeting get away from him. He kept the whole thing as clean as a hound's tooth, and what's more, there won't be any fighting afterwards. He told me so himself. He don't believe in it. It wasn't his boys that started that row the other night. It was a lot of hotheads who'd got all stirred up at that Abolition meeting. They went to a low tavern and began to brawl."

His wife sniffed. "Well, I don't see yet why John happened to be in a low tavern with a lot of Abolitionists, even if there *had* been a meeting. There must have been some of the Major's friends there, or there wouldn't have been any fight."

There were some things a woman could never understand. "John couldn't help it," Mr. Palfrey said patiently. "He went there for the Major, to see how the lower element of the town was taking it. Politicians have to know these things. And John's going to get somewhere in politics, or I miss my guess."

Mrs. Palfrey moaned slightly. "I wish he'd stay out of politics, if it's going to be so rough. I'd rather he stayed right in the saltworks with you. I wish everything would quiet down, like it's always been. I don't like all these changes. I want things the way they've always been."

The Old Liberty Tavern was not one of the fashionable hostelries of the town. Twenty years ago its site had been in the busiest, most populous section, north of the new Canal but near enough to call the brisk trade of the canallers, and not far from the old stone bridge where Genesee Turnpike crossed Clinton Square and struck west toward Auburn and Rochester. Salina Street split the square, running north to Salina Village and the saltworks, a street lined with coopers' shops and rough-built dwellings, a tough neighborhood, stirring with men and horses and the noisy, lively, raw business of the village.

Salt boilers and wagoners, boat hands from Buffalo or Albany, and farmers from Liverpool or Messina Springs or Cicero, trundled over the bumpy road. Passengers from the coach line stopped at the Empire House on the corner of the Square. Teamsters with creaking loads of empty barrels dropped in at Old Lib for a snort of blackstrap. Drovers with a hundred sheep on their way east, lumbermen floating a raft of white pine on the Canal, peddlers with packs, stopped for a night's rest. Politicians with segars in their mouths, butchers from near-by Robbers' Row with their cutting knives stuck into the belts of their bloody aprons, hobnobbed over the bar. Pimps and drabs from the houses that lined the Canal, bruisers and bullies from the saltworks, gentlemen in nankeen breeches, and ladies with enormous bonnets and sleeves two feet across, people of all sorts and conditions stopped at the Old Lib, as everyone called it from one end of York State to the other. They dropped in, they bought a drink, they ate a meal and, according to their natures, either praised the pastry or complained of flies in the sugar bowl. Some of them hired rooms and stayed overnight or for ten years, depending upon their business or their circumstances. Whatever they did, everyone, as the saying goes, knew Old Lib and made use of her.

That was twenty years ago, in the twenties and thirties, that was, when no one to matter lived south of the Canal, because of the marshiness and the miasma that it bred, and the malaria that seemed to breathe from it. Now, in 1850, everything was changed. The marsh had been mostly drained, and, by ones and twos, courageous merchants of the village had ventured to build here a grocery store, there a lumberyard, yonder a dwelling house. When this migration started, everyone said that the fools would starve, or go broke, so far away from everybody. But that never happened.

Trade followed the frontier, as it were; the new stores prospered, and other men began to build more stores and more houses, until presently the south end of Salina Street was as lively as the north end had ever been, and, later still, became the only place to be if you had a store to build or a hotel or a market or whatever. The homes of the first settlers retreated gradually to the west and east, out along Water Street or Clinton Street, along the outer reaches of Warren and Fayette and Montgomery. It was the last word in elegance and snobbery, as some said, when wealthy men—the town now had its rich as well as its poor—began to build what they called country residences up the long muddy hill that had always been known as Foot Street, and now was being refurbished and dressed up under the new title, James Street.

The coming of the railroad had much to do with this new life in the village. It brought trade, and trade brought people, so that, no matter how hard the politicians argued or the Salt Point Boys fought, when the time came to incorporate the straggling settlements into one city, Syracuse swallowed them all, Salina Village, Lodi, Salt Point and all the rest of them. Syracuse, with twenty-odd thousand souls, with thriving stores and mills, could boast of a dozen more or less respectable hotels newer than Old Lib, mostly clustering around the railroad depot in the very middle of Washington Street, where the proprietors could fight hand to hand for the passenger trade when trains stopped for dinner.

Old Lib was out of the swim. There she was, perched on the wrong side of the Canal, with trade flowing south instead of north, and nothing left for her except the rag, tag, and bobtail of salt boilers buying whisky after work, cheap-John canallers—the packet-boat passengers mostly went to the Empire or the Globe or the Syracuse House—and the lower and more questionable citizens of the town. Old Lib was now more famous for her gambling hell in the back room than for her pastries; no one cared about flies in the sugar bowl as long as there was plenty of redeye at the bar. The old place was going downhill, everyone said, and the proprietor was glad enough to sell out when a man and his daughter from out Ohio way made him an offer. He took his money and bought himself an oyster shop on East Genesee Street, which was really the old Turnpike dressed up with a city name, and the Old Lib passed into new hands.

After the brawl of the night before, all the doors of Old Lib— to the barroom, to the parlors, to the gaming room—stuck or were ready to fall from their hinges at the lightest touch. Old wood cracked easily under the weight of furious men, and there was a lot of work to be done before Old Lib would be straightened up and decent again. Ord shoved the door carefully, eased it open a bare ten inches, and slid through. All his motions were smooth and easy, beautifully timed and controlled as though his muscles were especially oiled and used to moving him about as lightly and springily as a cat.

Inside Mahala's sitting room—it was the old back parlor of the hotel, but none of the visitors was allowed to enter it nowadays—Ord found North and his daughter waiting. It was a cool night for early October, with a smell of frost in the air, and the huge old man was sitting comfortably before a small, flat-faced iron stove, his boots hoisted to rest on the ornamental fender, while its pleasant heat filled the room. His daughter, in a low rocker, had drawn a little away from the stove's glow, and was sewing with bright-colored silks on a stretched canvas. They both looked up eagerly as Ord came in, a question written on their faces.

Ord closed the door carefully behind him and said, "Evening." His eyes rested on Mahala as he spoke. "I can't ever get used to seein' you so domestic and ladylike, Haley," he said, teasing her, coming over to inspect the picture she was embroidering, a scene of funeral urns and weeping willows, with mourning figures in black clustered around a carved tomb.

Mahala's eyebrows lifted, the corners of her mobile mouth stirred. "I ought to be allowed some female accomplishments, even in a tavern," she said on a satirical note. Then, impatiently, "How was the meeting? We've been waiting to hear."

Ord sat down on an ottoman at her feet, took the embroidery frame from her hands and began to look at it. "Mourners and weepers," he said, following the design with a delicate forefinger. "Graveyard scenes. What do you want to sew that for?"

Mahala was not deceived. "I do mourning pictures because that's the way I feel about the world. It needs to have somebody mourn for it." Her face darkened as she spoke. Then she said crisply, "Somebody'll be mourning for you, Dal Ord, if you don't quit fooling and tell us about that meeting."

Ord grinned at her and said impudently, "There's nothing to tell, ma'am." Then he, too, dropped his light manner. "It was just what you might expect. Hall packed with Salt Pointers, and a bunch of local gentlemen up in the front rows to give it tone. Burnet and Noxon and some of their men on the platform. Speech by Burnet. Speech by Noxon. Speech by another man. It was that fellow," he said carefully, watching Mahala's eager face, "the same one you saved from the ruckus the other night. His name's Palfrey, and he seems to be one of Burnet's pet young bucks. He made quite a rousing oration," Ord said, his eyes never leaving Mahala's face. "He told the workers to look out, or the escaped niggers would have their jobs. It seemed to convince 'em more than anything that was said to 'em."

Mahala picked up her embroidery frame and began to take exquisite, small stitches. She said without looking up, "You could tell from what he said last night that he was a slave catcher." She drew her thread through carefully, and held the frame under the light to see the effect. Her voice was quite expressionless.

"It's a pity you had to save his life." Dallas Ord was laughing. "It would have been one less trouble for all of us. Unless, of course, he's aroused your maiden's heart, with his helplessness." Now he was teasing her again, his face bright with mischief.

Mahala said bitterly, "You needn't worry about my maiden's heart yet awhile." She put down her work and looked at Ord. "And he's not helpless, either. Nor he won't be. You were laughing when you called him a trouble for us, but you never spoke a truer word. That man's going to be someone to reckon with, or I'll miss my guess. Maybe it wouldn't do us any harm if I did play up to him a little. We ought to know what he's going to do."

The Southerner scowled. "I can find out what he's going to do without your getting into it," he said.

For the first time, Moses North spoke. Until now he had let the two young ones squabble. Now he stirred in his padded chair and said easily, "I don't know but Haley's right, though. It might cause less suspicion if a girl sort of shined around a young man than if another man was to keep an eye on him. We've got to go at this thing smart and careful—especially now when we're just getting going. It wouldn't do any harm to know what the other fellow's doing, too."

"They aren't anything to worry about yet," Ord said positively. "I made a good start with 'em." He smiled as he remembered it.

"I got up and spoke in the meeting, and now they think I'm quite a lad. They want me to come back and talk to the boys about the southern point of view."

Mahala was excited by this. "Tell us everything that happened. All about the meeting." She leaned forward to catch every word of his description. When he had finished she asked, "You're sure they meant it when they said they didn't know where the station was? Could they have been trying it on, to see what you'd say?"

Ord didn't think so. "They're not bright enough. The Major wasn't so ready to answer my question, but Noxon spoke too fast for him. I'd go bail that they really don't know—yet—who's running the slaves through, or where they're hidden. But they're going to try to find out."

"By keeping their eyes on Dr. May and Loguen," Mahala said scornfully. "Everybody knew they'd do that. That's why we've let everyone see them; made everyone think they were the important ones. If your fine Patriots will just keep suspecting men like that, we've nothing to worry about."

Moses North said, "It won't be so simple after a while. They'll catch on to the fact that May and Loguen don't ever *do* anything. Then they'll begin to wonder who really *is* doing it. That's when we've got to take care. We're new here, and folks would be quick to suspicion us."

"Not while we're just tavernkeepers, everybody's friends, not taking sides, not saying anything special about it." Mahala was still scornful.

Her father said, "It's not what we say, it's what they might see someday, if they hang around us too close. That's what we've got to look out for."

"There's the Canal," Ord reminded him. "That's going to be handy, if we get in a pucker. And then this old house is pretty big, and people don't often stay here. You needn't worry," he said with some impatience. "There's going to be no trouble with this end. If I can carry the Negroes this far, you shouldn't fret about sending them to the lake."

Moses North got out of his chair, stretched like a giant, and said he was going to bed. "You young fry can stay up all night, if you're a'mind to. I'm old enough to know better." He patted his daughter's shoulder and tramped out of the room.

There was a silence, after the old man left. In her chair, in the yellow circle of light from the lamp, Mahala sewed quietly and steadily, not looking up. Dallas Ord walked to the window, looked out over the dark stirring of the Canal beneath, then drew the curtain and turned back into the room. "Mahala!" he said abruptly.

Still she did not look up, or seem to have heard him. A faint smile curved her lips as she worked. She said, as though she was talking to herself, "I'd like to have been at that meeting. I'd like to have heard the elegant southern gentleman impressing all the salt boilers and ward heelers with his beautiful manners, and that queer way he talks. I'd like to have seen you making speeches to them and naming their new society. I'd like to have seen you cheek by jowl with young Mr. Palfrey, planning to catch the wicked slave runners and Abolitionists."

They'll take to Dal here, she thought. They'll trust him for the very reason that we were afraid to trust him at first. He's southern. Everything about him shows it; his talk, the way he acts. When Martin first brought him home, I was terrified. I thought it was a trap. I thought Dal was a decoy, trying to find out about the stations on the Railroad, the way they so often try. I warned Martin against him.

Martin had said, "Haley, he's the best of us all. He's been through fire and water for the cause. Some of the religious folks up here are afraid of him, and Coffin says he's a bad man, but they take the slaves he brings just the same. He's carried nearly a thousand Negroes up from below the Line. There's no one like him."

Mahala hadn't understood it. "But why should he be an Abolitionist? He was born owning slaves. His people are slaveowners. I should think he'd be on their side."

Her brother shook his head. "He got mad. They sold a Negro he'd grown up with and was fond of. His uncle owned the man, and wouldn't give him up. So Dal ran the slave out, himself. After that, he swore he'd free every slave he could get at. And he has. Dal's reckless," Martin North said, as though he wasn't as foolhardy as they came, himself. "He'll take any chance. He don't care what he does, as long as he gets the fugitives through. But you needn't doubt him. I'd trust him with my own life. And if I died, I'd know he'd never rest until he'd paid the score."

Ord did not move, but said again almost harshly, "Mahala!" This time she looked up, and he asked, "Why are you so interested in this man? You've talked about him in a strange way."

Still remotely smiling, the quiet girl went on with her work. In a moment she said, "It's a good thing to recognize your enemy—even if you like him. I know my enemies right off. I know the people that could never see what I see, or feel what I feel."

Ord said very softly, "You seem to take quite an interest in this new enemy of yours."

This time Mahala looked up. "Why shouldn't I?" she asked, her voice edged with anger. "Why shouldn't I talk about him, if I want to? Why shouldn't I like him, too, if he's pleasant? There's not much danger of my forgetting what I'm here for. I'm not likely to forget. And that's all that matters to you."

Without a word, Dallas Ord turned and left the room. Alone, Mahala continued to sew for a time. At last she folded her work and put it away in a painted Indian basket. Then she took the lamp and went up the stairs to her bedroom.

CHAPTER THREE

AFTER WALKING through the ruin and destruction of Old Lib's public rooms, it was a shock to find himself in anything as—he almost said elegant—but, well, gay and welcoming as Mahala North's private apartment. John Palfrey fairly gaped at it. On near inspection, the word "elegant" certainly did not apply. There was nothing sumptuous here, nothing very costly. But the green curtains that hung at the windows gave it quite an air. There were several pieces of polished mahogany, and a center table with a fringed cover on which sat an astral lamp. The walls were green, too—the girl must have a fondness for the color—and there were a number of colored lithographs and an old-fashioned mirror. A small cast-iron stove—from the Lennox Furnace, out east—had been fitted into the old fireplace, but since today was warm and brilliant, the stove was unlighted, and bore a glass jar filled with asters and zinnias, and the green curtains swung in a light breeze from the opened windows.

It was rude to go on staring like a zany, and John Palfrey recovered sufficiently to make his manners to Miss North, who advanced to greet him. Old Moses, towering behind them—the man must be six inches higher than Palfrey's own six feet—was beaming, and uttering loud words of welcome.

"Well, well—we're happy to see you again, Mr. Palfrey. Glad to know you've recovered from your injuries." He laughed so heartily at this that Palfrey felt hot and said, rather stiffly, that he had not been injured.

"Nothing to matter, I'm glad to say. I didn't see the man coming, in that dark room, and he caught me off guard. Otherwise I don't think I'd have had any trouble with him."

Ord's soft voice said lazily, "You shouldn't have. He was pretty elderly, as I recall. Not good wind. Weighty but not agile. I simply dodged him, myself."

Palfrey turned in surprise. "Were you in the fight? I don't remember seeing you."

Ord made no direct answer. "You didn't come into the card room, I believe," he said politely, and went to draw up a chair for the visitor.

John Palfrey sat down, wishing that these two men didn't have to be around all the time. He'd hoped to see the girl alone. What he wanted to say to her wasn't clear in his own mind, but there must have been something, because he was disappointed to find her in company. Why was the man Ord always with her? Who was he, anyway? It might be a good plan to learn something about him, if the Major was going to take such a shine to him. Another reason for knowing about Ord pricked at the back of Palfrey's mind.

He said as casually as possible, "Major Burnet was very much gratified by your speech at our little meeting, Mr. Ord. He'd be glad to have you take a real part in the movement. He was talking to me about it afterwards. He was saying that he hadn't caught the name of the place you came from."

That wasn't exactly a subtle approach, but Ord appeared not to mind. He smiled as usual—the fellow always seemed to be amused—and his answer told nothing, when you came to think about it. He said, "I believe I told the Major I was from Virginia. I've got small business interests there. But at the moment I couldn't give any fixed address. I'm looking about for a place to settle permanently. I may be able to say that Syracuse is my home."

Palfrey couldn't go on questioning, after that. He said, without hope of learning anything, "You mentioned the salt business?"

"I'm interested in it." Ord didn't seem embarrassed. "I may buy some salt here and sell it in the South. I might pick up a little money that way."

You couldn't get hold of the fellow. Palfrey gave it up, and turned to Mahala North. While the two men were talking, she had sat quiet, her long white hands folded in her lap. As peacefully as a dove she sat there, but it seemed to Palfrey that in her very stillness there was something powerful, pulling at all three men as a magnet pulls and pulls at a handful of pins lying in its field, until one by one they begin to move toward it and touch it. Thinking of her this way, he knew suddenly that every man in the room was conscious of this pull, and was obliged to resist it with all his strength. When she spoke, in her low voice, the attraction grew stronger. Palfrey couldn't help leaning forward in his chair, so that he was nearer by that much to this mysterious force. And although the southern man never moved even when she spoke, Palfrey felt something in him stiffen, grow alert, as it heard Mahala's voice. Ord's pointing toward her, too, Palfrey thought with certainty. He feels it every time she moves.

She only said, "I was wanting you to come back, Mr. Palfrey. You were something I rescued out of a shipwreck, and I wanted to look at what I'd found, by daylight."

Her eyes are green, Palfrey thought, scarcely hearing her words. The lashes are black and very long and straight, so that unless she looks directly at you, they seem to curtain her eyes. He heard his own voice say, foolishly, "And do you approve of the wreckage?" He didn't really care what Ord might think of this nonsense.

Mahala's smile was no more than a slight curve at the corners of her mouth, but this faintest change in the carved beauty of her face gave it a look at once challenging and inviting. She said with deep amusement, "I'm afraid it's too valuable for me to keep. From what I've heard, it seems to be state property."

All three men laughed at this sally, and as they laughed, Mahala's eyes moved to rest upon each of them in turn, regarding them with intelligence, as though she had some special thought to communicate to each of them. Palfrey was the only one who replied audibly. Ord's answering look, from his black, unreadable eyes, was enough answer for her, it seemed. The girl's father only laughed, as though everything she said or did entertained him.

Palfrey said, "I assure you that I'm really private property. And I think I ought to offer a reward to my rescuer. It won't be at all adequate, but would you consent to go to the lecture this evening? I just heard there was one, and since you're a stranger in the city, I thought maybe you'd enjoy seeing how we amuse ourselves here."

Mahala considered the matter, her eyes remote now, as though she had withdrawn from the company to take counsel with herself before she answered. "I might go," she said at last vaguely. Once more, her eyes made a circuit of the men in the room. "I have another engagement, first," she said, and smiled at Dallas Ord. "I've promised to see Mr. Ord off on the cars this evening. He's going south for a visit to his small business interests in Virginia."

Ord's eyes held steadily upon her. "I shouldn't think of preventing your attendance at the lecture," he said, always easy, always polite. He never showed whether he was pleased or angry with what anyone said. "It's really not important to go to the depot. I've taken trains alone before, you know."

Mahala shook her head at him. "You know that I never break engagements," she said softly. "I never forget anything, and I never break my word." The gleam of amusement came back into her face. "We can settle this by all three of us going to the station. Mr. Palfrey would be pleased, I know, to see you off."

Palfrey was obliged to swallow this as well as he could. He had no desire, certainly, to attend upon a stranger. But after all, he thought with some satisfaction, Ord can't like it any better than I do. I'm spoiling his pleasure, if he's spoiling mine. Maybe he'll refuse to let us do it.

Dallas Ord, however, had no intention of refusing. He rose and bowed to Mahala. "I'm flattered," he said, and now he, too, was smiling. The look of gay comprehension he sent to Mahala said that he saw her little trick and was amused by it. Damn it, John Palfrey thought, watching these two as though they were fencers, thrusting and parrying before his eyes. Ord is too intimate with her. He acts as though he understood everything about her. Everything they say to each other sounds like a reference to something else they've said before. I'm glad he's going away. I hope he doesn't come back.

Salina Street was filled with blue dusk when they left the Old Lib and turned south to cross the Canal. At the packet landing on the other side of the water, a boat, glimmering white in the darkness, was unloading its passengers under a flaring gaslight. Ladies were being handed down the gangplank, their gentlemen were hustling about attending to luggage. Boys in buttoned roundabouts were shouting the names of the local hotels.

"Empire House! This way for the Empire House!"

"Visitors for the Syracuse House!"

"Globe Hotel!"

The street beyond them, however, was quiet. A neat buggy, a surrey with a fine span of horses, a couple of Democrat wagons, were moving under the pale rays of the street lights, the horses' feet making a peaceful clop-clop on the macadamized paving. On the brick sidewalks men and women moved singly or in pairs, but not many were abroad on this autumn evening. The air was still; there would be frost tonight for certain. It was a good time to stay at home and rake the lawn. A veil of pale-blue smoke hung in the darker blue of the night, trailing over the city its fragrance of leaves burning and wood ashes that meant the end of a summer.

On the veranda of the famous Syracuse House, just across the Canal, there was the usual gathering of talkers, men who came every night and sometimes every day, to pick over the day's tittle-tattle of news, of small happenings, of larger politics; to expound and explain and exhort. Around these notable personages was also the usual fringe of hangers-on, listeners, men who had nothing to say in a discussion, no opinions worth hearing, but who rarely failed to be there, catching the crumbs of glory that fell from their betters. The new arrivals from the canalboat were beginning to cross the street now, burdened with carpetbags and parcels. The idlers on the porch held up their interminable wrangling to watch the newcomers pass; then the talk went on.

As Mahala and the two men stepped down from the wooden canal bridge and crossed the open space of the Square, a bell began to toll not far away, its strokes falling slowly and sweetly upon the evening air.

Dallas Ord looked inquiringly at Palfrey. "Church on Thursday night? Prayer meeting? This must be a religious town."

"It's the train," Palfrey explained. "Prayer meeting's on Wednesdays. The depot bell always rings fifteen minutes before the train leaves. It's to make sure the passengers get there on time."

Ding, dong, dong. He'll soon be gone, Palfrey was thinking as he spoke. In fifteen minutes, I'll have her all to myself.

Apparently unconscious of the curious eyes that followed her, Mahala walked between them with effortless grace, straight and tall, carrying her head up and tilted a little back, smiling at Ord or at Palfrey as they spoke, as serene as a cloud, not noticing any constraint between the two men.

"We needn't hurry," she was saying to Ord. "The depot's only around the corner, but we'd probably have time to walk a mile. The cars are apt to sit in the depot for an hour after the bell rings."

Ord said, "I'm not in any hurry to leave," and took Mahala's arm as they stepped from the uneven brick sidewalk down to the dusty street.

East Washington Street, at the Salina end, was no more than a split alley, breaking apart to skirt the white frame depot that stood squarely astride the railroad tracks in the middle of the street. As they picked their way around it, the station bell continued to toll, clear and unhurried, dropping its single notes upon them from a belfry that made the depot, with its classic façade, look like a church strayed into the highway. At the eastern end of the building, an engine puffed white smoke from its flared smokestack. The engine driver, in a blue smock, was tinkering with something around the wheels, and the conductor, in a frock coat, with an immense gold chain slung across his stomach, was passing familiarly among the crowd, talking to friends, cracking jokes. In spite of the ringing of the bell and the gathering of the passengers, the puffing engine showed no sign of starting. It might go in a minute, or in an hour, or it might sit there all night before it budged.

Palfrey was impatient to have this leave-taking over and done with. "Maybe Mr. Corning, the conductor, will know when they plan to leave. It's time, now."

"No hurry," Ord said lazily. "There's never any hurry about the cars. It took me nearly two days to come here from Buffalo. That's why I'm trying the eastern route this time. I won't have to change cars but once, at Utica. The Albany boats generally go somewhere near on time."

"You're bound for Virginia?" Palfrey's curiosity pricked again. Everything about this man was vague. You could never get a definite answer from him.

He didn't get one this time. "I'm going as far as New York, anyway," Ord said, and smiled at Mahala as though she knew all about his plans. "I never know for sure just what I'm going to do."

"That must be a difficult way to run a business," Palfrey couldn't help saying.

Ord was unruffled. "It surely is." His southern accent was stronger than usual. "It's a no-account way to do things, and no mistake. Now if I could only settle down and become a solid citizen in my community . . ." He let the sentence trail away into his untranslatable laughter. His eyes were on Mahala as he spoke.

Mahala gave him a slow look, then turned to the cars, where a new activity was stirring. "I think they're going to start," she said calmly. "The engineer has got into the engine."

Ord became suddenly active. "The time's come," he said gaily, picking up his bag. "I've got to leave this paradise among cities, much as it pains me." Once more he touched Mahala's arm and guided her along the platform to the spot where a crowd was beginning to enter the train. Incontinently he began to sing in his soft-whispering voice, "'O where are you going?' Lady Nancy she said, 'O where are you going?' said she."

A woman ahead of them turned to stare at this odd behavior, but Dallas Ord paid no attention. His face lighted with pleasure, with a reckless kind of amusement, as though he was uttering a dare to them all, and particularly to the girl at his side. The song had three more lines, and his voice, scarcely louder than ordinary speech, seemed to Palfrey to fill the whole depot.

> "'I'm going, My Lady Nancibel,
>   Strange countries for to see, see, see,
>   Strange countries for to see . . .'"

Mahala let him finish his song. "You needn't worry, Lord Lovell," she said satirically. "I plan to live until you return."

How he remembers everything, she thought, looking at his vivid face. How he reminds me, with everything he says, of what we both remember.

The three of them, Dal and Mahala and her brother Martin, standing together under the lanternlight in the barn. The picture rose in her mind so sharply that she could almost smell the fragrance of hay in the loft, hear the gentle stamping of the horses on the barn floor. Martin had been in a wild mood that night, she remembered with a pang of longing; one of his reckless, daredevilish moods, when no plan had been too dangerous, no scheme too crazy for him to try. And Dal was as bad. The two of them, close as brothers, with Mahala between them, loving both and ready to listen to their stories or help their work, but always fearing for them, trying to keep them out of danger, scolding when the scheme was too rash.

"They're waiting for you tonight," she had said to them, laying a hand on Thunder's bridle. "They know you came in today. They know you brought that Negro through. They'll be watching every road. It's foolish to go on tonight."

Martin had picked her up and whirled her around, dancing and frolicking in the dark barn. "Ladies' Chain! Grand right and left! Swing your partner!" Dancing together, whirling together under the pale light, they were as like as twin colts; the same in height, the same in color; Martin's red curls beside Mahala's, their eyes beaming at each other, the same green, wearing the same smiles of gay abandon.

Dal had caught her hand, his arm went around her, dancing her away from Martin down the barn floor.

"First lady swing with Captain Jinks;
Now with the one that never drinks . . ."

His voice sang the old dance call as he swung her beside him, his dark head beside her red one, his face alive with mischief.

Martin came forward, bowing low.

"Now with the one that carries the chinks;
And *now* with the dude of the ballroom."

They stopped at the open door, all three together, laughing and breathless in the sweet evening air. Mahala said, "You boys are crazy," and stood between them, linking her arms in theirs so that the three were joined together. She said, "I can't help it if you *will* get yourselves killed, when you won't listen to me."

Martin said to Dal, "The old lady's nervous tonight. Do you think we'd better fetch her smelling salts?"

Dal said, "She's getting old, that's the trouble. She ought to be in bed." Together the two men picked her up, carried her tenderly, despite her struggles, and deposited her on a pile of hay. "There, she can get her rest. We'll tell you about it when we get back."

Before she could move, they had run to the carriage and jumped in. The horse's hooves clattered on the boards as the light rig backed out of the barn. Mahala hurried to the door.

"Boys, I'll be waiting up for you. Be sure you come in and tell me about it."

Dal's voice floated back, singing to her.

> "Lord Lovell, he stood at the castle gate,
> A-combing his milk white steed,
> When along came the Lady Nancibel,
> A-wishing her lover God-speed, speed, speed,
> A-wishing her lover God-speed."

The buggy whirled out of the drive into the road. Thunder was wild tonight, too, ready to run like mad. Dal's singing drifted behind them.

> "'O where are you going, Lord Lovell,' she said,
> 'O where are you going,' said she.
> 'I'm going, my Lady Nancibel,
> Strange countries for to see, see, see,
> Strange countries for to see.'"

Mahala did not seem upset by Ord's performance in the depot. Instead, here again, Palfrey thought fretfully, was this private understanding. She knew what Ord meant by his outrageous singing. He had communicated something to her, and she had answered him. And neither of them minded the goggling stares of the other passengers, pushing against them as they edged their way to the car steps. It was a relief to have Ord make a quick business of his leave-taking. He became perfectly proper now; shook hands with Palfrey, said how grateful he was for this pleasant acquaintance. To Mahala he merely bowed, his face as blank as possible. Immediately after, he climbed the steps and disappeared into the car. For a wonder, the train actually got under way at once; the train shed was filled with steam and smoke, with the chuffing of the engine and the grinding of wheels as the cars began to move. Then it was gone.

Palfrey stared after the dwindling lights on the end of the train with a relief that surprised him. Why should he care because this stranger had left; why did it matter? Why was it a pleasure to know that he would not see Dallas Ord again, or hear Ord's soft, teasing voice speaking to him, speaking to Mahala? It's because I don't understand him, I don't place him, Palfrey told himself, struggling against the real facts. Major Burnet's taken a shine to him. It isn't safe, in our position, to accept strangers on faith.

You're lying, an accusing voice replied to him, deep in his mind. You're glad Ord's gone because you're jealous of him. You don't want him to be near Mahala. You don't know what he means to her; what she feels about him.

Impulsively he spoke to the tall girl at his side. "Mr. Ord seems to be an intimate friend of yours—and your father's." The words sounded rude as he said them, inquisitive. He looked anxiously into her face and saw nothing but a calm amusement.

"We've known him well, for some time" was all she said.

Palfrey couldn't keep the words back. "I gathered from his manner that you were all very familiar together." He hesitated a minute, then went on stubbornly. "Perhaps I ought to ask whether this gentleman has some claim on you. I wouldn't want to intrude."

For a moment she did not answer. Under the wavering gaslight at the end of the depot, her face, pale and unsmiling, told him nothing.

She said, "Mr. Ord makes no claim upon me. He is a friend from the past."

There was no particular expression in her voice as she spoke, and it seemed to Palfrey that her words were strangely chosen.

Ord made no claim, she had said. He was a friend from the past. What did she mean by that curious statement? Palfrey could not tell, and it was impossible to press the matter further. It did seem clear that, at least, Mahala was not engaged to marry Ord. She could scarcely have disregarded that sort of claim. Which, after all, was the important thing.

I'm going too fast, he thought, trying to quiet the turmoil in his mind. It's no affair of mine if she's interested in another man. I've only just met the girl. I'm merely curious about her and about Ord. I merely want to understand the situation.

The voice in his mind jeered at him again. You're lying, the voice said irrepressibly. You're lying, but you can't fool yourself. Palfrey gave up the contest and looked at his watch. "We'll still be in time for the lecture," he said, guiding Mahala out into the street. "I believe it's one of Dr. Dodd's lectures on psychology. That's a kind of magnetism. A great many of the people in town have been going to them. They seem to think he's quite a genius."

Mahala looked at him. "I don't know much about such things," she said, watching his face. "I'm not a fashionable person, you know. Maybe you shouldn't take me there. People may think it's strange to have you bring a person like me to a social affair."

Palfrey felt rising anger. "Why shouldn't you come with me? I'm honored," he began, and felt his face flush as he spoke. Perhaps he had been tactless in asking her to attend this performance. Perhaps, in spite of her assured manner, she was really uneducated; perhaps she had never been present at such a lecture. She might be embarrassed. Or perhaps it was the thought that she would be mingling with the fashionable people of Syracuse. After all, he knew nothing of her background beyond that she was the daughter of a tavernkeeper. What she had been, what she had done before she came to the city, he had not the faintest inkling. The thought crept in: Perhaps she is not, really, a respectable person. That may be the reason for her embarrassment. She may feel that she should not mix with proper people, with good women.

Anger—which he did not stop to examine—rose, and his flush deepened. Why should he suspect such a thing? She had shown him nothing—nothing at all—that would lead anyone to make such an accusation. She was strange, her manner was unusual, she was like no other woman he had ever known, but she was good; she was a decent woman. Controlling himself, he said, "There's nothing to alarm you in a lecture like this. There's no reason why you shouldn't go with me. I'm proud to have you. And if it doesn't interest you, we can leave." His face, as he turned to speak to her, was warm with emotion.

People did stare when they entered the lobby of Malcom Hall. Friends bowed, looked covertly or openly at Mahala, turned back to talk amongst themselves. Even Major Burnet, who was a friend to all and sundry, looked at him, bowed and continued to stare. Ladies, he noticed, were taking in every detail of Miss Mahala North's pearl-gray *barège*, her small velvet bonnet, the shining loops and braids of her brilliant hair. The gentlemen, after having looked away, looked back again, this time in frank appraisal of the lady's charms.

And to Palfrey's surprise, none of this ordeal left any mark upon its object. Mahala was as cool, as composed, seemed no more aware of the battery of eyes than if they had been turned in the opposite direction. She did not blush or simper; she did not appear nervous. Moving beside him in the crowd that was pressing up the stairway to Mr. Malcom's hall, Mahala looked around with interest, gazed at her new fellow townsmen, asked questions about the magnetic exhibition to be given upstairs.

Palfrey was the nervous one. His explanation of Dr. Dodd's celebrated experiments was not altogether clear. "He gets people to come up on the stage and look at a piece of bright metal for twenty minutes. Then, if they seem to feel the power, he puts his hands on their hands in some way, and makes them shut their eyes. After that, they seem obliged to do what he says."

"What does he say?" Mahala wanted to know, moving up a

step behind a trailing electric-blue moiré gown on a vast member of Syracuse's elect.

Palfrey said vaguely, "Oh—makes them twirl their hands around fast." There seemed to be some sort of confusion behind them at the foot of the stairs. He turned to look, hoping that there wasn't going to be anything unpleasant tonight. A colored man was trying to make his way through the crowd, and was not succeeding. Folks weren't feeling cordial to Negroes now. The fellow looked perfectly hopeless as the ranks closed against him. He ought to have known better than try to come into such a place as this, Palfrey thought. Even the Abolitionists knew enough to keep niggers out of public places.

At this moment, Mahala followed his gaze and saw the darky standing at the foot of the stairs. He had given up, and was only wringing his hands and muttering to himself, as though he was lost. Nothing, then, could have been more surprising to Palfrey than to see Mahala turn rapidly to him and to hear her say, "I've got to go down. That's our Negro down there. He must have been sent to find me." She did not apologize or ask his assistance, but began to push her way down against the crowd, which now turned to stare at her all over again. Palfrey followed, badly upset.

He overtook her at the edge of the crowd, where she was speaking swiftly to the frightened darky. As Palfrey appeared she said coolly, "I shall have to go home. I'm very sorry. This is our servant, Gasberry, and he says that my father is feeling ill. He wants me to come home."

The Negro looked at her, still evidently frightened at what he had done, then stared in terror at Palfrey; but he did not say a word. His mistress said to him, "You go home now, Gasberry. Tell Mr. North I'm coming straight away." To Palfrey she said again, "I'm very sorry I can't attend the lecture. My father sometimes has these spells. You needn't see me home. I can go alone."

Naturally Palfrey couldn't allow this. "I'll come with you," he said rather stiffly. "It's too bad you have to leave." Then, as

Mahala did not speak, he said, "It's strange. I thought your father seemed perfectly well when we left."

Mahala's face froze. "It's a sudden attack," she answered briefly. They walked back to the hotel almost in silence, and swiftly. Palfrey was wondering at her cool acceptance of the emergency. She walked rapidly, but she was not pale, she was not weeping. The only sign her face gave him was a sternness, a set look about her mouth, as though new determination had entered her mind. She must be devoted to her father, he thought, watching the clear, pale face. She's a strange girl, he thought; she wasn't nervous about what people might think of her. She didn't care what they thought. She's almost angry with me now, for coming with her. She doesn't even care what *I* think, he said to himself as they turned in at the doorway of the Old Lib. This last thought left a soreness behind it. She hasn't asked me to help. It's as though she wants to get rid of me. But I'm going to see her again, he thought stubbornly. I'm going to know her. I'm coming back tomorrow.

CHAPTER FOUR

FROM THE DOORWAY, as he said good-by, Palfrey could see the usual collection of shabby loungers in the bar of the Old Lib. He noticed that Mr. North was not behind the counter. The tavernkeeper's place was being taken, at the moment, by his Negro boy, Gasberry Robinson, who still looked frightened. Palfrey had no chance to see anything else, for Mahala closed the door in his face after the briefest farewell, and there was nothing for him to do but turn around and go home. The whole affair seemed strange, to say the least.

With the door safely closed, Mahala hurried straight through the parlors, through her own private rooms, and back through the dark and twisted passageway to a room behind the cavernous kitchen. The door of this chamber was closed, and she did not attempt to open it. Instead, she raised her hand and rapped four times, lightly, on the panels. After a moment's pause the lock snapped and the door opened a crack, then wide enough to allow her to enter. The small room, lighted dimly by a barn lantern, seemed full of people.

Rising above them all, like an ancient hemlock in a forest of second growth, Moses North's shaggy head dominated the group. His daughter went directly to his side and stood there, looking over the scene. Immediately before her, a white man, wearing a long, dirty, linen duster buttoned over what appeared to be his work clothes, stood twisting the handle of a buggy whip. He was so dusty that a light powdering of gray made his long face as pale as a ghost's, except where lines and wrinkles stood out like black crayon markings, and where his eyes, which moved constantly from one person to another, peered out of black-rimmed sockets. The man appeared to be extremely nervous.

Grouped near this man were the other members of his party. Three Negroes—ragged, disconsolate creatures they were—stood together, like cattle in a thunderstorm, pressing against each other for comfort, not speaking, not trying to tell whatever wild and incredible tale they might have had to relate. Neither were they begging for anything, nor asking any further help. They merely stood together, as though the conference in this room was but one more in an endless series of such hasty, hole-and-corner discussions to which they had listened as they were listening now, without taking any part, without having any more voice in the settlement of their affairs than if they had been children or animals. From time to time they raised their dark eyes and gazed meekly at the white people in the room. But they never spoke.

There were a man and two women, one of whom was carrying a small baby wrapped in a torn woolen shirt. The man was youngish, perhaps thirty, tall and well-made, with a powerful, flat-featured black face and with arms so long that they hung nearly to his knees as he stood. One of the women was old and small, wizened and toothless, with a face like a sad little gray monkey's. The other woman was younger but, perhaps because of their terrible journey, her expression was worn and hopeless, and she was as thin as a shadow. Her skin was almost completely white, her eyes brown, her hair only slightly curly, so that she could have passed as a white person, and it was strange to see her nursing a black baby. She was so frail that the weight of the child in her arms seemed more than she could carry, and her thin shoulders were bowed with it.

Besides the Negroes and the man with the whip, there were two other persons in the small room. Seated in the only chair, his silver head shining under the yellow light from the lantern, was Dr. May, his face as gentle as an angel's, his voice, with its broad New England accent, taking the leading part in the discussion. Standing near his chair, the darky preacher, Loguen, tall, thin, bent over to catch every word the old man was saying.

Mahala's entrance broke the flow of talk for a moment, and in the pause she asked, "What's the trouble?" Her manner was perfectly cool, and she did not seem surprised at the presence of strangers in the room.

Her father said, "Chaskey, here, thinks the marshals are after him. He says he was followed all the way in from Cazenovia."

"Did the marshals see him come here?" Mahala asked quickly.

The man in the duster said in a high voice, "No, ma'am. I'm dead sure I lost 'em before I come over the Canal. I turned into an alley, down on the Turnpike, before I come to Salina Street, and waited till I seen 'em go by. I wouldn't have come here if I'd knowed they was still after me."

Mahala's face was grim. "How long did you wait before you started up again?"

The man shifted his feet. "Well, I waited quite a spell. Anyways ten minutes. And I didn't hear a thing of 'em. Not a single rig went after me. Only folks walking in the streets."

As though the man hadn't spoken, Mahala said to her father, "He's left his team hitched right by our back door, where anyone can see it. And as I came in, there was a buggy pulled up across the street with two men sitting in it, looking over this way. I think they must have realized he'd slipped them, and then waited to pick him up. They may decide to come in and search any time now."

The man Chaskey said nervously, "It can't be the same fellows."

Mahala's voice was like an icicle. "Did the man following you drive a buggy with one tall bay horse?"

Chaskey merely gasped and stood twisting the whip in his hands. The whole matter was beyond him, now.

Dr. May's voice was soothing. "Haven't you got some safe place to hide these travelers until the search is over? That would be

[63]

the best plan, I think. Meanwhile, we can be arranging means for getting them out of town."

Old North looked at his daughter. "We haven't had time to rig up anything very much. We weren't expecting deliveries for a week or so. Mr. Smith sent word he was holding several parcels until the excitement had kind of died down. I don't understand how this man happened to come tonight."

Poor Chaskey was on the griddle again. "Well—it wasn't exactly Mr. Smith that sent me. My father was keeping these folks"—he nodded his head toward the silent group in the corner—"for Mr. Smith. But he heard the marshals were looking around Cazenovia today, and he said we'd got to get rid of 'em. You can't blame a man for not wanting to be caught," he said, looking from face to face hopefully. There was no mercy in any of them.

Dr. May said, like a hanging judge, "We blame no man for refusing to risk his fortune in this fight. But we do blame anyone who has promised to stand with us, and then deserts us at the peril of a fugitive."

To Chaskey's relief, Mahala cut this sentence short. "We'd better move," she said, stooping to pick up the lantern. "Father, you take Dr. May and Mr. Loguen out by the canal door. They can walk along the towing path and around to Foot Street. They mustn't be seen here. Chaskey'd better go in the bar and be drinking. And don't you say a word," she said, pouncing on the man so swiftly that he jumped. "You've done enough harm, without doing anything more. Just go in the bar and order a drink, and say nothing. We'll see you before you go." She went to the door and stood, holding the lantern high for the others to see their way. At last the three silent Negroes came forward and stood waiting, a step behind her, for her to command them. "Follow me," she said, and the little procession moved quietly into the darkness of the house.

The marshals wore badges, but they didn't have a search warrant. Moses North asked to see it, and caused them some embarrassment, but he didn't make any trouble about it in the end. He merely laughed until they began to feel somewhat foolish, and then said they were welcome to search his hotel if they wanted to. "You'll find a lot of broken chairs," he said jovially. "It's too bad you boys don't happen around when there's some use for you. We had quite a shindy here the other night—it'll cost me something before I've got fixed up after it—and do you suppose any United States marshals bothered to come in and calm things down? There wasn't any that I could see."

Deputy Marshal Guppy was an occasional customer at Old Lib. He looked sheepish. "It ain't our job to stop fights, Mr. North," he explained. "We're only hired to look for stray niggers."

North roared at this. "That's right, boys. You keep right out of trouble, and you'll live to grow up, I shouldn't wonder. You won't wear yourselves out finding niggers in this neck of the woods, though. It's going to be a nice peaceful job for you."

The other man wasn't so friendly. "We followed a rig all the way from Cazenovia to your house. It's hitched up right near your barn. We've been advised that the man was carrying escaped slaves in the back of his wagon." He looked at North suspiciously.

The old man laughed again. "Well, you go find 'em. But mind you," he said, laying a huge hand on the marshal's shoulder. "Mind you don't go arresting my boy Gasberry. He's a free nigger, and I've got his papers, and I'm not going to lose him just when I've got so much work to do."

Guppy said placatingly, "Sure, sure. I know Gasberry. He's the boy that serves the bar sometimes. I guess I can tell him. Although," he added regretfully, "these coons all look alike to me. I don't know how folks can tell 'em apart, no more'n puppies in a basket."

In the bar, Chaskey was the first sign of success. The marshals fell upon him furiously. "Here's the man." In a minute they had him by the shoulder. "Where have you put 'em?" they shouted in unison.

Chaskey carried the thing off better than Moses North had expected. He shook off the detaining hands and said, in quite a belligerent voice, "Here, you. Keep your hands off me."

Parsons, the strange marshal, put the question. "We have information that you were transporting runaway slaves in your wagon from Cazenovia to Syracuse. We demand that you give 'em up, or take the consequences."

Chaskey stared at him. "I ain't got any runaway slaves. If you don't believe me, go search my wagon. I don't know what you're talking about." And he turned back to his drink as though the whole affair disgusted him.

North slapped him encouragingly on the back. "These gentlemen have made a little mistake," he said, as though Chaskey needed pacifying. "They seem to have the notion that you're a Woolly Head, Chaskey; a regular old Amalgamator! They've been poking around in your wagon and they didn't find any stray niggers there, so now they think you've got some hid in your pockets. You'd better turn 'em wrong side out, to convince the United States marshals that you're a good orderly citizen." His laughter could be heard half a block.

Parsons said threateningly, "You'd better tell us where you've hid them, Chaskey. It's a big fine, if you're proved to have defied a marshal."

Guppy was a peaceable man at heart. "You tell us how come you drove in here, lickety-larrup, all the way from Skunk's Hollow, if you didn't want anything but a drink you could have got right to Lincklaen's in your own town?"

This was a reasonable question, and Chaskey looked for a minute as though he couldn't answer it to anyone's satisfaction. Moses North's roar of laughter came to the rescue. "Great suffering snakes, Chaskey! Can't you tell these gentlemen what you want on Pearl Street that you couldn't get so good in Cazenovy?" He poked the unfortunate man in the ribs, and leered amiably at the marshals. "You'd ought to be ashamed, embarrassing a man like this. Is it part of a marshal's business to pry into a feller's private life?"

Guppy was uncomfortable. After all, there wasn't any sign of a nigger around now, and they'd feel pretty foolish if they searched the whole tavern—with Moses North whooping and hollering after them, more likely than not—and didn't find anything. He looked hopefully at Parsons. "He seems to be all right," he said.

Parsons looked sour. "I didn't expect him to have the niggers with him in the bar," he said. "He's probably hidden 'em here in the hotel. We're going to search it." Doggedly Guppy turned to follow. Parsons was from Rochester, and was known as a hard man. It wouldn't do to have him report his partner as fainthearted in his first search. "I s'pose we got to," he said apologetically to Moses. "No hard feelings."

The search party found Miss Mahala North seated in her own bedroom, wearing a distracting green dressing gown and brushing her long red hair. She greeted them with surprise, and allowed them to search—somewhat gingerly—amongst the garments in her clothes press. "You'd better look under the bed," she suggested sweetly. "That's the place I'd probably hide a fugitive from justice." Helpfully she held aside the dimity bed skirts and curtains. "What—nothing there? How surprising." William Guppy was red as a beet before he got out of the room. He wasn't used to poking round in a lady's chamber, especially one as fancy as this, with its frills and furbelows, and the bed piled four feet high with feather ticks and pillows.

Beyond the Norths' own rooms, there were only two or three that showed the effect of their recent tenure. The rest of the rooms were what they had been at the Old Lib for the last twenty years: dark, dismal, smelling of must and damp wallpaper and unaired bedding, the furniture rickety and old, the windows blue with grime. Room after room, Guppy and Parsons went through them all, looking into closets when there were any, peering under beds at the dust of ages, rapping on the stained walls for secret panels. There was, apparently, nothing to be found. The attics had been recently disturbed to receive the accumulation of three-legged chairs and broken tables that were the aftermath of the barroom fight. Aside from this, there was nothing out of the ordinary. And the cellars, with their sweating walls and dirt floors where mice ran and spiders spun their webs, yielded no fugitives. In the end, after a warm half hour, the two officers gave it up and went down to the bar to wet their whistles, as Moses North suggested.

"You boys deserve it," he said kindly, leading the way. "After all the work you've had for nothing, you need a drink. Here, Gasberry," he shouted to the boy behind the bar. "Fix up something reviving for these gentlemen. They've had a hard night."

In her bedroom, Mahala stood behind her curtains, watching the marshals of the United States leave the bar and make their way, rather uncertainly, to their buggy. Mr. Guppy, released from the strain of duty, was feeling expansive and loving toward the whole world, and even the dour Mr. Parsons was distinctly mellower. It took them five minutes to say good-by to their friends at the bar, and when they reached their carriage it was a lucky thing that the horse knew enough to start up and trot without too much guidance. Mahala stood like a statue until the horse's hoofbeats were faint in the distance. Then she moved swiftly back into the room. With one motion she snatched the feather tick, as light as a cloud, from her bed. Under it, with her face pressed close to the edge for air, the young Negro woman was lying, her child held carefully so that it should not smother. As the puff of feathers was lifted from her, she still did not stir, but lay motionless looking at Mahala, her eyes sharp with fear.

Mahala said, "It's all right now, Daffney. They've gone. You can get up and have something to eat. You must be hungry." She bent over the child, to look at it as it slept. "He's very good," she said softly. "He never cried at all. It didn't hurt him, being covered up so close?"

The dark, mournful eyes looked at her. "I give him paregoric," the woman said simply. Then she asked, "Where's Blasi?"

"They're all right," Mahala said briskly. "I'll get them out, and then you folks want something to eat. You look starved. How long is it since you had a square meal?"

The woman was still fearful. "Is the paterollers gone?" she wanted to know, slipping out of the bed, holding her child clutched as though she was still ready to run or to hide once more.

Mahala said, "You sit down and I'll get the other two. You're safe now. The marshals have gone and everything's all right. After you've eaten, we'll find a way to get you out of town." She moved swiftly to her clothespress. The door stood open as the searchers had left it, so that a number of dresses were revealed hanging neatly against the back wall from a row of hooks. One of the hooks, as she twisted it, turned under her hand like the knob of a door, and, as it turned, the whole back wall of the closet swung forward on a hinge, revealing a small space behind it. For a moment, as the inner door stood open, there was no movement from the dark cubby beyond. Then at the sound of Mahala's encouraging voice, something stirred within; a shape emerged from the darkness, then a second figure. Mahala motioned them into the light.

"Come out quick and get some fresh air. You must have been like to smother in that hole. We're going to fix a better place, as soon as we get settled here, but this was a hurry-up call. You come out and sit with Daffney," she said encouragingly, as the tall black man and the withered old woman crept out of their hiding place. "You all wait here, and I'll go fetch you something to eat."

The man said, still hesitant, "That was a mighty close call, Miss Haley. Them paterollers done thumped right on the wall by ma head. I don't know is they all gone now." Stuffy as it had been, the black hole seemed safer than the lighted room and any assurance she could give them.

Mahala made up her mind. "I'll get father to come up and stay with you. If the officers should come back again, he'd help you to hide. Then you won't be afraid."

Not even the terror of these refugees was able to resist Moses North's reassurance. "I tell you folks you're safe as a church here. As snug as a bug in a rug. Now that those men have searched this house and not found anything bigger'n a black beetle, this is the very best place you could be. You just sit by and take some comfort while Mahala rustles up a meal of victuals. When you've got something hot in you, you'll feel sprier."

The new freedom of sitting down familiarly with white folks was still beyond them. Mahala, coming back with a tray of food, solved the problem by leading the three fugitives into another room and leaving them to themselves. She found her father comfortable in a rocking chair, his hands folded across his stomach, his eyes closed. She shut the door quietly and spoke to him.

"That was all right for once," she said abruptly. "We fooled them this time, but I don't want to cut it so fine again. We've got to fix up a bigger place, for one thing. The closet won't hold but two people. And I was afraid the girl and her baby would smother under that feather bed. Did you expect anyone to come through tonight?"

Moses North opened his eyes and began to laugh. "No. I never had a mite of warning. It was a slip-up. Mr. Smith sent word from Peterboro yesterday that he was holding his fugitives for a week, until after this ruckus had quieted down. I was figuring to get our arrangements made while he was waiting—so's to be ready for him. But this little twirp, Chaskey, got white-livered and decided to dump his visitors all of a sudden." The whole incident amused him. "He won't do it again in a hurry," he said, laughing to remember. "He was scared out of a year's growth when those marshals commenced to talk to him."

Mahala said, "He's a fool and a coward. We oughtn't to trust him again. I thought Mr. Smith picked his men better than that."

Her father said soothingly, "We all make mistakes sometimes." Then he hitched his chair around nearer to hers and said, "We'd better settle something. How do you think they should travel?"

"I've got it all planned," his daughter said. "I thought it out while I was waiting for those men to go." Her father leaned forward to listen.

The early boat of the Express Line got away by five in the morning and, as people said, the boats might be slower than the cars, but they did leave somewhere near the time they said they would. Runners for the canalboats, bawling through the windows of the railroad depot, made a great point of this to lure the impatient folks waiting for the trains. "Save your cash by going on a nice, clean boat that starts right on the minute, and takes you out to Buffalo for two dollars and a half, with good meals thrown in." But it was not often that they could persuade the speed-crazy passengers to make the change. People would wait all day for the train to start, if they had to, rather than travel at six miles an hour on a boat. The packet companies were hard put to it to make a living, the boats were getting dirtier and shabbier every year, and the meals, for all that the runners said about them, weren't much to brag of. However, since the boats were seldom crowded, it was easy to get passage at the last minute, and that was sometimes a convenience.

Mr. Darius Millholand found it an easy matter on this particular day to reserve the captain's own quarters, in the little cuddy up forward, for a lady traveling to Buffalo with her infant and a Negro servant. The lady was poorly, he explained to the captain, handing him an extra greenback to pay for his trouble. She'd been sick and gone up to Saratoga to take the cure, but it hadn't done her much good. She was a southern lady, going back home by way of the West, and, since the cars made her sick—as they did some unfortunate people who couldn't stand the jar and the noise and the speed—she was taking the Canal as far as Buffalo. A friend would meet her there and put her on board a boat on the lake for the rest of the journey. Mr. Millholand hoped Captain Jonas would see that the lady was left to rest quietly without being disturbed during the journey.

The captain was only too glad to agree. Extra-fare passengers didn't turn up every day. He said the lady could eat right in her room, if she wanted to, and Mr. Millholand, who seemed to be a lavish person, paid an extra dollar for that privilege. The lady's bags were brought on board, and Mr. Millholand handed her tenderly up the gangplank and showed her to her cabin.

The lady, Captain Jonas noted, was fashionably dressed, and wore a bottle-green veil hanging from her flowered bonnet. The veil was not too thick to prevent him from noticing that she was a nice-looking female, but thin and sickly to his eye, and nervous-acting. He assured her, as they proceeded to the cabin, that she needn't worry about traveling on the Canal; it was the safest mode of travel in the world; no fuss, no muss, steady as a rock, clean and salubrious. The lady nodded without speaking, and leaned more heavily on the arm of Mr. Millholand, who was escorting her. Her Negro servant, carrying a closely wrapped bundle of a baby, followed after like a black shadow. In the captain's stateroom, Mr. Millholand fussed over the accommodations, felt of the bed, peeked into the single cupboard, sat on the single chair, poked his head out the window. Finally he expressed himself as satisfied, and advised the lady to lose no time in getting straight into bed and resting, after the effort of coming aboard. Mr. White would surely meet them in Buffalo, he reminded them. They had nothing to worry about. They would rejoin their friends there and continue to their destination. After that, he and Captain Jonas departed, and heard the key turn in the door as soon as it was closed behind them.

"The lady is excessively nervous," Mr. Millholand said, shaking his head. "It's lucky for her that she's able to spare no expense in her journey."

Captain Jonas, remembering the two extra dollars, promised again to see that she had every attention, and he and the gentleman parted affably. In a few minutes, the packet *Silver Queen* pulled away from the landing and began to glide down the Canal behind its tandem of heavy grays.

Mr. Millholand, after glancing idly around at the crowd on the packet landing, walked without too much haste to O'Reilly's Telegraph Office, upstairs over Mr. Pierce's China Hall, and sent a message to a friend in Buffalo. The message read: "Shipped 2½ bales wool today, canal packet *Silver Queen*. Invoice number one. Please handle and reship to destination, per our correspondence." Then he descended to the street and repaired to the bar of the Old Lib tavern for a little snort of whisky. He was not known as a heavy drinker, and this was early in the morning for it, but there are some days when a man's nerves need a tonic. Chatting over the bar with the convivial Mr. North, Mr. Millholand's nerves were restored to their normal quiet.

By six o'clock in the morning, the streets of the town were filled with men going to work, walking along by ones or twos, with their tools slung over their shoulders and a pail of lunch in one hand. They went up Salina Street to the north, if they were working in the coopers' shops, or west toward the lake and the springs, if they were working at the saltworks. Others had farm lands on the outskirts of the town, and their way led along the Turnpike, which cut on a long slant from Clinton Square northwest toward Auburn and the Finger Lakes. In such a procession, no one paid any attention to one more worker following the same way, and there were enough Negroes in the city by this time so that the tall black man, swinging a tin pail in one hand and carrying a scythe over his shoulder, aroused no curiosity.

His work appeared to be out quite a distance. One by one, the other workers dropped from the Turnpike and followed side roads or weedy farm lanes away to the fields where they were going to work. The solitary Negro plodded along the road, still carrying his scythe and pail, walking with his long loping stride as though he had learned that gait the way a horse learns a steady, all-day trot, eating up the miles until the city of Syracuse was out of sight behind him. The sun was nearly overhead, and still he had not come to any farm where he stopped to work. Occasional wagons passed him, going his way, and once a man hailed him and offered to give him a ride, but the Negro only shook his head, without speaking. At last, opposite a farmhouse, he did pause and stare at it carefully, as though he was learning its outline by heart.

It was a large brick house, standing alone and out of sight of any neighbor. Its barns were commodious, its whole appearance well-tended. But the Negro was staring at a row of white brick, set in as a trimming just below the eaves. After a time, he seemed to make up his mind and turned into the driveway, following it on back to the big, hip-roofed barn. Perhaps his work was with the creatures, instead of in the field, for all that he carried a scythe. Any watcher from the road would have seen no more of him that day. A little later on, a well-found Democrat wagon, loaded with sacks of oats, set out from the barn and spanked smartly down the road leading to the west. A lady in a Quaker bonnet saw it off and handed up a bundle of food for the driver. Auburn and Rochester lay along that road, or the farmer might have turned off to the north and gone toward Mexico or Oswego to sell his oats. The Quakers in that region were known as prosperous farmers and extremely upright men.

Moses North called his daughter from the kitchen where she had been conferring with the cook, and led the way to her private sitting room before he told her what he knew.

"They've got away all right," he said with satisfaction. "Millholland didn't have any trouble with the boat captain. I went out on the bridge and watched the boat go, and Millholland came over afterward and told me about it. The captain was so tickled to get an extra fee that he wouldn't have minded if he'd been asked to carry a batch of monkeys."

Mahala asked anxiously, "Do you think he suspected that

Daffney was a Negress?" That had been the crucial point, of course.

"Millholand didn't think so. He said the man acted real impressed with her fine clothes, and he said the story about her being at the Springs went down smooth as butter."

"Did he ask to see old Cindy's papers?"

"No." The big man laughed. "He won't bother 'em. Or if he does, it'll be only because he's hoping to get another dollar out of 'em. They're all right, and White'll meet 'em in Buffalo and see that they get across the Bridge."

"What about Blasi?" Mahala asked.

"Well, we won't know for sure until the Meekers send us word," her father said. "It ought to be safe enough. Mr. Meeker's a good man, Dr. Clary says. Always willing to take a trainload through, whenever they come. It's all right, Haley," he said with assurance. "We've got through this pucker, and the next time we'll have it all planned, and be ready for 'em. You're a smart girl to have figured it out so quick."

Mahala looked at him without smiling. "I ought to be smart." She turned away to stare out the window into the autumn sunshine. "I've done it enough times," she said, watching the roof of a canalboat floating slowly past her window. "I've had harder jobs than this—and I wish I had a harder job now," she finished, as though she couldn't keep the words back. "This isn't enough. This is all waiting and watching," she cried out in anger. "I've got to do more than this."

Martin, she thought—feeling the tremor that always shook her at his name—I've got to work for you, Martin. This cause was your life. Now it is my life. I can't rest. I can't wait. I've got to work for you.

If Martin was here now, how he would be working, how he would be fighting. He would be bringing in fugitives, as Dal was. How many times he had come home, late in the night, stealing softly into the house so as not to arouse the rest of them, but always going down to Mahala's room. She would hear his light

[75]

tap on her door. She would spring awake, if she had been sleeping. She would hear his voice whispering softly, "Haley?"

Then she would hurry to let him in. "Who is it?" she would ask, as though she didn't know. It was a part of their game together.

"A friend, with friends," he would always answer, in the old password of the Abolitionists.

When she opened the door he would slide in, as stealthy as a shadow, his face bright with excitement. "We got them through," he would tell her. "They gave us a run for it, but we turned off on Hangdog Hill and got away from 'em. They went right to Hopper's farm and searched for us. I heard 'em, as plain as day. But they didn't find us."

Sometimes he would bring Dal with him, and Mahala would tiptoe down to the kitchen to get them warm food. While they ate they would discuss the run. "That was a close shave, Dal," Martin would say to his friend. "I heard hounds on the other side of the river and I didn't know for sure whether you'd got across ahead of 'em. I was scared for a minute."

Dal would laugh at him. "We waded the brook for half a mile before we touched shore. They never did pick up our trail."

Mahala would say, sighing with relief, "Thank God, you're back."

They always laughed at her fears. "We were safe enough. You've done as dangerous things, yourself. You carried that Negro baby onto the boat in your own arms, with its mother going along as your servant. The marshals were right on the wharf. If they'd caught you, they'd have jailed you."

"That was nothing," Mahala would retort. But, oh, she would be thinking; oh, God, suppose the marshals got *them*. I was in no real danger. It was nothing. But they might be caught any day, any night. Each time that one of them comes home without the other, my heart dies. A thought so terrible that she could not face it crept into her mind. Which one could I lose—and live? Martin is my twin. We have been so close all our lives, like halves of an almond fitting together in our minds, in everything we thought or did. But Dal? If I should lose Dal? He knows everything, too. Everything I think; everything I feel. He is as close as Martin. Closer, a voice in her mind said. He is something more than Martin. He gives you another kind of love that you can never live without. If it were Dal who did not come back, you could not breathe, your heart would stop beating, there would be nothing left of you. You would be cold and alone for the rest of your life. Martin is you—but Dal is the air you breathe. How can I make such a choice, Mahala's heart cried out. Such a choice is unbearable. I cannot lose either of them.

"We're three of a kind," Martin would say, laughing at her, his eyes as green as a cat's.

"A friend, with friends," Dal would say, looking at her and his eyes saying, "More than a friend. Ten million times more than a friend."

Her father touched her arm, bringing her back from her reverie. "You'll do more," he said, as though he understood her outcry. "You'll be called on for all you can do. The Lord don't let things go to waste. He'll find work for you."

CHAPTER FIVE

WHEN MAHALA'S NOTE reached John Palfrey on the morning after the lecture, he wasn't sure exactly how he felt about it. Her behavior the evening before had certainly been curt. She had said she was sorry to leave; she had offered the excuse of her father's illness. But at the same time she had seemed eager to go. Anxious to go, Palfrey thought, twisting the note between his fingers. Anxious—well, perhaps that was the answer. Her father was suddenly ill, the Negro boy had said. Naturally she was in a hurry to get to him. But for all that, there was something queer about it. She hadn't acted distressed, as he would have expected her to be. She hadn't turned pale, or threatened to faint, as so many females would have done. There were no tears in her eyes, no ghastly pallor, no trembling hands. She had become suddenly— what was the word?—businesslike, was all he could think of. It was as though she had been called by urgent business. She had grown tense, set, stern; all the softness and lure had gone out of her, and its place had been taken by her mind, acting swiftly.

This was a foolish way to think of her, Palfrey admitted to himself. You couldn't ever tell how people were going to take things. Mahala had had bad news; she had been shocked. And because she was no fluttering young girl but a responsible woman, who had probably gone through this same experience a dozen times, she had gathered her forces. That was what made her seem strange to him. He had resented it because, in the twinkling of an eye, her attention, that current that seemed to flow toward him from her, that magnetism he had felt pulling at him when he saw her, was snatched away from him and transferred to something else.

Why was he getting into this affair? he wondered, tearing the note into little pieces. Why should he care what a strange woman—and God knew what kind of woman, at that—should think about him? It would be better, probably, not to see her again. His friends in town were already sufficiently surprised to have seen him with her at the lecture. Any man who was seen with Mahala North would be conspicuous. He took up his pen and wrote, "Dear Miss North," at the head of the paper. Then he flung down the pen, got out of his chair, snatched his hat from the hatrack, and hurried out of the office.

The boy, Gasberry Robinson, who met him at the door of the Old Lib looked frightened, as usual, when Palfrey asked to see Miss North. He left the visitor standing in the deserted parlor while he scuttled across to Mahala's sitting room. The sound of voices came to Palfrey dimly as he waited, then footsteps, and presently the boy came back, breathless, to say would the gentleman be so good as to step this way. In the green room, the first thing Palfrey saw was old Moses North stretched out on a sofa in the corner, his immense frame draped with a knitted afghan, and looking as strong as an ox. Mahala, appearing suddenly as the door opened wider, came forward and took Palfrey's hand, and at that moment he forgot about everything else.

She was more beautiful today than he had ever seen her, Palfrey thought foolishly, staring at her pink dress, at her red hair, at the flounces that made her waist seem so incredibly small, at the deep V of her bodice, where skin as white as milk made the hollow between her swelling breasts. If she had seemed remote and stern last night, this morning she was gayer than he had thought she could be, smiling, her eyes filled with laughter as she looked at him. And this time there was no mistake; all her attention was meant for him.

I'm glad that fellow's gone, Palfrey thought, and was once more annoyed with himself. What difference did it make to him that a perfect stranger, a man he'd never seen three days ago, should be out of his way? How could Dallas Ord, a Virginian who might never come to Syracuse again, have any part in his life? He knows Mahala too well, that honest voice said in the back of his mind. He's too free with her. He understands her.

But she was not being difficult this morning. "My father's better today," she said, leading the way to the old man's couch to show him off as though he was a great baby. North grinned at her like an urchin. There was something irrepressibly young and boyish about him, for all his great size and his gray, godlike beard. Under penthouse lids, his eyes beamed, as blue as glass marbles, and a fan of smiling-wrinkles creased their corners. He didn't laugh like a man who had been dangerously ill.

"Glad to see you, Mr. Palfrey. There's nothing the matter with me, but Haley, here, likes to fuss over me. To hear her go on, you'd think I was about to pass over to the Summer Land." He roared with laughter at the idea. "If I get a bellyache, she puts me to bed and nurses me fit to kill. Women are all like that, my boy," he said to Palfrey, his eyes gleaming. "You want to watch out for 'em. If they ever get ahold of you, you're done for. Swaddled and laid in a manger, that's what happens to you, as true as you're born."

Mahala said, "Ask him if he felt that way last night, Mr. Palfrey. Ask him how he'd have got along without me last night. After everything's over, men like to pretend that they don't want a woman around, but when they're sick they sing a different song." She was smiling at her father, and this time, although it was plain to see that these two understood each other deeply, Palfrey didn't mind. It was charming to see the girl and the huge old man teasing each other, bickering with their words, but beneath the words, passing to each other a wordless message of understanding. There was nothing in their communication that excluded Palfrey; he was made free of their bond so that, seeing it, he almost shared it with them. We are friends, they seemed to be saying, but you might be a friend, too. Warmed suddenly by this feeling, Palfrey sat down with them and began to talk.

"It's a pleasure to see you so well, Mr. North," he said, watching Mahala take up her embroidery frame and lay the strands of silk against it. "I was concerned about you last night. I wanted to do something to help, but Miss Mahala wouldn't let me."

Old North said comfortably, "She never will let anybody else take care of me. She thinks she knows more than the doctors—and sometimes I guess she does." He chuckled. "But it's just like her to shuck you off when she got Gasberry's message. She don't waste any time, Mahala doesn't. She rolls up her sleeves and goes to work, whatever it is."

Mahala looked up directly into John Palfrey's eyes. "I must have seemed very rude, I'm afraid," she said in the voice that he had been hearing all through a wakeful night. "I knew exactly what I had to do, and I was in a hurry. But you must have thought I was ungrateful, after you'd asked me to go to the lecture with you. That's why I wrote this morning. I wanted to apologize."

Under her gaze, Palfrey felt as though he was floating about a foot above his chair. "It wasn't that," he managed to say. "I wished you'd let me help, that was all. It's a great relief to know that your father is recovered this morning. I wish you'd let me do something for you," he said, like a schoolboy, and sat looking at her as though he was under a spell.

Mahala said gently, "You can talk to father. He gets restless when he's laid up. He always wants to know what's going on around him. You tell him some news and make him calm down."

Mr. North didn't seem anything *but* calm, Palfrey thought, but it was pure pleasure to do whatever she suggested. "I'm not up on the news this morning," he said. "There isn't much going on at this time of day."

Mahala drew her thread through the canvas and held the frame away to inspect it. "You might tell us some about the new

Patriots' League," she suggested idly. "That sounds as though it was going to stir things up."

Palfrey sat back in his chair. The sound of her voice, with its deep timbre, wove a pleasant haze around him so that he was not able to think, or did not want to think, but only to listen. "We haven't done much yet," he said lazily. "We've got to organize ourselves and lay out a plan of campaign. Then perhaps we'll be able to accomplish something." It did not occur to him that he had never learned how these people stood on the slavery question.

Moses North moved on his couch. "You've tackled a big job, from what I've heard tell," he said thoughtfully. "Lots of folks are pretty stirred up about this law. It won't be easy sledding."

Palfrey frowned. For once, he was reluctant to talk business. It stood, in the hard and knowing part of his mind, for anger, hatred, fighting; for plain reason and unreason; for prejudice and fanaticism. It brought him back, painfully, from the mood of soft enjoyment he had been feeling. He sighed as he said, "You're right about that. The people of this country have gone crazy with this abolition idea. This is the greatest country on earth. We've got everything. Land enough, twice over, timber and coal and iron and gold and silver. Everything any country could want. We're going to move into the West now, and develop it. We're building railroads faster than any country. We're getting rich and prosperous and happy. There's nothing we couldn't do and be if these crazy men would let us alone."

Mahala said softly, "Maybe they think there's something wrong that's got to be fixed first, before we can grow. Maybe they don't want to upset things, but only to make them better. That's what they *say*," she said, underlining the word. "I've heard some of them talk. I heard the speakers the other night at their meeting. They seemed to be very earnest."

"Oh, they're earnest," Palfrey said impatiently. "They mean what they say. But that doesn't make 'em right. They don't see that just to change one thing—slavery—they're willing to ruin everything else. They're playing with fire. They don't know what a risk they're taking." He had grown warmer as he spoke, and now he was leaning forward, talking to Mahala as though it was of the first importance to convince her.

Her father broke into their argument. "Well—it does seem like a pity to get everyone so riled up they can't enjoy life. What I say is, keep out of arguments and be happy." His voice boomed in the sunny room. Mahala looked up at him and bit her lip.

"Father's right," she said, smiling again at John Palfrey. "Women oughtn't to try to talk politics, he always says. Tell us what the Patriots are going to do to catch the slave stealers."

Palfrey shrugged his shoulders. It was all very well to say, "Be happy; don't argue." The truth was that when the whole country was kicking and screaming the way it was now, no sensible man could forget it. For those first minutes in the room, the mere sight of Mahala, the sound of her voice, had bewitched him; put every other thought out of his mind. But now it had all returned: anger, worry, responsibility. He moved restlessly in his chair. "I ought to be going back," he said, the frown deepening. "I've got a thousand things to do. We've had word that a party of fugitives has been seen in the city. The marshals are after them, but we might have trouble at a time like this."

Old North sat up, too. "That's right," he said. "We know about the marshals, don't we?" He turned to his daughter. "We had 'em right here at the hotel yesterday. I guess they mean business, all right."

Palfrey was instantly alert. "You had them here? Why did they come? What did they do?" His voice rang again with the commanding tone Mahala had heard when he spoke at the protest meeting.

She said, "They came just when father was beginning to feel sick, and they stayed and poked around all over the place, swearing that a man here in the bar had been transporting fugitives. But of course they didn't find any, so they went away."

"Did they bother you?" Palfrey asked in a voice like a knife.

Moses North laughed deeply. "They bothered me some, because my insides were beginning to act like destruction, but they didn't do anything but inspect the property. That, and drink a quart of good liquor. It wasn't anything, as far as we're concerned," he said, comforting Palfrey's anxious look. "It was just that a young fellow from out Cazenovia way came piking in here as though the devil was after him, and the marshals naturally concluded he was up to something. When they found he was just out for a stroll on the tiles, they was fit to bust." He laughed again, and this time Palfrey did not laugh with him.

"The report about the fugitives is true. They were reported to have come to town from Cazenovia. We're still watching for them. But I won't have officers troubling you." He looked anxiously at the girl.

Mahala did not raise her head. "Now that they've looked under my bed and behind the woodpile, maybe they won't have to worry about us any more."

Palfrey was furious. "Do you mean to say that those men dared to come into your room to search? I'll speak to the Major about that right away. You needn't worry about seeing them any more. I'll have their hide for it." He was terribly disturbed. Men, a couple of tough officers, searching this room, searching Mahala's bedroom. Insulting her, perhaps, treating her like a common woman of the town, questioning her, making free with her. He fairly choked on it.

She said softly, "Don't be upset. They were only doing what you've told them to do. If they're told to hunt fugitives they've got to search for them. We're common people. We run a hotel. We have to expect that they'll search here. I only hope," she said, looking up at him, "that now they've satisfied themselves we're not harboring stray slaves, they won't keep coming back again."

Palfrey said, "They won't," and before he could say any more, Moses North reared his great bulk from the sofa, peeled off the swathing afghan. "Maybe it's good for some folks to repose on a

[84]

divan, but it ain't for me. If I stay here any longer, I'm going to have the epizootic for sure." He stood, towering over Palfrey's chair. "There's times when a man's got to assert himself before a woman runs him crazy for his own good," he confided. "You stay a spell and keep Haley's attention occupied while I get away, and I'll do as much for you someday."

Mahala started to speak, then let it go, spreading her hands helplessly. It's no use, her smiling face said. You can see how it is. John Palfrey, looking down at her, thought, That's how she speaks without words; that's how she makes you feel that you're sharing her mind. It's me she's talking to, now. Not her father; not Dallas Ord. For once, I'm the person who understands. The door shut with a bang after Moses North, and Palfrey thought, We're alone for the first time, really. The lecture didn't count.

The green curtains swung in the breeze and the room was a dazzle of sunshine. Beyond the window, a canalboat was passing. They saw its cabin roof drift by and heard a brown-haired man at the tiller, singing as he steered. His voice floated up to them.

"Madam, thou art tall and slender
Ho, ho, hi, ho, hum;
And I know thy heart is tender,
Ho, ho, hi, ho, hum!"

Unconsciously, Palfrey sighed. "Sometimes, when you see those boats go by, it makes you almost wish you could run away. Just forget everything, drop all your work, and escape on a boat headed for nowhere."

Mahala said dreamily, "You could, if you wanted to. But the boats would always come back." Then another idea occurred to her. "Why don't you go west—to California or Oregon Territory? You were talking about the West. I should think you'd want to go out there and make your fortune. I'd go, if I was a man."

"I would, if you'd go with me," Palfrey said, and waited for the heavens to fall upon him. Good God, he thought in the confusion of his mind, what am I doing? What if she says yes? Another voice answered, You've wanted her ever since you first saw her. You'll want her more, all the time.

The heavens did not fall, but it was not, actually, a relief when he saw that she had taken it as a joke. "I could dress up in men's clothes and go to California to dig for gold." She was laughing at him, teasing him as she teased her father. "Do you think I could fool people into thinking I was a man?"

He said slowly, "You wouldn't have to dress like a man to please me." You want her, the voice was repeating, over and over. Get her now, while this other man is away. Don't waste your chance. You'll never rest until you have her.

Mahala was still laughing. "That would be a fine scandal for the city of Syracuse. Mr. John Palfrey, the aristocratic young lawyer, has run off, bag and baggage. The baggage is Miss Mahala North, the mysterious newcomer from Ohio. Mr. Palfrey's name is never to be mentioned again in polite society."

Palfrey said, "You *are* mysterious. I wish you'd tell me about yourself. I don't know a thing about you."

"References given and received," Mahala said, and the laughter had gone out of her voice. The smile that curled her lips was ironic.

"You know I don't mean that," Palfrey said urgently. "I don't care about anything—except that I'd like to know you better. Sometimes I don't understand you at all. And other times, you treat me like a friend."

Mahala turned her head away sharply. "I'd be a very strange friend for you to have, Mr. John Palfrey," she said in her low voice. "You'd be better off not to know me at all. We'd never really understand each other." She looked back with eyes suddenly clouded. "We're too different; too far apart. A million miles apart. We have no business with each other."

Palfrey said, "I have business with you." He got up and stood over her. "You don't seem to be a million miles apart from that fellow Ord." His voice held a bitterness that surprised him. "Perhaps you understand him."

Mahala gave him back a look he could not read. "Perhaps I do," she said, and rose to face him.

For a moment they stood, their eyes locked together in a kind of battle. Palfrey wouldn't give in. Anger filled him, furious anger, and yet it was not anger with this girl. It was against something else, some barrier that stood between them, something that he must beat down before he could reach her. He said between his teeth, "You'll understand me, before I'm through."

Mahala broke the spell. Suddenly, she smiled and held out her hand. "What are we quarreling about?" she asked him, laughing, brushing the moment behind them as though it had been a cobweb. "How foolish, when you've come here to see me for the first time. I have a very bad temper." She spoke as though it had been all her fault. "I try to conquer it, but it's because of my red hair, my father always says. You must forgive me."

Palfrey couldn't stop looking at her, and he couldn't speak. Here was the mystery again. For all her sweetness and apology, she had retreated, gone far away from him. He was a stranger again, not her friend. She had said they were a million miles apart, now it was true. He reached out and took her hand, merely to see if it was possible. Mahala said, "We will shake hands and forget it. I'm very much complimented that you've come to call."

Palfrey dropped her hand. "I didn't come to call," he said rudely. "I came because I wanted to see you again. I'm going to keep on coming. You can't get rid of me."

Mahala dropped her gaiety. As she looked at him, her eyes darkened until they seemed to be no longer green, but black. She said somberly, "Very well. In that case you ought to know what you're doing. I am the daughter of a tavernkeeper. This is a shabby, low hotel. Respectable people seldom come here because there are better hotels, and our reputation is not good. I help my father run the hotel because he needs me. I am not a fashionable person, and your friends will be shocked to see you with me. They were shocked last night at the lecture when they saw me. You will cause a scandal, and your friends and family will suffer. You are an important man in this town, and the scandal will hurt you. Now are you satisfied?"

Palfrey said, "I'm perfectly satisfied." He broke off, and they stared at each other like enemies. He said in a moment, "I want to know what Dallas Ord is to you."

Mahala's head went back. As Palfrey watched her he thought, It's as though I'd struck her. What is it? What does this mean? Why does she feel this way about him?

"Dallas Ord is—my friend," she said, and raised her hand to her face. All the fight seemed to have gone out of her.

Palfrey touched her arm, felt the soft flesh warm under his fingers. "It doesn't matter what he is," he said more gently. "I don't care at all. He can be your friend and I'll be your enemy— but I'm going to have you." He didn't wait for her to answer, but turned quickly, took up his hat and walked out of the room.

In the entry the tall shape of Loguen, the Negro preacher, stood aside to let him pass. That's a strange thing, Palfrey thought, looking sharply at the man. What's this nigger preacher doing in a canal hotel? He's supposed to be a minister. He's a friend of Dr. May's. Why should he be here? A cloud of suspicion which he did not examine rose in Palfrey's mind. He said sharply, "This is the entrance to Miss North's apartment. Are you looking for her?"

The tall Negro bowed politely. "No, Mr. Palfrey. I seem to have lost my way. I was looking for the colored boy, Robinson. He's a member of my flock." Loguen shook his head. "I'm afraid this isn't a good place for him to be. He don't come to meeting like he should. I'm going to talk to him about it."

Relief flooded Palfrey's mind. Of course, this was the explanation. Loguen was a well-known man, a self-educated fellow, an escaped slave, it was said. But a number of the prominent men in the city had taken him up and made a fuss over him, and he had great influence among the colored element in the town. Right now, of course, he had become so conspicuous as an Abolitionist that it was hard to remember that he also had duties as a pastor. That was his errand now.

Palfrey said, "I see. Good morning," and went on through the empty public rooms to the door. Gasberry, unaware that he was being sought, ran to open it for him. Palfrey gave him a coin. "Mr. Loguen's looking for you," he said, and saw terror make the boy's eyes roll.

They're an inferior race after all, he thought, going down the steps and turning south toward the Canal. Loguen may be more intelligent, but most of 'em ought to be under somebody's protection. As he passed over the bridge, a freight boat, loaded with salt boxes, slid beneath him, going west. Palfrey thought, I wish I was on that boat—with her. I wish we were starting for California. The boat slipped away below him, emerged into the wider waters of the packet landing. A woman, steering in the stern, waved a blue apron. We can't be enemies, he thought, watching the boat glide away from him. I'm in love with her.

In her room, Mahala listened to Palfrey's footsteps retreating down the passageway, to his voice speaking briefly to someone, to the outer door closing. Why am I doing this? she asked herself, staring at the closed door. I have no right to know John Palfrey. How can I feel a softness toward him, when he is my enemy? Why do I like him when I should hate him? He is falling in love with me. That is what he was trying to tell me. I must stop him, she thought, twisting her hands together. I mustn't let this happen. Dal is the one I love, her thoughts ran on feverishly. Dal will always be the one.

But Dal has forgotten you, a voice said in her mind. Dal has never forgiven you. Dal will never want you again. And if Dal has left you, why is it wrong to turn to another man who does want you? You know why, a second voice said, accusing her. Martin would know why. You and Dal were joined together for always. Dal was Martin's friend before he knew you. After he loved you—before Martin died and you lost Dal—you three were of one mind, working together, thinking together, loving each other. Now, how can you speak of loving another man? I am not loving him, Mahala answered the voice, defying it. I am doing my work. I am seeing John Palfrey because it is useful to my work to know him. I am not falling in love with him. I am only doing my work.

Dinner, at two o'clock in the afternoon, was the important meal of the day. Mr. Amidon Palfrey took his place at the head of the table, his wife at the foot. Between them their daughters, Emily and Francelia, as pretty as peaches, advanced demurely to their chairs on one side of the table. On the other side, young Thomas sat below his father. The remaining seat was empty. Mr. Palfrey frowned at it, then sat down, lifting his gray beard neatly and tucking his napkin into his collar.

Mrs. Palfrey looked at her husband. "He hasn't come in yet," she said, nodding toward the vacant chair. "He got up early and went out before I could speak to him. And now he's late to dinner."

Mr. Palfrey frowned more deeply and began to ladle rich beef soup out of the tureen into the soup plate on top of the pile before him. Young Thomas started to speak, looked at his father's face and thought better of it. The girls, however, chattered irrepressibly.

"Everybody's talking about it," Emily said, leaning toward her mother. "We've just been over at Amelia's, sewing on her album quilt, and all the girls were talking about it. Everybody saw them," she went on, heedless of her father's repressive countenance. "Everybody wanted to know who she was. They said she was dressed *elegantly*." Emily sighed to remember it. "They said she had on a pearl-gray *barège,* cut very low"—she rolled her eyes at her father—"and a velvet bonnet with flowers. *Very* striking, they said she was. Archie Darrow, Amelia's brother, was there and saw her, and he said she was a *stunner*."

Mrs. Palfrey wailed, "How did he ever meet her? Where did

he ever get in with such folks? He's never run with queer people. He's never paid any attention to girls. And to be seen, publicly, with this creature—"

Her husband said, "Now, Emma. No hysterics, please. I shall see John when he comes in and ask for an explanation. I've no doubt he has a reason for it. When a man's in politics, he has to acquaint himself with people he wouldn't know, otherwise."

Francelia wouldn't swallow this. "What's a canal hotel got to do with politics? Archie says that he's seen this girl at a tavern over north of the Canal. Liberty, or Freedom, or some such name. He says this girl is the daughter of the man that's just bought the place. He's seen her down there, right in the parlor where the men were sitting. There's nothing political about that."

Mr. Palfrey said, "Francelia, I'll thank you not to discuss such matters. They're not for young girls to speak about."

Francelia pouted. "I guess it won't hurt me to speak about them, if my own brother can take them out to a lecture, before the whole town of Syracuse."

Her mother was horrified. "Celia! That's no way for you to talk to your father. When I was a girl, I wouldn't have dared to talk to my father so. And what's more," she said, wiping her eyes, "I wouldn't have soiled my mouth talking about such a woman. Your brother may be willing to lower himself, but you don't have to," and she broke down altogether.

His brother's entry, young Tom thought, hearing the front door slam, couldn't have been better timed. Now they'd have a dust-up, and no mistake. He sat up straighter, not to miss a syllable.

John said, "I'm sorry to be late, mother. I was detained," and sat down as though the whole family wasn't goggling at him, and his mother openly sobbing into her lace handkerchief.

Mr. Palfrey decided to have it out, then and there. "John," he said heavily, "you are breaking your poor mother's heart."

John looked up inquiringly. "Really?" he said, as though the whole thing was a joking matter. "I must have done it in my sleep. I haven't seen mother since yesterday."

This was too much for Mr. Palfrey. With great dignity he rose from his seat. "We'll discuss this matter in private," he said. "Please come into my study at once," and he stalked out of the room.

John shrugged his shoulders, glanced at his mother, then pushed back his chair and followed his father. The study door slammed ominously.

Fortified behind his large walnut desk, Amidon Palfrey addressed his son. "I am deeply shocked," he said, looking sternly at John Palfrey's set face. "I am wounded and surprised that a son of mine would disgrace me and his whole family by appearing in public with a fallen woman."

In the silence that followed this speech, John Palfrey faced his father. At the old man's words, John's face had set like stone. At his sides, his hands clenched themselves into fists. When at last he spoke, his voice was controlled, but as cold as ice. "I'm sorry, father. I can't allow you to speak of Miss North in those terms." He paused, and the two men stared at each other steadily. John said, "I don't like to remind you of this, but I'm a fully grown man, capable of making my own decisions—and my own friends. If I choose to escort any lady to the theater, that's my affair. I can't discuss the matter with you or with anyone."

There was no going beyond these words. This man would not be browbeaten like a child, or even persuaded. He had given a final answer. A warning. Come any closer, interfere with my life, and you've lost me. Your child is gone. I am a man. I go my own way.

Amidon Palfrey felt old. He said, bowing his head, "I'm discussing it as your father, John, for your own good." It was an admission of defeat. Regret flickered in John Palfrey's mind.

"I know you're doing what you think is your duty, father," he said, but his voice was still cold. "I'm sorry to cause you distress.

But I intend to see Miss North when I please. You and mother may as well know it."

His father couldn't help saying, "But, John—her father's a tavernkeeper. It'll be a scandal—"

John Palfrey cut him short. "I said I wouldn't discuss it, and I won't. If you and my mother would prefer to have me move elsewhere, I'll be glad to do it."

The old man said, "No, no—we don't want you to go." Before he had finished, his son turned away, crossed the room and opened the door.

"Tell mother I'm in a hurry. I'll get my dinner downtown," he said, and the door slammed.

When Mrs. Palfrey came in to see how things had gone, she got no comfort from her husband. When John set his will, they both knew there was nothing to be done about it.

CHAPTER SIX

By December, the Patriots had had all the general meetings they wanted. They had told their story to the multitude, they had gathered a good working body of adherents, they had organized themselves into a practical agency, they felt, for combating the Abolitionist evil. Even the Abolitionists themselves had given over public meetings, for the time being at least. They had called a second meeting, after the first protest, and formed their committee called Vigilantes, and the Committee of Thirteen, which caused the Patriots a good deal of amusement. But they seemed to have calmed down otherwise. There was talk in the town, of course. There was always talk, and a good rousing opposition, such as Major Burnet and his cohorts presented, gave the gossips enough to gabble about for the whole winter.

It was said that slaves were being passed through the city; it was said that there were stations in every part of town; it was said that there was a tunnel for the fugitives, a cave, a secret chamber, a black wagon to carry them through the streets after midnight. It was said that white men blacked their faces and pretended to be Negroes, to play a joke on the Patriots. It was said that Dr. May kept a dozen black men in his own house and smuggled them away in his own carriage. It was said that Mr. Loguen disguised fugitives to look like himself, and sent them through on the cars. It was said . . . it was said. Everything possible was said, over and over again, until people in the city were tired of hearing about it, and little boys on street corners whistled when Mr. Noxon went by.

Both sides, therefore, welcomed the announcement that a grand Abolitionist Convention would be held in Syracuse, early in January. The Abolitionists were in high feather, because a lot of notables had promised to come and address the meeting, and that ought to make new converts. The Patriots welcomed it because it gave them something to chew on. It would ginger things up, they said, talking it over in the bar of the Syracuse House, over a hot toddy. The boys were getting a little bit relaxed. They hadn't seen enough action to keep 'em on their toes. Mr. Noxon said fretfully that he couldn't see what action a lot of preaching fanatics would give the boys, unless the Major planned to raid the meeting. Major Burnet had other ideas.

"It'll be like this," he said. "Unless I miss my guess, the local Woolly Heads will want to do something to show off to their fancy friends. I've been told they were thinking of staging some sort of special doings on this Underground Railroad of theirs. If they do, it'll be our chance to shine."

"Where is this Underground Railroad?" someone asked. "I've heard a lot of talk about tunnels and so on, but nobody ever seems to know just where the things are located."

The Major said impatiently, "That's all bosh. They don't have to dig holes in the ground when they can sneak right through a town in a Democrat wagon. They may have caves in the hills. I've heard that Gerrit Smith has had one dug near his place. But what we've got to watch out for is niggers passing through the city. We'll have to organize watches to spy on 'em. We'll have to watch the roads and the cars and the Canal. It ought to be easy," he said, his enthusiasm rising. "You can't change the color of a nigger's skin. He's got to stay black. We can't help catching 'em."

"Who are you going to watch?" Palfrey asked. He'd been offish lately, the Major had noticed. Probably it was because of that girl he was running with. It was taking his mind off his work. The Major looked at him sharply.

"What's the matter with you, Johnny?" he asked. "We've been

talking about it for ten minutes. You've been mooning around so lately that you don't know what's going on."

Someone said, "He's in love," and got a hostile stare from Mr. Palfrey. He's a prickly cuss, they said to each other afterward; stiff-necked, quick-tempered. Now he said morosely, "You've watched Dr. May and Reverend Loguen for three months, and you've had your trouble for your pains. What makes you think it's going to be so easy to lay your hands on these fugitives?"

The Major couldn't afford to have his best lieutenant out of temper. He said soothingly, "Maybe we've stuck by them too close. Maybe we ought to change off and keep an eye on Leavenworth or Wilkinson or some of those men. They never had much to do with this outfit until the law was passed, so I thought that maybe they weren't very serious about it." He laid an affectionate arm around Palfrey's shoulders. "You aren't losing interest in the work, are you, Johnny?" he asked. "We need to have you with us. You're the smartest man in the outfit. And you've got a big job to do. Unless you've lost your interest in politics," he added softly.

"I haven't lost interest in anything," Palfrey said, staring down into his drink. "I'm just tired, I guess. But I'll do whatever you suggest about this meeting. I think you're right that they may plan some smart move to impress their visitors. They like to have visitors know that Syracuse is a radical town." He looked up, his anger rising to think of it. "It wouldn't be a radical town if it wasn't for a bunch of jug-headed fly-by-nights who are trying to ruin the nation. Most of the citizens of Syracuse are decent people, willing to obey the law. We're growing every day. We're getting more mills, more stores. New business all the time. We'll be bigger than Albany or Rochester, if some of these fools don't get us into trouble. Who'll want to move here, if he hears that we have niggers running through the town every day? Workmen won't stay here, if we get so many runaways that wages go down."

Major Burnet patted his friend's back, like a teacher whose

favorite pupil has made a perfect recitation. "That's the talk, Johnny," he said. "Here, let's have another drink to Johnny." He called to the bartender. "If the businessmen in this town can hear you talk like that," he said with deep approval, "there won't be any more converts to the radicals. And there'll be one new man in the State Legislature, or I'll miss my guess."

"That's all right, but what are we going to *do?*" Perley Deacon persisted. "Fine talk won't get us anywheres. And we've just admitted that we haven't done any good by watching Loguen and Dr. May. We've got to be smarter than that."

Major Burnet said, "We're going to be. We've appointed a lot of special deputies for the marshals, for one thing. We're going to keep watch on the roads. We're going to keep our eyes on every nigger in this town, to see if he's harboring or helping a fugitive. We've got a lot of ideas," he said, nodding over his drink. "You'll see. We're going to make these Amalgamators sit up and take notice."

"Ideas are all right," said Perley doggedly. "What I say is, we got to be practical. We got to *do* something. What I say is, we got to think where they'd hide anybody, and then watch *that*. I know what *I'd* do, if I had a bunch of niggers to hide," he said darkly. "I know right where I'd put 'em."

"Where's that?" half a dozen voices demanded.

"Down along the Canal," Perley said triumphantly. "There's a hundred places along there that nobody'd ever think of looking. And that's where I'd look," he said, glaring at them as though they were the nigger stealers. "I'd get me a warrant, if I had to, and I'd go through those dirty old dumps like a tornado."

The Major nodded slowly. "Maybe you're right, Perley," he said, frowning. "Maybe you've accidentally got hold of a good idea."

"It's a tramp," Mrs. Butterfield said, planting herself before Mahala as though she intended to stay all day. "He knocked on the door and wanted to come in. I says to him, 'We'll feed you if you'll chop that pile of wood in the woodshed. But we don't feed no tramps that don't work.'" She folded her large red hands across her apron. "*And*," she said firmly, "I ain't going to have dirty old tramps tracking across my kitchen floor, not after I just got it mopped. But this feller says he wants to see you before he'll do a tap of work. That's the way they all are, nowadays. Hoity-toity, too good to do an honest day's work. And you and your pa are so softhearted, you'll take in anything on two legs, if he can tell a sad story for you."

Mahala put down her embroidery. "I'd better see him," she said quickly. "Did he give his name or anything?"

Mrs. Butterfield followed her, grumbling. "He didn't give nothing. He just laughed in my face when I told him to go to work, and he said he wanted to talk to you, right off. The nerve of some folks," she said, waddling down the hallway to the kitchen. "I wouldn't let him in, you can just bet. I left Minerva right there to keep an eye on him. He's probably skedaddled, by now."

In the dark of the porch, a scarecrow figure, fluttering muddy rags, said softly, "Do I have to chop wood, Mahala?"

Mahala said, in a breath, "Go down to the canal door and slip into the cellar. I'll meet you there." Then she turned and went back into the house. Mrs. Butterfield was gratified to see the shabby creature disappear.

"Well—for once you turned somebody down. You're getting a little sense."

Mahala said sharply, "That was Mr. Ord you were being so sharp with. I've sent him in the other way. I don't want anyone to see him come into the house. Now—you and Minerva fix me a tray of food for him, and if anyone asks you if that tramp came in, you tell them I sent him away."

Mrs. Butterfield's jaw dropped. "Good Land of Goshen. I never knowed him at all. The poor gentleman," she said, all sympathy. "He must be starved, he looks so poor. Is it on account of slaves he's bringing?"

Mahala said, "I don't know yet. I didn't expect him, and I

don't know what he wants." She paused a moment to look thoughtfully at her cook. "You told me you wanted to help us save these Negroes. You said you and Minerva wanted to work for the cause. Now you've got a chance. We may have trouble getting fugitives through, if he's brought some. The marshals are all over the place lately."

The large woman said fiercely, "I'd like to see 'em get anybody out of my kitchen! I'd take a broom to 'em."

"That may not be enough to keep them out," Mahala said. "You'd better be fixing the food. I'm going down to see Mr. Ord." She hurried through the pantry into a littered woodshed at the back of the building. Moving aside a barrel in the corner, she revealed an open space in the flooring from which a ladder led to the darkness below. Taking a candle and a handful of lucifer matches from a dusty shelf, she started down the ladder.

Swiftly, in the wavering light of the candle's flame, she moved around the cellar room. It was large, a cave of blackness except for her small light; the floor was of bare earth, littered with an accumulation of rubbish, broken furniture, old boxes, broken bottles and, in the far corner, an immense pile of stovewood rose to the rafters. Rapidly Mahala examined the room, flashed her light near the woodpile. Nothing had been touched. No one had disturbed the careful disarray of the place. Satisfied at last, she went to the door and opened it. The space beyond was better lighted. Two or three windows, coated with ancient grime, let in a dismal twilight, and in the shadows near the outside door a darker shadow moved toward her.

She fairly ran toward him. "What's happened to you, Dal?" she cried, as her hands reached out to touch him. "What's the matter? Why are you here like this?"

Ord caught her hands, took the candle from her and set it on a box. Then he stood looking down at her. "I'm lucky to be here at all," he said, his eyes still searching her face. "We're in trouble." Then, as though his inspection had shown him something new, he asked sharply, "Has anything gone wrong here? Has anything happened? Are you all right?"

For a moment Mahala clung to his hands without speaking, only looking up at him as though she could never stop. Finally she said, "I'm all right. Tell me what's happened. Where have you come from? Where are your people?"

Ord hesitated a moment. "Is it safe to talk? And I've got to have food—"

Instantly Mahala recovered herself. "Oh, Dal—you're sick. You're starved. If you're alone, come upstairs and let me put you to bed." She was clinging to him, her arms seeking to support him.

Ord said, "I'm not sick. I'm tired. And I've got to find a way to get some Negroes away from here. I must go back to them as soon as I can. The marshals know we're somewhere around here, and we've got to move before they find us."

"Come upstairs then." Mahala was in command of her forces now. "You'll have to talk to father, and perhaps Loguen or Dr. May. They'll think of something. But first you've got to have some food and decent clothes." She began to lead the way, not to the room at the back through which she had entered, but to the rickety stairs that led up to the kitchen entry. "I thought at first that you had some of them with you. We've got a place fixed behind the woodpile. But if you're alone, there's no need to use it. Go straight through the kitchen." She was whispering now as they reached the top of the stairs. "Mrs. Butterfield didn't recognize you. She's got a tray of food ready. Take it, and go up the back stairs to my room. There's a door at the back of my closet, if anyone should come. I'll go and get father."

Moses North, slipping after his daughter into the upstairs room, took Ord's hand in both of his. "Boy—you've given us a scare. We hadn't had any word from you for three weeks. I'd heard from Smith that he was expecting a large party from Dr. Langdon in Elmira, and I suspected it might be you, but when we didn't see you, I thought you'd gone straight up to the lake. I thought you'd be well over into Canada by this time."

Ord passed his hands over his face, wearily. "I ought to have been there. Everything's gone wrong, this trip. We had to get off from the cars, half a dozen times. They've got officers and deputies and marshals all over the place. We managed to slip through near Peterboro, and sent word to Mr. Smith. He had one of his men take us to this cave he's got out in the woods, and he sent us food. But every time he tried to get us out, the marshals came after us. We stayed there nearly two weeks, until finally some of the people got so sick that I had to chance it. I thought we'd be caught a dozen times."

"Where are they now?" Mahala wore her old look of sharp concentration.

"In the ravine beyond the upper end of Foot Street. Sixteen of them. There's some cover there—not much. They'll have to move before night, and they've got to get into a warm house." He paused for a moment, then he said grimly, "One man and two women are sick, and a baby died just before I left. We've got to move them."

There was no exclamation, no outcry, as he told his story. Moses North and his daughter heard him quietly. They had heard as bad before, their faces said; they had met situations like this before, and conquered them. Now they sat calmly as Dallas Ord began to eat from the trayful of food before him.

North said, "It's risky using the cars from here. Mr. White would give us passes, all right, but Burnet's crowd has been watching the depot day and night. They'd spot us in a minute. And they're just primed to make a capture right now. They've been sniffing around Dr. May and Loguen so long without finding anything that they're getting provoked."

Ord grinned, his dark face lighting with wickedness. "My friends the Patriots," he said with his mouth full. He turned to Mahala. "You don't mean to say that our elegant young Mr. Palfrey hasn't been able to do better than that? Or has his attention been so taken up with Miss North that he hasn't had any time to catch miscreants?" He was laughing at her now, softly and gaily, as though he hadn't a care in the world except to tease her and make her blush.

"We haven't got time to fool," Mahala said with impatience. "They've been keeping their eyes on this place, too. I've seen them hanging around for weeks now. And lately they've been searching houses along the Canal. Palfrey will be here tonight, himself. We've got to move before anyone sees anything. We haven't got time for your nonsense." Her color was high as she spoke, and Ord went on laughing as though he couldn't get over the joke.

"I suppose they've ordered their bright Mr. Palfrey to keep track of suspicious characters like you," he said. "Her eyes are turning green, Moses," he told old North. "That means she's getting mad. There must be more to this than I thought."

North chuckled. "Mahala's redheaded," he said. "She flies off the handle easy." Then he sobered. "Maybe I ought to get hold of Loguen and Dr. May. We'd better think of something before those poor critters freeze to death. You look kind of peaked, yourself."

Mahala said passionately, "He's sick. He's tired to death. He ought to get straight into bed and let us take care of these fugitives." She turned angrily away from his smiling face. "He won't let me do anything for him."

Ord pushed back his tray. "I'll let you do a lot, my dear," he said softly. "You won't have to complain of that." He was quieter now. "Maybe you'd better get those men," he said to North. "My Negroes'll die, if I leave 'em out in this snow much longer. And I've got a crazy idea." His thin face lighted with excitement. "I'll want Loguen, particularly, and I want a man that has livery hacks, five or six of them. I think I see how we can get out."

Mahala went to the door with her father. "Henry Bowker's the only Negro that runs a livery. Loguen knows him, of course. He could stop by and get him. They ought to come into this house separately. Bowker can wait in the bar, and Mr. Loguen can come upstairs to us. Be careful about Dr. May. It's hard to explain his being here, if anyone should see him."

Moses North said, "Yes—yes," and closed the door quietly behind him.

Mahala said to Ord, "I'll get you some dry clothes. You'll catch your death of cold in those rags."

Ord stretched out a hand and caught her wrist. "Wait a minute. I want to look at you again." His eyes held hers until she could bear it no longer.

"No—Dal. Let me go. We can't talk now," she said, pleading. "We've got to hurry." She was trying to draw away from him. "We can talk after we've got these people safe."

Ord's face was somber, the expression in his black eyes unreadable. "Something *has* happened," he said, watching the color flow into her face. "I thought it had. You can't ever lie to me, Mahala. I know you—and you know me. We can't hide anything from each other. And we can't ever get away from each other, even if we try." His voice died away in the silent room.

Mahala bent her head. "No," she said in a whisper. "We can't."

Ord's hand tightened on her wrist, then relaxed. "You go and find me something dry to wear," he said, his light tone returning. "If I'm going to confer with the clergy, I'd better be respectable or you'll be ashamed of me. They're used to seeing you around with the town beau, and it might be a shock to 'em to look at these rags. It might lower your social standing."

Mahala said, "You're a fool," and went quickly out of the room.

Loguen, answering the summons, understood the situation immediately. "You can't leave them in that ravine. There's not enough shelter, of course, and then Burnet's men are too active. If they've followed you into town, that's one of the first places they'll search. We ought to move right away." He pondered the problem. "Have you any plan?" he asked Ord. "Our usual facilities aren't in good working order, right now. The Patriots," he said, showing his white teeth in a smile, "are serving their country with a good deal of zeal. They want to show that Syracuse is a law-abiding town."

Ord, decently clad once more, was brisk. "I've got an idea," he said, leaning forward. "It's risky, and it might not work, of course. But it would take care of the whole party; get them through town and out toward Oswego before the marshals knew they'd been here." His face wore its reckless look, as though the very danger in his scheme excited him. "This is what I want to do." He looked from face to face as he spoke. "A baby died this afternoon. We've got to do something about that, anyhow. Well—let's have a funeral."

"Go on," Mahala said, as he paused. Her attention, every atom of mind and feeling, was centered on Dallas Ord.

Ord said, "A funeral is perfectly legal." He looked at Loguen. "A dead baby's got to be buried. And nobody questions a party of mourners, driving out to a burial."

Loguen considered. "We could take the dead child to one of the colored families that live out on the edge of town. Dr. Clary would certify the death. Then we could start the procession with a number of closed carriages, and drive right through the city." He looked back at Ord, to see if he had taken his meaning correctly.

Ord nodded. "That's it," he said. "It's nearly dark now. If we could act at once—"

The tall Negro got to his feet. "I think that's the best plan we could devise," he said mildly. "It's a risk, of course. Someone might interfere, or they might see the fugitives getting out of the woods. But I don't see any other way to get so many persons through town at a time like this. I think we'd better chance it. I'll go downstairs and talk to Henry Bowker. He's got enough rigs to take care of us, and he'll be glad to do it. If Mr. North will get word to Dr. Clary, we can begin at once." He spoke carefully, as always, choosing his words with precision, as though he was making a speech. His dark face showed no sign of fear or excitement.

Moses North got up too. "I guess you're right, reverend," he said. "It's kind of rash, but that's like all of Dal's schemes, and the wilder they are, the easier he works 'em. Don't you think so, Mahala?"

The tall girl asked one question. "Will you be driving out with them?"

Ord frowned. "I don't know. I'll go along and get them out of the ravine and start them off. But it might be better to have only Negroes in the carriages, in case someone should stop them."

Loguen said, "I should accompany them, of course. As a minister, it would be quite natural that I should go to the cemetery with the body and the mourners. I think that would be best."

Ord agreed with him. "I hate to drop out now, but I think that would be safer. I can rejoin them at the next station."

Mahala moved toward the door. "I'll have to get food ready, and I expect they'll need warm wraps." She looked at Ord. "Which way will you take them from here?"

Ord said, "Mexico, I think. Or Oswego. That's the safest way to the lake, if we can't use the cars. Wilbur will take them overnight, tonight, and see that they get on to the next station. We can wire Masterson to have a boat ready on the lake, when we need it. The Underground will get the train through yet," he said, with his old assurance. "The cars will start on schedule."

Indeed, it was as though a train had been set in motion along the rails. After the first few puffings and whistlings, it settled down to smooth travel. A message to Dr. May; a message to Dr. Clary. In the back parlor, Mr. Loguen gave orders to Bowker. In the kitchen, Mrs. Butterfield and Minerva packed baskets. Upstairs, from boxes hidden in the attic, Mahala sorted out warm clothing. Moses North hitched up his buggy and drove leisurely up Foot Street hill. Ord, muffled in a greatcoat, with his hat pulled down against the driving snowflakes, lounged across the Square, walked indolently across to Pearl Street, past the dingy whitewashed houses in the purlieus called Whitehall, picked his way through the paths that straggled by tumbledown shacks where Negroes and other inconsequential people lived, disappeared into the drifted and unsettled regions near the old reservoir and Prospect Hill. Beyond this waste lay the ravine and the wooded edges of the town.

Winter dusk settled lower over the city, lights shone from the windows. At a house where Negroes dwelt, Dr. Clary's old buggy stopped while the doctor went inside. Quite a congregation of darkies had gathered there, because there had been a death in the family. Passers-by, hurrying down into the more populous part of the town, said, "A nigger funeral," and went on their way, while the draped hearse and the little procession of shabby carriages, with their curtains buckled high against the storm, gathered to transport the bereaved family and friends.

Deputy Marshal William Guppy, swinging his arms to get warm while he kept an eye on the Old Lib, saw them pass, saw the Reverend Loguen's face under the street light. It was a cold night for a funeral, he thought, pulling his greatcoat closer against the northwest wind. I bet those niggers wish they were down south now, slave or no slave. A tall man with a wide-brimmed black hat pulled over his eyes went into the saloon entrance of the tavern, and Mr. Guppy thought with longing of hot toddy, of hot buttered rum, of a steaming milk and whisky punch. Being a United States deputy marshal was well enough in warm weather, he thought bitterly, but it was a cold job in winter.

Well, that was a funny thing, Palfrey thought, watching Jarmain Loguen's tall figure stoop to go through the door at the end of the passage. What in thunder was Loguen doing around the Old Lib so frequently? Twice, three times, he'd seen him here before; had spoken to him once or twice. Loguen hadn't seemed embarrassed, as he well might, considering the tavern's dubious reputation as a hangout for drinkers and roustabouts, and considering his own cloth and his fame as a Cold Water preacher. He'd said, as cool as you please, that he had come to labor with the Negro boy, Gasberry, who worked for Moses North. That was all right for once, but why did he have to visit the backslider again and again? And today, the Negro boy had seemed strange, or so Palfrey thought, looking after the two men, staring at the closed door through which they had passed.

Gasberry hadn't acted like himself—or even looked like himself. Usually the boy was so nervous, fairly cringing when he talked to a white man, twitching and rolling his eyes, and generally acting as though he wanted to run away like a frightened rabbit. But this afternoon he had stood quietly in the shadow by Mr. Loguen's side, his head bent so that you couldn't see his features plainly, but there was none of the nervous wiggling and twisting that usually made Gasberry look like a monkey on a stick. It was dark in the hallway, of course, which might account for it, but it had seemed to Palfrey that this Negro was darker-skinned than Gasberry; yes, a larger man altogether, heavier, more powerful. If Loguen hadn't mentioned his name, you'd have said it was another Negro, a stranger. Could it be that the Norths had a new servant? Or could it be . . . Stop. No. Palfrey cut the question down in his mind. No. Certainly not. But still, it was very queer.

At that moment, Moses North's voice boomed through the house, shouting the colored boy's name. "Gasberry! You—Gasberry Robinson! Come here, you useless coon! You come in here quick and tend bar for me. I've got to go out for a minute—" The door swung open while he was still talking, and Palfrey saw North's great shape, followed by a much smaller man, emerge from the lighted room beyond into the gloom of the hallway. North's voice went on, "Right this way, Dr. May."

It was at this moment that the two men realized they were not alone. North came forward two steps, then saw who it was. He said cordially, "Well, well. It's Honest John Palfrey, come a-sparking." His laughter filled the narrow space with sound. "Come in, John. Haley's waiting for you, I shouldn't wonder. Dr. May and I'll go somewheres where we won't intrude on you young folks."

"Thank you, sir." Palfrey took off his hat. "Good afternoon, Dr. May," he said, and tried to see what kind of expression he could catch on the face of the saintly man. Two ministers at once, he was thinking with astonishment. Two teetotalers in a saloon; two Abolitionists in a canal hotel. How would they explain this?

Moses North made no attempt to explain anything. "You two gentlemen know each other, of course," he said with perfect ease. "I'm the stranger in the party, so I won't try to make you acquainted. We're honored to have the Doctor visit our old place. I say it's mighty neighborly of him to come all this way to pay a call on a stranger."

The Doctor's beautiful voice said calmly, "It's not such a distance to come. I only live a little way up Foot Street, and you'll find our church handy for you, if I can persuade you and your daughter to attend."

Old North said, "You'll have to talk to my girl about such things, doctor. She's really the boss of the family, now her mother's gone. We used to go to church regular, in Ohio, but here we don't seem to have got into the habit of it."

Samuel May said, "I'll give myself the pleasure of stopping to see her some other time when she isn't busy."

"Do. Do. She'll be happy to see you." North followed the minister along the passage as they spoke. At the farther end he turned to say to Palfrey, "You'll excuse us, Mr. Palfrey. The Doctor, here, only stopped for a minute, and he's got to go. You'll probably find Haley in her sitting room—that is," he said, laughing as usual, "you'll find her whenever she gets all her furbelows on. You may have to wait awhile. She didn't expect you so early."

Palfrey answered, but his thoughts were confused. In the green sitting room, the astral lamp was already lighted in the early winter dusk. A fire was burning in the Lennox stove. On the cushions of a low chair near the center table, Mahala's embroidery was lying, the needle still thrust into the cloth as though she had been interrupted in the middle of a stitch and had left hastily. The room was quiet and peaceful, but somehow the rest of the house seemed to be full of movement; footsteps passed and repassed the door while Palfrey sat there. A door slammed at the back of the house. Someone ran up the stairs.

Time dragged slowly. Inside his own mind, Palfrey was fighting with an ugly thought. It was preposterous, he said to himself sternly; ridiculous, disgusting. He was naturally suspicious, had always been so, suspected everybody and everything. Now, because that was his nature, he was actually beginning to suspect these people; this place. No, he said to himself again. It's nonsense. Moses North is a newcomer here. He has nothing to do with the people in this town except as a tavernkeeper. And, as a tavernkeeper, he was bound to have all sorts of men passing through his inn. If a local minister—white or colored—wanted to make a little missionary visit to him or his servant, it was entirely natural and reasonable. If his Negro boy was nervous one day and calm another, why, that was nothing extraordinary, either.

When you examined the evidence coldly, he said to himself with some relief, there was nothing to be suspicious about. Had he, for a moment, suspected the woman he was in love with? As he turned his thoughts deliberately to Mahala, a wave of emotion, a warmth, almost a weakness, flowed over him. In love with, he thought, his spirit fairly groaning; so horribly in love with; so hopelessly, so wildly; so lost and sunk in it. What would she say if she knew he had felt that moment's suspicion? She would turn on him, John Palfrey thought, remembering her. She could be fierce, God knew. She could be angry. She could be soft and warm, too, he thought with longing. She could ravish his heart. But he never knew how she would be. She would not commit herself, she would give him no answer to his pleading. If he had let himself be refused, she would have refused him, but he gave her no chance. He had said that he would have her, somehow, someday, and, by God, he would.

Her step sounded at last, outside the door. Her hand touched the knob, turned it. He heard her say to someone, "Now you go along and do what I said." Then she turned and saw him, standing by the table waiting for her. "Oh—I didn't know you'd come," she said, and stepped forward into the room. "I thought you weren't coming until after supper." She looked at him inquiringly. "How did you happen to be so early?"

Palfrey said slowly, "You don't seem overjoyed to see me. Am I interrupting something?"

Mahala smiled, moving forward and sitting down in her low chair. "Yes. Something very important. I've spent the day trying to clean out those glory-holes in the back of the house. We thought we might have more chance to rent rooms if we cleaned them out a little. They were really shamefully dirty." She held up her narrow hands and looked at them as though she expected to find cobwebs on them. "I've had everybody in the place down scrubbing for me. Even father," she said, laughing to remember it. "You ought to have seen him."

"I just saw him as I came in." Palfrey's voice sounded strange to him. "He was in the hallway with Dr. May." Then, when Mahala seemed to expect him to say more, "How does it happen"—the words fairly pushed themselves out of his mouth—"how does it happen that you have so many eminent ministers visiting you today? I saw the Reverend Loguen too, as I came in."

Why am I saying this? his anguished spirit cried to him. Why am I asking her what will make her detest me, what will make her resent me? What will make her, his warning inner voice said, want to get rid of me—if what I thought is true.

Mahala looked surprised. "Why shouldn't he call on us? We used to be Unitarians, out in Ohio, and he thinks we ought to go to church here." She looked at him, shrugging her shoulders. "I told father that the Unitarians were too fashionable for us in Syracuse," she said in her sardonic way. "Out there, it didn't make any difference if you dug ditches, you could go to any church that suited your fancy. Here in the East," she said, laughing, "think what the Episcopalians would say if we wanted to join their church. We'd better keep away from them all."

"What about Loguen?" The words were wrenched out of Palfrey. I've got to know, he kept telling himself. I can't help it. I've got to know what she will say.

"Well—what about him?" Mahala asked reasonably. "He's come here to see Gasberry several times. I suppose he has to visit his flock. And if that lazy darky acts in church the way he acts here, he won't be much use to them." She was apparently amused by his questioning. "You seem to have religion on your mind today," she said, rallying him gently. "Have you been converted recently?"

It's all right, the voice in Palfrey's mind was singing like a choir of angels. She doesn't know what I'm talking about. If there was anything queer going on, the rest of them might know about it, but she didn't. And she was being sweet to him, joking with him, not angry as she might have been. Palfrey felt suddenly as though he had escaped from a great danger by the very skin of his teeth. In a gush of relief he went quickly to Mahala's side and laid his hand on her arm. "I'm only converted to one thing," he said deliriously. "To you, Mahala."

She was not expecting it, so that when he caught her up suddenly into his arms, holding her, pressing his mouth against hers, she was unprepared, helpless before the rush of his passion. Against his body, Palfrey could feel her, after the first startled moment, struggling, her hands pressing against his shoulders, straining to draw away. He let her go long enough to say, "You're mine, Mahala. You're going to marry me."

He heard her voice, scarcely more than a whisper, and whether speaking to him or not, he could not tell. "No. No. No . . . This is not what I said I would do. This is more than I can bear. No. No."

She was fighting against him now, struggling so that he had to let her go. He said, still clinging to her hands, "Don't hate me, Mahala. Don't fear me so. You know what I feel. You know what I want."

For a moment she stood with her hands over her face so that he thought she was weeping, but she made no sound; no tears flowed through her fingers. When she dropped her hands, he saw merely that her face was as white as paper, her eyes dead black, as he had seen them once before. She said, "If I made you do that, John, I never meant to. I want you to forgive me."

Palfrey was stunned. "Forgive you," he repeated stupidly. It was one more strange thing, lost in the confusion of his feelings. "How could you make me do anything I didn't want to do? Why should you ask me to forgive you? I want you," he said desperately. "You know how I feel. You know what I want. You know why I had to kiss you."

Mahala, still looking at him from black, fathomless eyes, said, "Yes, I know. But I can't let you. Never again. I'm not meant for you, John. It's wrong," she said, suddenly wringing her hands as though a pain had stabbed her. "It's all wrong. We can't go on this way."

Her distress, her self-reproach, broke Palfrey's heart. He took her hands strongly between both of his and spoke to her as he would to a sobbing child, "You *are* meant for me. You can't help it. There's nothing for you to accuse yourself of. I don't care about what anyone else thinks. It's only us that matters. And we're going to go on this way, whatever you say—because you can't make me stop. I'm going to take care of you. I'm going to marry you, and take you away from all this."

He would have drawn her to him and kissed her again, but a voice sounded outside the door. The old door creaked on its hinges and swung inward. Moses North's voice said, "Haley's entertaining a suitor, my boy. We'll come in and pay our respects."

What Dallas Ord made of the scene in the room, no one, of course, could know. Palfrey and Mahala were still standing, drawn a little apart now, but facing each other, Palfrey deeply flushed and Mahala as white as marble. And even the air of the room, Palfrey thought with a kind of grim pleasure, must be full of the electricity of their feeling. But if Ord saw anything unusual in the scene, certainly neither his manner nor his words gave any evidence of it. He entered, smiling, and crossed the room to bow politely over Mahala's hand.

He knows, Mahala thought wildly. He knows that John kissed me. He knows everything. He always knows. He always remembers. And I remember, too. The thought turned like a knife in her breast. I remember that you have kissed me, Dal. I remember the first time, when we lay beside a stream, watching the water flow past us, waiting for a fugitive to come through.

There we lay together, talking a little, laughing a little, and then suddenly you reached out and touched my face with your hand, and that was like a kiss, before your lips touched me. The lightest way you ever touched me was like a kiss. You said so little, always, in love. There was too much to say for words to carry it, so you didn't speak. John claims me. He says so often that he wants me. That he is going to have me. You never said that. You knew, always, that we were a part of each other. There was no reason to claim me. You touched me, you kissed me, and it was like dying. The sun went out, the earth vanished under me. I was on a star, in another world; there was a new heaven and a new earth.

Dal, she cried out in her heart, how could you leave me? How could you stop loving me? How could you hate me, whatever I did or said, after what we had? I have been punished enough, she pleaded with him silently. You have watched me starve to death, for a year. I have begged you to come back, and you refuse me. You will never forgive me, she thought, looking at his calm face. You know what I am feeling now and yet you give no sign. You will never forgive me. I have lost you. If I take another man now, you will not care.

"It's as though I'd never been away at all," Ord said in his soft southern voice. "These are the last two faces I saw in Syracuse. Now they are the first two I see when I return. What a coincidence," he said, and smiled at Mahala with that old maddening look, as though he was saying something under his breath which only she might hear.

Mahala drew her hand away from him. "I'm glad you're back, Dal," she said, but there was a curious note in her voice. In the moment of Ord's entrance, she seemed to have slipped away from all of them. She could not be touched. A moment ago, Palfrey thought, I was going to kiss her again. Now she does not know me. But she knows Dallas Ord. Jealousy, like a poison, poured suddenly into his veins. I'll take her away from him, he thought while the poison gathered in a solid lump below his breastbone. He'll never have her.

Ord was chattering as though the situation was entirely casual. "I came by way of Buffalo," he was explaining. "The train was two days making two hundred and sixty miles. I doubt if I'll ever get warm again." Laughing, easy, he moved over to the stove and held his hands toward it to warm them. He was thinner, Palfrey noticed. His face was gaunt, as though he had been utterly exhausted by the journey. Perhaps he's sickly, Palfrey thought, grasping at foolish straws; perhaps that's why Mahala's so attentive to him.

She said now, "Was your business successful?" Again, there was that strained note in her voice. What does she care about his business? Palfrey thought with impatience. He's one of these southern gentlemen who don't pay any attention to business. Probably he's got a hundred slaves to do all his work for him. Slaves; his mind stumbled over the word, then remembered what it meant to him. If Ord's a slaveowner, and he's such a close friend of the Norths, they can't be running fugitives. For a moment a wave of pure relief, almost of gratitude to Dallas Ord, filled Palfrey's mind. I can stand anything but that, he thought thankfully. I don't care if Ord's in love with her. I'll take her away from him. But the other thing *must* be all right.

He shook Ord's hand cordially. "It's nice to have you back. We'll hope to see you at some of our meetings. Major Burnet's been asking if you didn't plan to return." He smiled at Mahala. "I'll be going along now. I only came early to see if you felt like going out this evening. There's going to be some sort of concert at the Lyceum, and I thought we might go."

Mahala said doubtfully, "I don't know. Now that we have a guest—"

Ord wouldn't hear of it. "You mustn't let me spoil your innocent pleasure," he said in his teasing way. "I wouldn't for the world." His eyes, as he looked at Mahala, were as black as jet, almost glittering, Palfrey thought, watching his handsome, reckless face. He knows Mahala won't go and leave him. He's simply deviling her. Before Palfrey could say anything to resolve the situation, however, Moses North broke in.

"I'll tell you a fine entertainment that we can all go to," he said persuasively. "The Woolly Heads are having a big meeting tonight in Market Hall, and we could all go to that. It's going to be very elevating. Dr. May told me himself this afternoon that he thought it would do me good to attend. We can all go and be converted to the great cause. You, Mr. Ord," he said, rumbling with laughter, "you ought to be a fine, tough subject for the slave stealers to convert. And Mr. Palfrey, here, is going to fight 'em, so he ought to hear what they've got to say."

Mahala said, "No," violently, but the others immediately agreed. It was better than having her stay at home to entertain Dallas Ord, Palfrey thought. It was better than not seeing her. And if she went with him, no one could suspect that she had joined the cause. He would see Burnet and advise him to attend, also. That would make it obvious that they were all going to observe, not to take part.

He said, "I'd be very much interested to hear what they have to say. We might get some pointers on how to beat 'em, if we heard their talk." He looked at Mahala, to see how she was taking it.

Apparently she had given in. "Very well," she said. "We'll be ready when you come."

Even so, it was hard to leave her there in the room with Ord. What would he say to her when they were alone? What was there between them? Palfrey thought heavily, crossing the Canal and turning east toward Warren Street. What does she say to him? What does she feel toward him? He won't see her as much as he thinks he's going to, this time, Palfrey said to himself, swinging through the snowdrifts on the sidewalk. I'll take her away from him.

CHAPTER SEVEN

"THESE BENCHES are hard enough to paralyze a man," Moses North said in what was meant to be a whisper. He shifted his great weight on the creaking board, and sighed audibly. "I don't know what it is about Abolition that calls for so much talk. They get to going, and they can't seem to remember the ends of their orations." His daughter said, "Hush," and they could all feel the seat tremble with his laughter.

On the platform, a great fuss was being made over Mr. William Chaplin, fresh from a Maryland jail for having given two escaping fugitives a lift in his carriage through the outskirts of Washington City. Mr. Gerrit Smith had bailed him out for $20,000, and told him to skip to Syracuse. A grand reception had been held for him in the Congregational Church a few days before, and people were still inclined to make speeches over him in the Anti-Fugitive Slave Law Convention. Mr. Chaplin said modestly that he had only done his duty, and added, with great feeling, that he would rather be 'laying in his grave, or in the dank dungeons of the Maryland jail, than not to have aided these poor, noble creatures.' There was loud applause after this remark, and Mr. Chaplin's hand was shaken, publicly, by Mayor Hovey, who was in the movement now, body, soul and britches.

Mr. Frederick Douglass took the stage, looking like a lion—a Nubian Lion, Dallas Ord said slyly—with his bush of black woolly hair, his lordly dark features and his magnificent voice. Things went better while he was speaking. He'd been all over the country, the audience whispered from row to row; he'd been to England to make converts and raise money, and the lords and ladies had made a great pet of him, even though he was a Negro. He'd traveled all over America—not the South, of course, where they offered a reward for him, dead or alive—preaching and exhorting for Abolition. He'd debated against Captain Rynders and carried the meeting into a frenzy of excitement with his famous question: "Am I a man?" Rynders was completely routed, and Douglass became a hero to the Abolitionists. He had also—and this caused some feeling amongst the brethren—broken sharply with Garrison and the Disunionists, to take his stand with old Ga't Smith who believed in political reform. It was said that Douglass ran a station on the Underground, in Rochester.

"I'm a Peace Man," he was saying in his rich voice. "I believe in peace. I want peace. But I believe we ought to say to the slaveholders in the South: 'Gentlemen—'" his voice underscored the irony of his words—"'Gentlemen, we fear for you. We are obliged to warn you that you will risk bodily danger, if you try to come and capture fugitive slaves in this state!'"

The crowd in the room roared approval. "Amen . . . hallelujah! Go it, Douglass . . . we'll take care of the—" The last word of this threat was lost in the general uproar, fortunately. Most of the audience were churchgoers. But you couldn't expect men as excited as this to preserve perfect decorum. Even old Gerrit Smith nodded his shaggy head and clapped with the crowd.

Douglass's great voice rose again. "If it were a struggle between a fugitive and a slave catcher, I would strike the manhunter down, with as much composure and thoughtlessness as I would a bloodhound!" The audience was completely carried away.

This kind of talk led to argument. There were Garrisonites in the assembly. Someone shouted, "No union with slaveholders!" And a storm of talk rose, this time from the body of the hall itself. Radicals always had to have their say; it did no good to exclude them from the program. Now they bellowed their opinions. Secede. Let the South go its own way. Let the Constitution go to smash, if it held with evildoing. Let South Carolina nullify, if it wanted to, and Massachusetts and New York would nullify too, rather than belong to the same union with the slaveocracy. There was a great uproar for a few minutes, and it took all Gerrit Smith's power and eloquence to get the meeting back in hand. He believed in constitutional reform, political reform, but not in disunion. Now, however, he was wise enough not to argue the point. The crowd wanted violence. He led it to a more popular subject.

"Resist the slave catchers," he said, whipping up their fury in a safe direction. "Resist them to the last man! It is our duty to peril life, liberty and property in behalf of the fugitive. . . ." This was better. The crowd settled down to listen to the rest of his speech.

I wonder what John is thinking of this, Mahala thought, looking at Palfrey from beneath her eyelashes. I wonder how this seems to a man like him. He doesn't believe what they say. He doesn't feel what they feel. He's angry, she thought, stealing another look at the set frown on Palfrey's face. He thinks these men are crazy. He thinks they're trying to ruin his country. If I weren't here, he'd get up and tell them so, the way he did before. He thinks these men are fools, and he's impatient with fools. He's honest. He thinks that what he feels is right, and that whoever thinks another way is a fool. He could never understand them. He could never understand me. Not even if I told him why I felt this way.

Before her mind's eye she saw a large house standing alone on the slope leading to a river. The windows of the house were closed. The doors were closed. Outside the house, mist drifted up from the flowing water, and with it mingled an acrid odor of gun smoke. Inside the house, as the picture rose in Mahala's mind, a woman with red hair crouched on the floor beside the body of a man. She was holding the man's head on her lap; her arms were clasped around him as though their grasp could hold him with her forever. As though not even death could take him from her.

The man's face was ashen. His eyes were closed, and the lashes lying against his pale cheek looked like the false lashes on a doll's waxen head. From a wound, hastily bandaged with a linen sheet, a great stain of blood reddened and widened on his breast. The spaces between his breaths became long and longer. After a pause that seemed to last forever, there came a last, a final breath like a sigh. After that there were no more. But the red-haired woman—Mahala—sat there, her arms still clasped around the motionless figure, her head still bent to gaze at the white face, her tears falling upon it. She did not stir or make any sound.

Finally, from outside the house, she heard two shots, then a pause and two more shots. At this sound, she looked up, away from the dead man in her arms and toward the window. The sun was just beginning to rise, shining rosy and jocund over the river beyond the house. In its rays, mist rose in twisting spirals from the glassy water. Birds in the trees were beginning to speak of day. A thrush, down beyond the bend in the river, was tuning its lovely liquid water-pipe; a robin, near the house, was chirruping. As the sun rose, the pink of early morning changed to yellow, the palest gold, which shone in long flat rays through the leaves. On the ceiling of the room, a quivering pattern of light painted itself against the plaster, reflecting the quiver of water as the sun fell upon it. Birds called louder now, singing all together in a chorus of pleasure to see the new light, to smell the fresh new day.

Slow words tolled like a passing bell through the mind of the woman who crouched, holding her dead in the silent room. An eye for an eye, a tooth for a tooth, a life for a life. I will repay, saith the Lord. I will stretch forth my hand and make of thee a burnt mountain. My brother, my other self, has been killed, and my lover will pay the debt. Go; go; go, the words drummed in her head. Go and kill. There was one moment, like a piercing light breaking through the darkness of her hatred, when the teachings of childhood broke upon her, and the words in her mind were changed, confused. Thou shalt not kill. No, she cried silently. This is a war we are waging. This is a holy war. To the death. To the last man. Dallas Ord once belonged to the enemy but now he has joined us. He is our man. My man. Martin's man. He will fight for us. He will kill our enemies. Another shot rang out somewhere beyond the house, and Mahala raised her head to listen. In the presence of mine enemies, she thought, staring straight ahead of her.

She did not move, but sat still clasping the body of the dead man. She did not stir until a footstep sounded quietly on the porch outside. The door opened; footsteps came into the room. Framed in the doorway, a dark young man stood, holding a rifle loosely in his left hand. He said, "They got away." He stood quietly, looking down at Mahala and the man she held in her arms. When he spoke again, his voice, soft and whispering, said, "Leave him now, Mahala. You can't do anything more." A hardness came into his tone. "You shouldn't have been in this. I wanted you to go away. I knew this might happen. They were bound they'd kill him."

Suddenly in her mind the bright blankness of pain was clouded with a wild storm of rage. As she looked at the man who had entered, his very features were blurred with the cloud of anger that swam in her brain. Martin is dead, is killed, is lying murdered at my feet, and you have let the murderer escape. You should have avenged his death, but instead, you have let his killers escape. You are as bad as they. You did not love him, or you would have taken blood for blood. You have betrayed him—and me, her wild thoughts raged. You are a traitor, a murderer, a false friend, a false lover. You . . . you . . . Words, frantic and insane, whirled in the red cloud of Mahala's brain. I will avenge my brother upon this traitor, a voice said in the cloud of anger. I will take my revenge upon this treachery.

Slowly, stiffly, like an old woman, Mahala loosed the body of the dead man, laid him gently on the floor and rose to her feet.

The face she raised to answer the newcomer was drawn with anger. When she spoke, her voice trembled with it. "They got away?" she said, echoing his words with such awful bitterness that he winced as though she had struck him in the face.

"They got away?" she said again, making the words an insult by her very tone. "*You* let them get away. *You* let them go—because they were your own people. You could have shot the man who killed my brother. But you let him get away. You told me you believed in our cause. You said you'd give your life for it. You'd give anything. Do anything. And I believed you because I was in love with you. And it was a lie. All lies. You pretended to my father that you were with him. You pretended to Martin—" She cast an anguished glance down at the still figure on the floor, then closed her eyes quickly. Her voice was broken now; tears were streaming down her face, but her words were a knife in the man's side.

"You pretended you were Martin's friend—and now he's dead, because you wouldn't harm one of your southern people. Not even when they had killed Martin," she cried out at him. "You betrayed Martin. You've betrayed father and me. I believed you because I loved you. You said you felt as I did. And it was a lie. I'll never believe you again."

The dark man said harshly, "You're out of your head, Mahala. I know you feel bad about Martin. You aren't responsible for what you say. You don't mean it. You know that I've never betrayed you—or anyone. Unless it's my own kin," he said with a bitterness that matched her own. "You'd better let me take you away somewhere now. You aren't fit to stay here."

"*You* take me away." Mahala's voice was only a whisper. "Do you think I'd ever go with you again? Do you think I'll leave Martin—and go with you? Because you can betray your friends, do you think I'll betray my brother? Do you think—"

While she was speaking the door had opened softly behind her, and in the doorway stood the immense figure of Moses North. His first glance had been at the dead man on the floor. But as

Mahala's words rang wildly in the room, he took a step forward. His hand closed on his daughter's arm.

"Mahala," he said sharply. "Stop this. Stop saying such things. Ord's done all he could do. You've gone out of your head." Then, as she continued to stare at Dallas Ord, he shook her arm roughly. "Mahala! Stop this. You don't know what you're doing."

"I know this," she said in a terrible voice. "Dallas Ord has been my lover and I would have married him. After what he's done, will he still dare to ask me to marry him? If he doesn't dare, I'll know I was right. His hands are covered with Martin's blood as surely as though he had shot him." Her eyes stared, as hard as green glass, at the man before her. Her voice whispered, "And if he does dare to ask me, how will he prove that he's not a traitor?" She held her hands out before her stiffly, palms up, as though she expected to have the answer placed in them. Her eyes never left Ord's face.

Dallas Ord met her gaze. He said slowly, "I say now that I *will* marry you—but not until I've proved you're wrong. Not until there's no doubt left anywhere. In you, or in your father, or in anyone." At the slight motion of her hand, he saw that she had shrunk away from him, and so he said, "If you think I have Martin's blood on my hands, I promise that I'll never touch you until that blood is wiped out."

Moses North said quickly, "Dal—that isn't so. Mahala's out of her head. You mustn't pay any attention to what she says. She doesn't mean this. You mustn't take it this way." His arm was supporting his daughter now, for she seemed to have broken suddenly, like a mechanical figure that has run down. Her father gathered her up and held her lightly and easily, as a grown man carries a child. Across her motionless body he spoke to Dallas Ord. "She and Martin were twins, Dal," he said, and his voice sounded like the voice of an old man. "Twins are closer than other folks. Right now, it's almost as though she'd been killed, too. You can't blame her."

Ord bowed his head. "I don't blame her," he said wearily. "I know she's out of her head. She'll be all right again after a while. But I meant what I said. I've got to prove to her—and to you—that I'm not a coward or a traitor. Tell her that when she comes to. I'm going now."

Oh, Dal, Mahala thought now, her mind going back to that terrible memory, so that she could see nothing in the meeting room except the slender figure of Dallas Ord sitting beside her. Oh, Dal, why did I say those things? Why did you believe I meant them? Why couldn't you understand that I was crazy when I said them? That Martin's death had shaken me out of my mind? I've told you a thousand times since then that I know you aren't a traitor. But you won't believe me. You won't forgive me for what a crazy woman said to you. You won't marry me. You won't let me touch you. You won't understand, or believe a word I say to you. All you'll do is go on working, running into every kind of danger you can find, trying to get yourself killed to prove to me what I never doubted—except for that awful morning when I saw Martin die. Why did it happen? How can I ever undo it? How can I tell if you still love me and want me to wait for you? Perhaps you want me to forget you and let you go. Perhaps you want me to marry John Palfrey.

At her side, Dallas Ord stirred and looked at her, as though he could hear the unspoken words in her mind. Softly he said, "You aren't keeping your mind on the cause, Mahala. You mustn't miss a word."

If any violence had been planned, any attempt to make a demonstration before the visiting celebrities, the worthies of the Anti-Slavery Convention must have abandoned it. Major Burnet and his allies were disappointed, and inclined to the opinion that their presence at the meeting—they had turned out in force, at Palfrey's suggestion—had scotched it. Whatever the reason, nothing exciting occurred, during the meeting or afterwards. The Patriots stalked out of Market Hall, commenting loudly on the foolishness of the whole affair, and the Vigilantes were left to compliment each other upon the excellence of their own speeches.

Palfrey, who was feeling restless and dissatisfied with the whole evening, walked back to the Old Lib with Mahala, her father and Dallas Ord. It hadn't been any good, he was thinking, as he paced beside Mahala through the snowy streets. It had been a bad evening; bad from the minute Dallas Ord stepped into Mahala's room before supper. It was always bad when Ord was there. You couldn't put your finger on what it was Ord did or said to make it bad. He was elaborately polite—too polite, Palfrey thought, kicking a lump of snow from the path—he was smooth and courteous. But he was always laughing, as though everything amused him in some private way. Half the things he said seemed to have a private meaning; seemed intended to convey a private message to Mahala. And she seemed to be answering him, too. She would get mad, for no reason Palfrey could understand, and fairly snap at Ord when she answered him. And that amused him more than ever.

Before Ord came—that moment when Palfrey kissed her, told her what he felt, what he wanted—Mahala was warm and alive to him. She tried to refuse him, but he hadn't let her. He'd never let her refuse him, he said to himself, taking her arm to guide her across the canal bridge. And now, at least, she knew in so many words how he felt toward her. How Ord felt, Palfrey didn't care. Mahala had once said, in that strange way as though wincing from a blow, that Ord was her friend. But that was a long while ago, when Palfrey had first known her. That did not matter now. Ord could remain her friend. What Palfrey wanted was more than friendship. He would show her that there was no social difference, or whatever made her say that she was not meant for him. I'll make her forget that, Palfrey thought, as the Old Lib came into view, with its sagging veranda banked with snow, its weathered sides, its comfortable old shabbiness. I'll take her to meet people. I'll show her another kind of life. I'll make her see that she *is* meant for me.

At the door of the tavern, North said politely, "Won't you come in, John, and sit with us for a while? It's not late. We might have a little glass of something, to celebrate the wanderer's return." He slapped Ord jovially on the back.

Palfrey looked at Mahala, but she had gone up the steps and was standing with her hand already on the latch, leaning against the frame of the door, too tired to stand alone. She did not look at him, nor add her invitation to her father's. She's worn out, Palfrey tried to assure himself. If she felt well, she'd want me to come in. She always asks me to come. But if tonight she wants to see Ord alone? This thought stabbed him so hard that he heard himself speaking in a voice he did not recognize. What he said came from some depth in his mind which he had refused to look into since this afternoon. Now, like a genie rising from its bottle, the words issued from his lips without having shaped themselves beforehand in his brain. "I'm afraid I can't stop, tonight. I'm told that our men have located the party of fugitives we heard about. We can't afford to let them slip through our hands. We've heard that some white men here in Syracuse are helping them to escape. I've got to do something about it."

Why had he said that? he wondered, watching Mahala's face. Why had some devil in his brain known that it would touch her? This afternoon he had felt an instant's suspicion, but he had only suspected that perhaps Moses North was trafficking with Loguen and May, as an agent. Now, what did he suspect? Ord, perhaps? Was that his weapon against Mahala's indifference? Or could it be that he actually suspected her of being associated with them? He would have given everything he owned to take those words back. He would have given still more to have throttled the instinct that made him speak. But he could not help himself; the words had to be said. As he watched her, Mahala turned to him, her weariness forgotten, a look of cool amusement on her face.

"Mercy, we mustn't keep you if you're going to do anything like that." She looked down smiling, tantalizing, and Palfrey returned her look with all the force of his being. She must see it. He was a man. He'd fight them all; fight her, too, if he had to, to get her away from this thing.

Ord was mounting the steps with his graceful, lounging gait. He said, "Men must work and women must weep. That's the way it always goes. Perhaps Mr. Palfrey'll come back tomorrow and celebrate, after he's captured the evil-doers. I'd be honored," he said, bowing to Palfrey. "Please make my compliments to Major Burnet and tell him I'd like to help him, too."

With an effort, Palfrey tore his eyes away from Mahala and answered Ord. "Thank you. I'll hope to see you again." To Mahala he said, "I'm sure Mahala understands why I can't accept tonight." Once more his eyes fairly pierced her. "I'll call tomorrow, if I may."

She can't be in it, he said to himself as he walked rapidly down the street. It's impossible. If her father's involved—or Ord, his demon said for him—she'd naturally cover up for them. But that's all the more reason why I've got to get her out of this place. It's dangerous. It's horrible, to have her touch this thing. It can't be true. It isn't true. How do I know that North is in it, or Dallas Ord? Ord's a Virginian, a slaveowner. He'd be the last man to want to run fugitives. No southern man would sympathize with such a thing. But some of them do, the demon whispered. Some of them have worked for the Underground, or it wouldn't be running today. Some Southerners are against slavery, just as some Northerners are for it. I'm a Northerner, he thought, frowning. I'm not actually in favor of slavery. I think it will be abolished sometime, peacefully, when we're ready for it. But right now I'm fighting to protect it. I won't let them ruin the country over it. It's no stranger, in a way, that Ord should fight against it than that I should fight for it.

And Moses North. The old man was from Ohio, and Ohio was noted and infamous for its hundreds of stations on the Underground. Every year thousands of Negroes escaped across that state to Canada, with white men to help them. North might have been one of those, come to Syracuse to work in a new place. And his daughter with him. But there was no proof of it, Palfrey thought in agony. I've got no reason to suspect this. I only suspect because I'm jealous of Ord. If it weren't for him, I'd never have dreamed of it. It isn't true, he said to himself again, tramping up to the Major's door. It isn't true. Or if it is, no one must get wind of it until I've taken Mahala away from them. Then, by God, if it's proved true I'll shut up the place, myself. There'll be one less station on the Underground Railroad.

"He knows," Dallas Ord's voice said, behind her. "There was no mistaking it, just now. And he wants you to know that he knows. What are you going to do about it, Mahala?"

Mahala walked slowly over to the stove and stood looking down at it, as though somewhere on the embossed black panels she might read the answer to his question. Slowly still, she began to strip off her gloves. She could hear Ord moving in the room behind her, closing the door, throwing off his greatcoat, moving a chair nearer the heat. She waited for him to go on speaking.

Ord said, "He's going to make trouble, Mahala." It was as definite as that. He was saying that the trouble was her affair; that John Palfrey was her affair. Perhaps, that she was to blame for it.

"I can't help it," she said at last. She would not talk to Dal about John Palfrey, she thought with anger. This is impossible. I don't know what I want. I don't know what to do.

Ord's hands lifted the cloak from her shoulders and laid it aside. His hand on her arm guided her to a chair. "You're drifting, my dear," he said in his old, taunting manner. "I never saw you so undecided before. Can it be that our handsome young politician has won you over?"

The anger she had been keeping barely in leash leapt out. "I'm tired of having you make fun of John Palfrey," she said furiously. "You tease me about him all the time. You make fun of him before his face, if he only knew it. You pretend to be nice to him, and make him think you're a sympathizer with his side. You're trying to make a fool of him. I'm tired of it." Her eyes blazed at Ord. "I won't let you go on. It's not decent."

The faint, characteristic half-smile died out of Ord's face, leaving it drawn, tired, white. He sat down, resting his elbows on the table, supporting his face in his hands, unutterably weary.

"I'm offered a choice," he said, not looking at her but staring down at the polished mahogany before him and speaking carefully as though he was reading from a speech. "I can do one of two things, in the circumstances. I can declare myself. I can be rude to Palfrey, let him see I don't like him; let him see I'm opposed to his politics; let him see I don't want him to come near you. In that case, I'd lose all use for our work, because Palfrey'd know what I was doing, after a while certainly. We'd be enemies; we might even fight. And if he knew that I was a slave-runner, he'd know pretty soon that you and Moses were, too. And that would end your usefulness. That would be the result of one way of acting. On the other hand, I can treat him the way I do now. I'm polite enough not to arouse his suspicions. If I'm smart, I may be able to keep in with the Burnet crowd and learn something about their activities which would be useful. Because I'm fairly civil to Palfrey, he can't make a fuss about me without betraying the fact that he's merely jealous over you. That's an advantage. And because I'm polite, he can't keep me from going along when he wants to see you. And that's an advantage, too." He looked at Mahala, his eyes as black as jet.

Mahala said bitterly, "I thought you just said he suspected us and wanted us to know it. If that's true, what difference will it make how you treat him?"

Ord laughed, without mirth. "I didn't say he suspected. I said he knew. He's got no reason, no evidence, nothing to go on. Therefore, because he also knows he's jealous, he won't say anything or do anything about it. It's just an instinct that will bother him and devil him, but he won't dare to trust it because there's no proof. And he won't do anything to hurt you because he's in love with you."

"You've got no proof of that." Mahala looked down at her hands. "That's just something *you* know—in the same way. It might not be true, in either case."

"I don't need proof." Ord wore the look that Palfrey would have called dangerous. He said in his soft voice, "No one has to tell me how you feel, Mahala, or how anyone feels toward you. I always know. I always will know—because I know how I feel, myself. And I know what to do about it." His voice was no more than a whisper. "He isn't going to have you, Mahala. You belong to someone else."

Suddenly, as though he had touched a brand to a pile of straw, Mahala was on fire with anger. "I belong to no one. No one. I could have belonged to you—but you wouldn't have me. Now, if this man wants me, that's my affair." They had both risen and she was facing Ord; her eyes, wide and green as beryl, were level with his, her face flushed, her hands clenched against her breasts.

Ord said without raising his voice, "No. That's *my* affair. And I say he'll never have you." He reached forward and took Mahala's wrist, drawing her close to him, holding her there while he spoke. "Have you forgotten about us, Mahala? Have you forgotten who we are? Have you forgotten what we've got to do? This afternoon, when you knew that twenty starved, sick Negroes were hiding in a snowbank, wasn't that your affair? Do you think you can grow soft and weak and forget what you're pledged to do? Do you think I can? Do you think," he said fiercely, "that I'll let you forget?"

Mahala was trying to draw away from him. "Let me go," she cried out to him, as though he was hurting her. "You don't have to remind me. I don't forget things. I did what I had to do this afternoon. But that's no reason why I should mistreat John Palfrey. He doesn't care what I do. He only wants me."

Ord looked at her sardonically. "You think that if he knew—really knew—that you were running a station on the Underground, he'd let you go on?" He looked at her accusingly. "Do you think he'd marry you if he knew you were a Black Abolitionist?"

For a time Mahala did not answer. Restless, she went over to the window and stood staring with absorption at the panes of glass. On this cold night, frost had formed over every pane, so that only a small round space of clear glass was left in the center of each. Through this narrowing peephole, the city lay black and silent beyond her. Somewhere, in a house on one of those dark streets, John Palfrey was, perhaps, asleep. Or perhaps he was peering through the rimed glass of his own window, looking north toward the Canal and the house she lived in. He might be thinking of her, remembering the words he had spoken to her that afternoon. Unconsciously, Mahala sighed. "He'd marry me if I'd have him," she said, speaking out of a dream. "He wouldn't care what I'd done. He might not even care what I believed. He'd only care if I loved him."

For the first time, Dallas Ord was shaken from his own control. "Don't talk like that." His voice was rough with anger. "You're being a fool, and you know it. This man may have caught your fancy for a moment because he's new, and he's crazy over you. But you could never love him. You could never marry him. If you did, you'd leave him in a week, and come back to me. There's no one else for you, Mahala, and you know it. There's nothing else you can do, but what you are doing. It's in your blood—and I'm in your blood. You can't ever get away."

"I *can* get away." Mahala matched his anger with her own. "You only want to control me. You only want to keep other men away from me. You don't want me for yourself. You only think of what you've got to do. That's all you really love. But I'm a woman," she said passionately. "It's natural that I should want something for myself. I do want it. I'll take it, if I choose."

As she spoke, the anger seemed to leave Dallas Ord and he was quiet again and smiling. "Ah—but you'll never choose," he said softly. "You think you could do it. You think you could leave me. But you're wrong. Wait and see. Try it and see. And you'll see that I'm right. I won't offer you any of the things Palfrey will offer: marriage, a fine house, money, safety. I'll only offer you danger and pain, and the suffering of a thousand slaves. I'll offer you a life of being hunted and shameful. I won't stay with you or comfort you. But I'll know every atom of you, all the rest of your life. And you'll know me. We're the same person, Mahala. We're one. Nothing can come between us. I'm not afraid of John Palfrey or anyone else."

Mahala hid her face in her hands. "You're cruel," she said and shivered. "Maybe I've had enough of this life. Maybe I'm tired of the fight. Maybe I want to get away from you, after these hard years we've had. I lost my brother in this fight," she said, pleading with him. "I've done his work as I said I would. I've served. Maybe I'm tired. Maybe now I want something else."

"Yes. You're tired," Ord said mildly. "I know how you feel. You think you can change in the twinkling of an eye and be another sort of person. But you can't. You've worked for Marty, but you've worked more for yourself. Because you're like him. You can't see the things we've seen and not give your life for them. And you've belonged to me for five years—and all your life before that. You can't change that, either."

"I've belonged to you—and you won't have me," Mahala cried wildly. "I've done what you said. I've waited for you and worked for you. Like a slave," she cried, laughing hysterically. "But you don't pity me as you do a slave. You won't have me. You won't touch me. You only keep me forever, as though you'd mesmerized me. If you'd take me—take me with you—do you think I'd want to marry John Palfrey?"

Ord did not speak or move. His face grew whiter, if possible, than before. The lines in his face deepened. Mahala suddenly pressed her body against him, slid her arms around his neck. "If I'm yours, prove it," she said. "Kiss me."

For the first time, color came into Ord's face, a dark tide, flushing his cheeks, making him look for a moment more vulnerable than ever before. Then his lips hardened into a line of pure bitterness. Carefully, not to hurt her, he disengaged her arms, moved away from her. When he spoke, it was like a whiplash falling. "Palfrey has kissed you. I don't want your kisses. When I take you, I'll have more than that."

He looked into her face that seemed blind with pain. "I'm

going now," he said. "Tonight. I'd better get away from here. We'll only quarrel if I stay. And if you marry Palfrey while I'm gone"—his voice was suddenly soft and light with his laughter—"I'll come back and take you away from him. It won't do you any good, Mahala," he said, his face alive with his old reckless arrogance. "You can try anything you like, but you can't get away from me." Moving swiftly, lightly, he went to the door and opened it. "I'm going now," he said, smiling at her as though he hadn't a care in the world. "Remember what I say."

The door closed behind him. He was gone. For one moment Mahala moved to run after him. Her lips opened to call. Then she pulled herself up. Staring at the closed door, her shoulders back, her head raised, she was like a statue of defiance. "He's left me," she said aloud. "He's gone away from me. I won't remember. I won't think of him. I'll be free of him." Then the strength seemed to drain away from her; her bones turned to water. Weakly, she groped for support, found a chair and sat down, shuddering. "Judas," she said in a whisper. "Judas."

CHAPTER EIGHT

"It doesn't sound to me like a polite journal for a pure young female to read," said Moses North mildly, leaning back and lighting a segar. "I don't know much about such things, but I've been told that young females were apt to faint if they so much as glanced at such a periodical. Their minds," said Moses, enjoying himself, "are popularly supposed to be so virgin white and fair that I understand they stain indelibly at the slightest touch of anything coarse." He looked at his daughter, grinning like a wicked old cherub.

Mahala turned the page of the newspaper. "As far as I know, you're right," she said, running her eye down a column of blurry type. "They ought to get a better printer. Some of the citizens are going to miss the best parts, if it's always as dirty as this. Shall I read some of it aloud? You might be interested in what it says about the notorious Miss North this week. It's usually pretty savage. I'd like to know who writes it."

"You'd better ask who reads it," Moses said, chuckling. "I'll bet a nickel John Palfrey don't. He'd be around with a horsewhip if he thought they were attacking you. Why don't you tell him?" he asked curiously. "Are you afraid he'll get the idea you aren't quite the proper thing, if he sees how they talk about you?"

Mahala shrugged her shoulders. "He must know it, by this time. Some of his loving friends must have mentioned it. Or his family. This rag goes all over the city to a lot of people who pretend they're shocked by it. I was waiting to see if he'd say anything about it. He hasn't, so far."

"He's probably got the pure female idea about you," her father said, dropping ashes on his vest. "Read it out, a little. I'd like to hear what they've got to offer."

Mahala scanned the page. "The first page has a lot of advertising of things to sell, guns and so on—for suicide, they say. And then a skit of some kind called the Happy Family. I suppose it's about people in town. It's a satire, but it isn't funny if you don't know who they mean. The real point of the paper is to scare people. Things like this: 'Now, John, if your wife caught you down back of the sawmill last Tuesday night, making love to Miss V. D., it would grieve her most to death. But, John, she mistrusts you. Beware, John, we will show you up to the public next week.'" She paused and looked up inquiringly at Moses North.

The old man laughed heartily. "I bet somebody didn't sleep well last night, after he read that. He probably hotfooted it down, the first thing this morning, to pay 'em off and get shut of it. Is it all like that?"

"Some of it." Mahala frowned over the inky print. She read again. "'You had better not be caught with that Dutch widow again, for if you do, old *Santa* will raise h—l with you, you degenerate son of a female dog.'" She turned the page, searching. "Here's the part about me. 'Miss N. wears her shoulders bare down to the edge of decorum. Now you dress a little more chaste, Miss N. Or if you should ever have *a fellow-feeling in your bosom*—don't tell of it.'" She threw down the paper in disgust. "That's vile. I wish John *would* horsewhip them, whoever they are." She was really angry, her face flushed, her eyes light with it.

Old Moses said, "Now, Haley—keep your hair on. You know better than to pay any attention to that sort of offal. It can't do you any harm, because it ain't true. And if it shocks John Palfrey so that he quits you, the sooner you know he's that kind, the better." He began to laugh again. "I expect you think your poor decrepit old father ought to grab for his horsewhip, too."

Mahala said shortly, "It wouldn't hurt you any. You've got so used to thinking about me as if I was really Marty, and a man instead of a woman, that if someone hit me you'd expect me to put up my fists."

Moses roared at this. "You're a caution, Haley." He swung around in his chair to look at her. "Are you really mad about it? Do you really want me to go out seeking whom I may devour?" he asked quaintly. "I'll do it, if you say so. I'm willing to die defending my daughter's honor, if you want it defended. But I thought you were too grown-up to pay any heed to such things."

Mahala said, "I'm not too old to get mad," but the sight of her father's real surprise was too much for her. She was obliged to laugh. "No—I don't want you to go out and kill anyone. You *would* kill them, if you fought with them, you're so big," she said, looking at his great frame. "It's all right, but I hope John Palfrey sees it."

"Hope John Palfrey sees what?" a new voice asked, as the door opened. "Gasberry said you were here, so I came right in." Palfrey stood in the door looking down at them.

Mahala rose to welcome him. How much easier he was now, when he came to them; how much more at home, more genial, more unconstrained. The naturally severe lines of his face seemed less sharp, the expression of his mouth softer, the look in his eyes so much more unguarded. He knows us now, Mahala thought, going to take his hat and greatcoat. He's at home here with us. He's happy here. Perhaps happier than he's ever been. How can I ever make him unhappy again? He's never trusted anyone in his life, in the way of friendship. He's never let down the bars before and loved anyone. Now—how can I bear to betray his new trust? How can I bear to teach him never to love again?

Palfrey was immediately curious about the tag-end of talk he had overheard. "What is it you hope I'll see? Mahala's voice sounded as though she was mad about something. What is it?" His eyes roved around the room, lighted upon the disreputable little journal. Instantly the gaiety left his face. His brows drew together. "The *Bastinado*—you were reading that?"

Mahala made light of it. "Someone sent us a copy. We were

looking it through." She did not say that she had found a mention of herself in it.

John Palfrey picked up the sheet and ran rapidly down the columns. "I haven't seen this one," he said. "I've seen others, and I'm going to make it hot for the people who publish it. It's plain blackmail, and I think we can send somebody to jail for it." He paused abruptly, to read the item he sought. When he raised his face, it was hot with shame. "There's no way I can apologize to you for this, Mahala," he said in his fighting voice. "I'll see that there's never any more like it, and I'll try to have the man punished. But that doesn't make it any less revolting."

Old Moses rumbled into his earth-shaking laughter. "Haley's too sensible to mind, really. She was hopping mad for a minute, just before you came in, and she was egging me on to go and horsewhip the feller that wrote that piece. But then her native good sense," he said, with a droll look at his daughter, "her native delicacy, showed her that it was no more use than plugging rags down a rathole. If they could write that once, they could write another one later, after they'd recovered the use of their arms from my kind attentions. I tell her the thing to do is to give no heed to it. It never pays to defend yourself against that kind of dirt. You only make it look as though there might be something to it, after all."

Palfrey was furiously angry. "You don't need to do anything about it. It's my job. And I'll see that it's done, the first thing tomorrow. There won't be any more *Bastinado*, after I've settled with them."

Suddenly Mahala was filled with remorse. "Don't do anything about it, John," she said, putting out her hand to touch his arm. "Don't get yourself into any trouble about it. Your friends would think it very strange if you touched a matter of this kind. Your family would be pained. I don't really care."

John Palfrey drew his arm away gently. "You'll have to let me do what I think best, Mahala," he said. "There are certain things I must do."

* * *

"This may be the last of the good sleighing," John said, tickling the high-stepping bay with his whiplash. The cutter slid beautifully over packed snow along the Brewerton Plank Road. "You can't depend on March. We often have a thaw and nothing but slush in the roads. Are you sure you're warm enough?"

From her nest of buffalo robes, Mahala assured him that she was. "I'm wrapped up like an Esquimau. I love sleighing," she said like a young girl. "At home, we lived too near the lake to have much cold weather. But I had a colt of my own and a little red cutter, and I used to love it."

Palfrey looked at her with curiosity. "You've never told me much about your home in Ohio," he suggested. "Did you have a hotel there?"

"No." Mahala's childish enthusiasm vanished. "We had a house."

Palfrey wouldn't give up. "What did your father do? What did you do? I wish you'd tell me about it."

Mahala's tone was forbidding. "I've told you all that's important. I did nothing, except what any woman does, at home. I kept house for my father—and my brother." She turned her face away quickly, so that Palfrey couldn't see it.

He said, "I didn't know you had a brother. Where is he now?"

"He's dead," Mahala said. "I don't want to talk about it. If you need a reference for my character, you'd better give me up and find a girl you know all about. I've told you that before."

Palfrey pulled the horse to a walk and reached over to find Mahala's hand under the fur robe. "Don't be angry," he said. "I know I say the wrong thing, sometimes. I don't mean to. It's only because I can't help wanting to know everything that concerns you. I don't care about the past. You could have taken in washings, and I wouldn't care."

"Maybe I did." Mahala couldn't help laughing. "Oh, it's all crazy, John. You've no business with me. I've told you so, a thousand times. You're getting yourself talked about. You're hurting your family and shocking your friends. You think you can make people accept me. You think you can push me down their throats and make them forget about the Old Lib. But it's no good. It's hopeless. I'll never marry you."

John said gravely, "I didn't hear what you said. I'll never hear you until you say yes. I don't care what anyone thinks or says. If my family disapproves of my choice, I'm sorry, but it won't make any difference. I know this is hard for you, Mahala—" he was pleading with her now—"I know how proud you are and how it galls you to have these people be rude to you. But they'll get over it. As soon as they really know you, they'll act differently. You'll see, tonight. Mrs. Bensted was delighted to have me bring you on this sleigh ride. You'll get to know people and then everything will be all right."

Mahala did not answer immediately. I'm a fool, she was thinking, her eyes fastened on the moon-painted snow slipping past them. I'm a fool and a cheat. I won't tell John what I am— what father is. He thinks he doesn't care, because the worst he can imagine is that we were poor, not fashionable. Perhaps not educated. He may even think I've been fast. Everyone else in this town thinks so. And he could even stand that. But if he really knew. Her thoughts turned black. If he knew what I'm doing, what I believe. If he knew about Dal. That's the wrong thing, she thought in great pain. That's my sin. I'm trying to get away from Dal, after all these years, because he hurts me. He won't give in to me. And I won't give in to him. I'm running away from Dal, her honest mind said. I'm pretending that it would be easy enough to get free, forget what I believe, give it all up and be like any other woman. John loves me. He'd make me happy and safe. There would be no more fighting, no more struggle. I'm tired of being an outcast, she thought, a foolish rebellion rising in her mind. I'm tired of being alone, of having no friends, no pleasure, no love. I want to live like other women. I'm tired of being a man. Marty, she cried out silently to her brother, Marty, let me go. Give me back my promise. Let me marry John Palfrey and be a woman again.

Palfrey's voice brought her back from the darkness. "Do I make you unhappy, Mahala?" he asked so simply that it broke her heart.

"No—never. Not you. If I'm unhappy, it's my own fault. And if you're unhappy, it will be my own fault, too." How can I ever hurt him, she thought with passionate remorse. He's so strong, so proud. It is far worse to hurt a strong man than a weak one. Far more dangerous, more damaging, because he is not used to pain. If John knew about me he would be humiliated, and I should have done this to him. If—when the time came—he would only be angry and fight back. That could be borne. But why must it be borne? she asked herself, as the temptation took her. Why should I not marry him and make him happy?

Bells jangled ahead of them, and a light showed from the windows of a rambling house. "There's the tavern," Palfrey said, pointing with his whip. "This is Brewerton. The lake's over yonder. We often come here for parties." The horse's hooves clopped hollowly over a bare patch on the plank road. Up ahead of them, a half dozen rigs were drawn up before the old hotel. Men and girls were getting out of the sleighs, with a great to-do of laughing and screaming and shouting. A man opened the door and stood outlined against the warm light within while he called out to the new arrivals. Moonlight was bright enough to see by, but someone came out on the porch with a lamp in his hand. Palfrey leaped out to hitch his horse, and a friend cried, "Who is it? Watt Duncan? No—John Palfrey. Hurry up and come in. It's cold enough to freeze the tail off a brass monkey."

Palfrey said, "We'll be there in a minute," and ran around to help Mahala unwind herself from her mountain of fur. "They're all here," he said, and she could see he was excited. He took her arm with a special protectiveness as he led her into the old tavern. Under the light, the expression on his face was wary. He's waiting for them, Mahala thought, smiling grimly. He's anxious to have them take to me. But if they don't, he's ready to fight them all.

A stout woman in a bright green dress hastened forward to meet them. "It's a mercy you got here," she said nervously. "You're the last ones. I was afraid you'd tipped over in a drift." She looked at Mahala with open curiosity. "I'm pleased to meet you, Miss North," she said and held out her hand doubtfully, as though she was afraid Mahala might injure it. "We've heard lots about you from John. My boys say he can't talk about anything else." She was laboring hard to be hospitable. "We've heard so much about you that nothing would do but you must come to our little party." She giggled out of sheer embarrassment. "I hope you'll make yourself at home."

Mahala felt sorry for her. "Thank you. It's very kind of you to ask me," was all she said. It was cruel to keep this nice old thing in such distress. Across the room, a bevy of girls were whispering and giggling at a great rate. Occasionally one of them stole a glance in the direction of John Palfrey and his Unknown.

Mrs. Bensted remembered her duties. "You come along and lay off your wraps," she said, bustling down a dark passageway to a lighted room at the end. "You can primp here." She indicated a mirror, and settled herself to miss no detail, while Mahala slipped off her cloak and settled her furbelows.

Dove-gray dress, Mrs. Bensted could report later; only cashmere, my love, nothing elegant about it, really. High corsage, as plain as a Quaker's, except for some velvet bands. The bodice long and pointed—her waist is very small, for anyone as tall as that. Skirt full, made with a deep flounce, and training a little. The *only* thing that was in the *least* elegant, one could fairly hear Mrs. Bensted report, was the fur; chinchilla, my dear, a huge muff, and a tippet around her shoulders. I suppose it was *stylish*— but a lot of our girls had fancier dresses; fringe and bugles, and ruchings and puffings. And all that red hair, so loud, if I must say so, under a gray velvet bonnet and veil.

Mahala didn't have red hair for nothing. It took less than an hour or even a half hour to see how things would go. When she and John appeared in the bare old assembly room a few of the couples approached, the girls evidently reluctant, the men with a do-or-die look about them, bound to stand by a friend in his hour of need. After the briefest murmur of civilities, they retreated, and John talked to Mahala with feverish attention. Later, when old Harvey Bennett began to play his fiddle and the squares formed for a dance, Mahala went forward dutifully with John, and they danced out the set, but it was not a pleasure. Mahala danced with a face like a marble angel, showing nothing. John did not trouble to conceal his anger.

That's enough, Mahala thought recklessly. The women have decided to freeze me. I've nothing to lose if I make them hate me more. And there is always a way to do that. In the next hour she had polked with every presentable man in the room, sat on the dusty stairs with three of them, had supper with a perfect crowd. John, to whom she returned frequently enough to make it plain to him and to all the others that he was the preferred partner, was suddenly in high spirits, and poor Mrs. Bensted scarcely knew what to do with a party that was going wrong.

In the dressing room, a handful of young ladies could be found at any minute, saying that of course they didn't *care,* but it was a pity to see John Palfrey make a fool of himself. And, of course, it meant nothing to *them,* but Davey Hollister and Myron Blane were acting like calves, the way they looked at that woman, tagging her around. And that anyone could *tell,* just to look at her, that Miss North was—well—just what they'd heard all winter.

Mrs. Bensted was ready to cry, with her own daughter as cross as two sticks, and her four sons acting as though they were possessed, chasing after John Palfrey's new girl. She told old Harvey to stop fiddling at twelve o'clock, although the lake parties usually lasted much later, and she had everyone bundled up and out of the place soon afterwards. There would be plenty to talk about in the morning.

Oyster suppers were quite the thing. Mrs. Adelbert Strever requests the pleasure of Mr. John Palfrey's company. John Palfrey tore the invitation up and then decided to go. After that sleigh ride, he wanted them to see that he was quite untouched by their attitude. He'd refuse the next one, which would say plainly that he could take them or leave them. Further, he might observe how the elite was prepared to feel about him. He sent a polite acceptance, and his family was relieved to think that perhaps John had learned a lesson—the girls had given a minute account of the Brewerton fiasco—and was willing to forget that woman and behave properly again.

"Boys will sow their wild oats," Mrs. Bensted said magnanimously to Mrs. Palfrey, settling herself before a heaped plate of scalloped oysters with all the trimmings. She took a mouthful and said, "Lovely oysters. What I mean is, my dear, John will get over it. You wait and see. My Oren took a terrible fancy to an Irish girl from over in Salina. Mercy!" She shook her head so that the rosebuds on her headdress wagged violently. "I was never so upset in my life. I didn't know *what* I'd do, and neither did Mr. Bensted. We talked to Oren, and it was so much wind blowing, for all the good it did. He acted like he was possessed about her. And then, all of a sudden, he got tired of her and we never heard another thing about it."

Mrs. Palfrey tucked her napkin into the blooming front of her steel-gray taffeta. "Goodness knows I hope you're right. Mr. Palfrey has talked to John and *talked* to him. But John won't hear a word against her. He acted real stiff with his father. If he's going to get over it, I wish he'd hurry up. It's making me so nervous I don't know where I'm at. It's the disgrace of it," poor Mrs. Palfrey wailed, her eyes filling with tears. "We've never had anything like this in the family. What will our friends think? I declare to you, Jessie, I'm ashamed to go out in company. I keep thinking what folks are saying about us. I can't hardly hold my head up."

Mrs. Bensted made every effort to comfort her. "Most folks just pity you, Emma. They know what you're going through. Of course, it's only natural that some of the girls got mad about it.

If you'd *seen* the way that woman acted with the men at our dance—" She shook her head and gave up trying to describe it further. "It was a caution. It wasn't any time at all before she'd begun flirting with the boys until they were just bewitched over her. They went right off and left all the nice girls they'd known all their lives, and trailed around after *her* as though they didn't have good sense. And you couldn't blame the girls for feeling it. My Ethel's practically engaged to Minot Corney, and he never came near her for a solid hour. Sat out on the stairs with this new girl, laughing and talking. You can bet that Ethel gave him fits for it, when he did come back. Lots of the girls weren't speaking to their beaux by the time we were ready to come home. And there was nothing I could do."

Mrs. Palfrey wiped her eyes delicately on the corner of her napkin. "It's wicked," she said through her tears. "I'm just sick about it. And it's not the least bit like John. He's always been so good before."

In another corner of the room, Ethel was airing her opinion. "I think it's perfectly *impudent* of him to come around tonight, as though nothing had happened," she said, casting an indignant glance at John Palfrey across the room. "It's a wonder he didn't bring his fine lady right here, to insult us again. But if he thinks I'm going to speak to him after what happened the other night, he's grandly mistaken." She drew herself up to look as firm as Gibraltar.

There was a difference of opinion about this. Little Annabelle Moss said she thought they ought to save him from such a horrid fate. "He's so handsome—and he's going to ruin himself. *I* think that if we were to make a fuss over him and let him see how *nice* girls act, after the kind of person he's been with, it might be a lesson to him."

Ethel snorted. "You've always been soft on John Palfrey. And you weren't at the sleigh ride, so you didn't see how gone he was on that red-haired woman. He acted right-down foolish about her.

And so did a lot of the other boys. I'll tell you, I gave Minot Hail Columbia for what he did. He won't forget it in a hurry."

Annabelle looked longingly at John Palfrey. "I don't see what she does to make all the boys so stuck on her," she said mournfully. "I've only seen her once, on the street, but I didn't think she was so good-looking. She looked sort of fast to me. All that red hair," she said, pushing back her own shower of yellow curls. "I thought she was queer, myself."

Francelia Palfrey agreed with her. "He's my own brother, but I think he's awful to take up with such a person. I was ready to slap him out at Brewerton, but he never let me get anywheres near him. I was mortified to *death*," she said bitterly. "I could have sunk through the floor when he came in with her and everybody turned to look. I don't blame anybody for not speaking to him. I won't speak to him myself." She tossed her head proudly. "He's disgracing the family, and I'm not ashamed to say so. I wouldn't blame you girls if you were to stop speaking to *me*, because he's my brother."

At this, all the other girls broke into a chorus of denial. "Goodness knows, it's not your fault. I guess you can't help it, what your brother does. We're just sorry for you."

In a group gathered around the decanters at the end of the collation table, Major Burnet was amused at the commotion his young friend Palfrey was causing. "I guess you've ruffled the dovecotes, as they tell about, John," he said, grinning and nodding his head in the direction of the ladies. "It's more like you'd robbed somebody's hen-roost, though. I didn't know you were such a devil with the ladies."

John said, "I'd rather not discuss it, Major. I fail to see why my private affairs are of so much interest to the people of this town." His face was grim.

Major Burnet agreed soothingly. "Sure, sure. It's just that folks like to talk. They can't help it. In a slow town like this, you've done 'em a real favor to give 'em something to chew about. They haven't had this much fun since Jackson was elected."

"If all this . . . comment destroys my usefulness for you, I'd be glad to resign," Palfrey said stiffly. "I wouldn't want public opinion to be turned against you on my account."

Major Burnet poured himself another glass of Madeira and sipped it with appreciation. "Old Strever's done us proud with his drinks," he said easily. "Lord, no, John. It don't bother me any, what folks say about you. I don't care. Not for these folks, anyhow. They don't add up enough votes to wad a gun. They're toney; they think they're the whole town, but they don't cut any ice politically, you might say. And the boys out on the Point don't give a damn who you're sweet on. Every man to his taste, as the old lady said when she kissed the cow."

Mr. Noxon slapped John on the back. "They'll get over it," he said. "Next week they'll have something new to talk about. You just tend to your knitting, and help us run the Abolitionists out of town, and these folks here will forget they ever said a word against you. The men won't say much, I'll bet you. A man don't look behind the door unless he's stood there himself."

I'd better not go straight up there, Mahala thought, sailing along Salina Street with her chin up, as two heavily plushed ladies glared at her in passing. Everybody's watching me, since that party. I wasn't as smart as I thought, to rile them up so. It hampers my movements when I've got business to do.

She picked her way across the icy flagstones in front of the Dillaye Building and reached the safer brick paving of the next block. No one will be curious if I'm merely doing a little shopping here and there, she decided. Women were always poking about in the shops, buying a little of this and a little of that. She saw the neat Palfrey carriage drawing up before the bank Arcade and hurried past it. There was a bookshop just across the railroad tracks and she turned in rapidly, asking at random for a remembered title. No, Mr. Stoddard was sorry, he said with an admiring look. He hadn't heard of *Genevieve, or The History of a Servant Girl*. It must be the newest thing, and they were apt to be a little slow getting the new books in Syracuse. But he would send for it, with the greatest of pleasure. Mahala thanked him and said it was not important. She'd heard it was a pretty thing. She promised to stop in again and look over Mr. Stoddard's stock when she had more time.

The carriage was still there, and two gentlemen were conversing with the Palfrey girls, vivacious and pretty in their sealskin jackets. Mahala crossed the street, feeling at least four pairs of eyes upon her back. Livingston & Mitchell's wasn't the most fashionable dry-goods store, but it was handy at the moment. She fussed over a selection of cologne water, keeping her eye peeled for movement in the street. Presently the young ladies alighted, parted from their admirers and went into the Arcade. Mahala rapidly selected a bottle of *esprit* of *mignonette*, had it wrapped, and emerged, carrying the parcel plainly in view.

Mr. Pierce's China Hall was only a few doors above, and there was nothing strange in her need for a spoon holder or a pin tray or an extra dozen tumblers for the hotel. The doorway leading to the stairs was inside, luckily, and no one saw her go up quickly and enter O'Reilly's Telegraph Line office. Or if they had seen her, and if Mr. O'Reilly should tell of her visit, there was nothing out of the way in the message she sent to Mrs. Eliza White in Buffalo: "Forwarding a package of woolen goods by five o'clock train this morning. Valuable. Please write if it reaches you safely." Mr. O'Reilly wrote down the message carefully and then began, with a great flourish, to tap it off on his new machine.

Mahala paid him and went down the stairs. In case anyone had seen her turn in at China Hall, she entered the store and bought the largest thing she could see on the shelves—a queen's ware soup tureen. It made a great bundle, but she insisted on carrying it home. People on the street might stare at the queer Miss North, lugging a great thing like that, but they would not suppose that she had another reason for her visit to China Hall.

And it was important that that train be met promptly in Buffalo. The Whites were very reliable.

When John Palfrey came running down from his office and insisted upon carrying the tureen, Mahala did feel a pang of guilt. His law offices were just across the street, and he must have seen her enter and leave. Now, not knowing that he had been tricked, he was braving the eyes of the village to help her. She sighed and said, "You oughtn't to do this, John. Everybody's staring at you. It will be all over town in five minutes. You ought to be more discreet."

Palfrey tucked the unwieldy parcel under his arm and guided her through the melting snow of Clinton Square. "I don't care what the people say. You know that. And you can't carry this heavy thing home alone. You should have brought Gasberry along with you."

Mahala sighed again. If she hadn't cared about Palfrey, everything would have been all right. Her father was in high feather about getting his fugitive off under the very eyes of Burnet's watchers, and Dr. May and his committee were loud in praise of their new stationkeepers. Dal would laugh at her remorse, and tell her she was getting soft. But there was John to think of. There was John—and there was Dal. And there was the terrible pressure of keeping the stream of hungry, terrified Negroes passing safely through this dangerous territory to Canada. I want too many things, she thought. I care for too many things.

Moses North was standing by the window of Mahala's sitting room, holding a letter in his hand. He turned when she entered, all breathless and rosy from the March air outside. Freshness and coolness seemed to enter the warm room with her, as though the wind had got tangled in her floating green veil. She looked happy today, Moses North thought, watching her bright face; as though this spring wind had blown away all the dangers and difficulties; as though she was a young girl again, excited and gay and ready for anything. It's not often I see her happy, her father thought. I've taken away her girlhood and everything carefree and foolish. I've made her into a man, and a strong man. But I've killed something—or I thought so. Is Palfrey giving her back what I've taken? Will she go with him, in the end, and find what she's lost? The stiff note paper crackled in his hand as he turned. He looked down at it, frowning.

Mahala was slipping off her cloak now, pulling off the little bonnet with its green veil, dropping her gloves and furs carelessly on a chair as she came forward to warm her hands at the fire. "It's blustery out," she said, smiling at her father. "The wind's enough to take your breath. But we had a fine ride, out the plank road along the lake toward Liverpool." The memory of pleasure still occupied her mind so that even now she did not scent the worry in this room, the bad news, the danger, the anxiety that seemed to Moses North to fill it like smoke. When her father did not respond immediately, she looked up in surprise and, seeing the letter for the first time, asked, "What is it? Who is the letter from?" Not even yet did she feel the danger.

Old Moses drew a deep breath. "It's from Dal, Mahala," he said, trying to speak so that the words would come to her easily. "He's in trouble. We've got to do something for him."

Happiness and youth died in her face. In an instant the worn, wary look took its place, the look of steeled endurance, of readiness, of tense apprehension. "Tell me," she said, and reached out her hand to take the letter.

Her father held it away from her. "I'll tell you what he says. He's in prison, Mahala. We've got to get him out, or they may lynch him. He's got into bad trouble."

She was as steady as a rock now. She took the letter from her father's hand and read it swiftly. When she raised her eyes to his, he could see fear in them, but behind the fear was rising her old furious anger, the fierce rage that made her fight each time the call came, that made her ready to do anything, take any risk. She said decisively, as though there could be no question about her decision, "I've got to go to him. I've got to get him out. Those devils will hang him without a trial, if they know what he was doing." She bent her head to study the letter again. "He can't say much here, of course, but it sounds as if they weren't perfectly sure about it. They're trying to prove it by some of the Negroes he was running. He's lost them all, of course." She looked at her father. "I've got to go right away," she said. "There isn't a minute to lose. When does the next train leave?"

Old North stirred at last. "I don't know about you going, Haley," he said anxiously. "You're only a girl. It don't do to have a woman running around trying to break a jail. And like as not you couldn't get him out, alone. I think I'd better go, instead."

Mahala said fiercely, "Don't be a fool. You can't go. Too many people know you down there. You've run too many slaves yourself in that country, and you've been caught, too, and only just got away. There's a reward out for you everywhere south of the Line. You couldn't step foot over it without being arrested, and then I'd have to get *you* out, too. I'm the only one that *can* go, and I'm going," she said, her eyes blazing at her father. "Do you think I can stand it to wait and hear, a month later, whether or not Dal Ord was hanged for nigger stealing? It's Dal, father," she said, her voice trembling for the first time. "Dal. He's going to be killed if I don't hurry. I'm going, I tell you. You'd better help me get ready. I'm going tonight, if I have to walk."

Moses North said uncertainly, "I don't want you to take such a risk. There's a lot of danger in it. He's in a country jail, locked in. How are you going to get him out? What are you going to do to help him? If they find out what you're after, they'll jail you along with him."

Mahala said sharply, "They won't find out. There'll be ways to do it. We've got money. I'll buy him off, if I can. I'll take a Negro with me, and he can pump the slaves around there. I'll find a way. You needn't worry about that."

Her father tried a last time. "What will John Palfrey think? If he was to know, he'd have me put in jail right here, for letting you go. I thought you were getting kind of fond of John, Haley," he said, desperately persuasive. "I thought you were kind of thinking of marrying him and giving up this risky business. I'd be willing to have you." He was almost pleading with her. "You're the only child I've got, now Marty's dead. I've let you see a lot of danger, because you were so set on it. But if anything was to happen to you, I'd never forgive myself. And John Palfrey'd never forgive me."

Mahala's face was dead white. "Don't talk to me about John Palfrey. What he'd think about this doesn't matter. I've got to go and get Dal. I've got to get Dal." Her voice broke over the words. "I've been trying to forget Dal, and now they may kill him. Don't waste any more time, father," she said, and it was a command. "We've got to move fast. Send for Gasberry, and find out about the train. I'm going, some way, tonight." She moved toward the door and stopped, her hand on the latch. "When you see John, tell him that a close relative is sick—in trouble—anything you like. I can't stop to think about him tonight."

North heard her light footsteps running along the passageway, away from him.

CHAPTER NINE

Six o'clock in the morning was dark enough to keep fellow passengers on the station platform of Jeffersonville, Ohio, from getting much of a look at the tall young fellow bundled up in a greatcoat, with his black wide-awake hat pulled down over his eyes. They saw him standing in the shadows talking to a Negro servant who was carrying his carpetbag. His manners, they thought, watching the abrupt gesture of a gloved hand, were imperious. The Northerners among them—Ohio was an antislavery region—decided that this was some haughty young blade of a southern planter, going home from college.

An old suit of Martin's, nankeen pantaloons and a fawn-colored coat, a pale-yellow vest of great elegance, fitted Mahala as though it had been made for her. Her hair, cut short, curled up in irrepressible duck-tails over her collar, but that was the fashion for young men. The matter of a youthful beard, which should have been there but was not, would be a danger. The only explanation for that would have to be age; she would have to pose as a spoiled baby—eighteen perhaps would be acceptable—a lad just come into his inheritance. She would have to rant and rave. She had been in college in the North, the story ran, in Hamilton College perhaps. She was sickened by all this low-class talk of equality and slave-freeing. In a rage, she had—or rather, *he* had, this petulant youth—left the school, shaken the dust of the crude and fanatical North from his boots, and come into the aristocratic South to buy a place and live among people who agreed with him. A comic, hotheaded creature, this young Mr. Martin would have to be; green and foolish and headstrong, easy picking for the men who would want to sell him a farm or slaves or horses. That would make him popular at once, make him conspicuous enough to keep wary eyes from watching too closely what his browbeaten Negro servant, Cuffee, might do with his spare time.

Mahala didn't feel like a daring young man, a gay sprig from college, when black Cuffee finally pulled the horse to a stop before a shabby tavern porch that evening. Seen through spring dusk, fifteen miles south of the river in Kentucky, the town of Darby was no more than a huddle of buildings in the midst of farmlands. Cuffee had pointed out the jail-house at the very edge of the village, at the top of a sharp little hill past which a stream ran down a small ravine into the woods. Mahala stared at it, her eyes fastened to the single light it showed through a barred window.

Was Dal there? Was he sitting, perhaps, at this moment, looking at the barred window, listening to the sound of hoofbeats chattering down the road outside? Was he wondering when she'd come? Did he really expect her, or had he given up hope after all this time, thinking that she had forgotten him? In her mind's eye she saw him sitting on a bare cot in his cell; he was leaning forward. For a moment, his head lifted as he listened to the clop-clop of the horse's feet. Then the sound died away into the night, he dropped his dark head down upon his hands, his body slumped hopelessly. No, it was nothing, he would be thinking. No one for me.

I've got to hurry, Mahala thought for the thousandth time. I've got to act quickly. I've got to get him out. Can I go to see him tomorrow? Would it be safe? How can I stay in this town without seeing him, without letting him know that I've come? No, the hard part of her mind said sternly. Tomorrow will not do. The next day will not do. You cannot lose everything by some foolishness. You must follow the plan. That is the only chance for Dal. He must stay there, not knowing that you have come, until the time is ripe. You must do what you have come to do. Be fortunate; be lucky; be clever, or you will not do even that.

The jail was out of sight now, around a bend in the road from the main part of the town. Something to be thankful for, Mahala thought, getting down stiffly from the buggy and crossing the tavern porch. Inside the smoky room, a dozen men turned away from the bar to stare at the newcomer. Now I begin to act, Mahala thought, swaggering across the floor to the bar under their curious eyes. Luckily, I've been in a tavern enough to know how to behave. She returned the stare of the gentlemen with interest, leaned her elbows on the counter and ordered a hot toddy.

In this part of the world, at least, a lordly manner was appreciated. Before she had finished her drink she was deep in conversation with some of the citizens of Darby. If a gentleman wanted to buy a fine plantation, they assured her, this was the place to come. When Cuffee poked his woolly head around the door to announce that he'd stabled the horse and brought the bag inside, young Mr. Martin was setting up drinks for the crowd, and damned his servant heartily for impertinence. His new Kentucky friends were inclined to smile at the boy's grand airs, but they agreed that his politics were sound. They arranged to meet him in the morning and show him the town.

Under ordinary circumstances, it might have taken longer to be accepted by the haughty South. What's your family? Where are you from? Rich or poor; handsome or ill-favored; oafish or elegant? How do you vote? All such questions would have to be given satisfactory answers before a stranger would be taken in by the tribe. But a young man, green as grass, with plenty of money and a hot head? Well—perhaps. Why not? The word went round, from the farmers who had been in the bar, from the overseers, from the town gossips who loved nothing so much as a piece of fresh news. A young tyke, they said, a young squirt, a redheaded boy from up north. But he's got enough sense to vote right—if he's old enough to vote. He's raving mad at the Woolly

Heads up where he comes from. He's so bellyful of talk about this damned abolition that he's picked up and come here to live. He says he won't listen to such rubbish any more; he won't live with such people. He wants to buy a farm—ah, there's the point. He's looking for something, with money in his pockets. The Yancey place; the Stewart place; the Elkins place; invite him to look them over. Ask him to come by and have dinner. Ask him to step in and meet the girls. Ask him to have a drink of old Kentucky whisky.

Before noon, young Mr. Martin from up north had been called upon by a half dozen citizens, and before night he had tasted the smoky liquor, bowed over the young ladies' hands, stuck his long legs under the most highly polished table in all Darby. His manners were well enough, the Darby ladies said; not like a Kentuckian's, of course; not courtly, but what do you expect from a Northerner? He scowled a good deal, and was more interested in what the men said than in the way the girls smiled. He had his mind set on something, the gentlemen agreed. And of course he was young. Not altogether dry behind the ears. And a hot-tempered boy, too, who swore at his servant so that the darky went in fear of him, and he couldn't say enough about the latest outrage of the North against decency and sound government. But he'd learn, everyone said indulgently. He'd pick up southern ways.

One day gone, Mahala thought, shutting the door of her musty room in the tavern that night. One day gone, and I haven't seen Dal; I don't know how he is; I haven't done a thing to get him out. She set the candlestick on the table and sat down wearily to pull off her boots. Men's clothes were a burden and a weariness. Men's ways were hard to learn. She was certainly forgiven much for being young, but there was always danger.

A knock on the door startled her for a moment, but Cuffee's voice made it all right. He sidled into the room and stood holding his cap respectfully. "I's seen those niggers," he said in his soft voice. "I's found out something for you, Miss Haley."

Mahala said quickly, "Don't call me that. Someone might hear." She rose and went over to him. "What did the Negroes say, Cuffee?" Perhaps, between them, they had done something today, after all. Perhaps Cuffee had been of some use, even if she hadn't.

Cuffee's dark face was doubtful. "They says the white gentleman's going to hang Mr. Dal, for *sure*," he said slowly. "They says he bin feeling real poo'ly. Lot's of nigras have run out of this town, they says, and the white folks is mighty riled up about it. They says h'it's goin' to be mighty hard to git Mr. Dal outen 'at jail-house."

Mahala steadied herself. "I don't care what they say, Cuffee," she said, gathering her courage into a knot in her mind. "I don't care how hard it will be. I'll get him out if we have to burn the jail-house." She stared at Cuffee for a minute. "What else did they say?"

Cuffee shook his head. "They's willing to help us, can they do it." He looked at Mahala, still hesitating. "They don't know *what* to do," he said at last.

"We can't wait long." Mahala began to pace the floor. "I can't do anything but pretend I'm going to buy a farm or a horse. If I asked to see the jail, they'd probably think it was queer. We'll have to follow our plan." She looked at Cuffee, to see how he was taking it. After all, he was the one who would have to suffer. "Are you willing to go through with it, Cuffee?" she asked him. "It won't be easy. They may beat you. And if they do, I can't stop them. I may have to beat you myself."

The Negro bent his head humbly. "That's right, Miss Haley. You can't do nothin' but what you're doin'. You got to act mean. But I's willing to try it." He looked up at her. "Mr. Dal got me out of slavery, and I'll git him out, if the Lord helps me."

Mahala made up her mind. "All right. We'll do exactly as we planned. Go out and make your arrangements tonight. Store the provisions. Get everything ready. Tomorrow I'm going to look at some more farms. As soon as I'm gone, you run for it. And be sure that someone sees you and raises the alarm."

Word of Cuffee's runaway came to her the next afternoon, by a galloping messenger. The man reined up beside her party as they trotted through watery fields under a warm spring sun. He said, not without some satisfaction because after all the stranger was a Northerner, "Your Negro's lit out, sir. The hotel people heard about it from some of their blacks. He told 'em he was going, and they told Bellum, that runs the tavern. They say your boy was going to slip away about noon."

If Mr. Martin turned pale at this moment, Mahala hoped her new friends would lay it to sudden anger at the loss. She rose in her stirrups and cried, "Great God Almighty!" with all the fury and authority she could summon. "Do you mean to tell me he's been captured right here in Kentucky?" she demanded furiously. "Do you mean to say those damned Abolitionists have come right down here and stolen my man?"

Her numerous hosts explained in a chorus. "He didn't say anyone stole the nigger."

"He run away, Jakes says. He told the other Negroes he was going to run for it."

"Don't worry, Mr. Martin. We'll catch him for you. We know how to take care of runaways in this state."

Young Martin looked bewildered. "Why should he run away here?" That was a natural question. "If he was going to run, why didn't he try it north of the river in Cincinnati?"

Mr. Merriam of Belle Isle, the big plantation of the neighborhood, said, "You probably kept too sharp an eye on him there. Down here, he was left alone and he thought he could make it."

Martin's boyish voice said roughly, "Someone must have told him he could get through. Is there a station of this Underground Railroad they talk about? Have you had any trouble here with nigger stealers?"

Merriam shrugged his shoulders. "No more than any town near the river. We're all bothered, from time to time." He looked at Martin doubtfully. "You may have heard about the Woolly Head we caught here recently. He's in our jail right now, waiting for trial. We caught him with a bunch of twelve Negroes, in a cabin back of my place. One of my boys had sense enough to tell about it before he got away." He looked at Martin for approval. "He won't steal any more property for a while," he said grimly. "We'll take care of *that*."

Mahala allowed young Martin to look helpless, for all his anger. At eighteen, it wouldn't do to be too knowing about such things. "What should I do now?" he asked like a puzzled boy. "I can ride after him, myself, if someone will show me the roads—"

The whole chorus drowned this suggestion. "No, sir. We're accustomed to dealing with this matter. As soon as we get back to town we'll question these Negroes your man talked to, and see if they know where he might have gone. Then we'll get the hounds and a posse. We'll have him back for you," they assured Martin kindly. The boy was all right, they thought. He was just too young to know how to handle a matter like this. As for their trouble, they assured him, it was their affair, too. No slaveowner could afford to let anyone's slave escape. It started all the darkies to thinking. It ruined discipline; made them discontented. Slave-owners were used to it. There'd be no difficulty. Luckily, they'd heard about this break early. The man couldn't be many miles away yet.

The afternoon was a wild confusion of galloping and racing, of hounds baying through the wet woods, crashing through the underbrush, following along the freshet-fed streams, throwing back their mournful heads to cry out, while the pack of riders followed, shouting, and Negroes armed with clubs beat through the bushes after them. Mr. Merriam of Belle Isle commanded the posse, and twenty eager citizens of Darby supported young Mr. Martin in the ruck. Dusk found them somewhat winded, pushing up a long slope through heavy woods. Just the place,

Mr. Merriam said, for a man to hide. There was a cave that everyone knew about, apparently. The local Negroes might have told Martin's man about it, and the poor fool might be hiding there. From the way hounds were giving tongue, they were right.

The poor devil was crouched like a rabbit behind a burdock, just by some rocks at the mouth of the cave. When hounds struck him, he covered his head with his arms and waited, with the hopeless patience of a tortured animal, until they were called off. At the sight of his master, he cowered afresh. Young Martin was in a towering fury. His light riding whip rained blows on his rebellious slave, his boy's voice stormed. When he was reluctantly restrained by one of his new friends, he cried in a fury that he would have the Negro put in jail. "I'll teach him to run away from me," he cried, trembling with his anger, as they all could see. "I'll put him in jail with the nigger stealer. Then they can both see how they like running north."

There was a shout of laughter and approval at this notion. "That'll be just the thing. Let the nigger stealer see how he likes sleeping with a nigger. And maybe it'll cure these boys from thinking they can get away when your back's turned."

The slave, Cuffee, was roped in a jiffy, his arms trussed painfully behind his back, his ankles tied so that he could barely hobble. Between two mounted men, he was fairly dragged back into the town, down the muddy road and around the bend to the jail-house. The crowd of loungers around the tavern saw him go; saw his young master gesticulating excitedly with his whip, saw the whole party sweep past. From behind fences, trees, bushes, from the half-shut doors of cabins, dark faces watched Cuffee's heavy figure stumbling along between the two horses, saw him fairly dragged up the steps into the jail.

Mr. Durkee, the jailer, did the honors with a flourish. There was not much to show the young northern gentleman; a bare little anteroom with a couple of rickety chairs and a table. A lantern hung from a peg on the wall, and a cuspidor completed the furnishing of the room. Mr. Durkee was, as he said, tickled to death about everything. He praised the posse for its efficiency. He thought the plan of putting the captured Negro into the same cell with the nigger stealer was nothing short of inspired. "That'll learn 'em something," he said several times, slapping his fat thighs as the full beauty of the joke overcame him anew. "That'll give 'em a taste of their own medicine. That'll fix our high and mighty gentleman. That's funny, that is," and he laughed all over again.

Mr. Merriam said impatiently, "All right, Durkee. Show him into the cell. Let's get it over with and go home. We can't stay here all evening."

Durkee was immediately busy. The large brass key was taken down from the wall. Mr. Durkee became every inch the jailer. Cuffee quailed before him.

"Git in there, you black trash. We'll show you how we deal with runaway nigras in Kintucky." Hobbling the best he could, Cuffee moved forward. The key grated in a rusty lock, the heavy door creaked open.

Mahala North, standing in the guise of young Martin, watched the door swing slowly inward, strained her eyes to see, and saw nothing in the darkness of the inner room. A single window, high in the farther wall, showed a pale square of evening, but the cell itself was washed in shadow. No one stirred. No one spoke. Trembling in the agony of the moment, Mahala took a step forward, staring over the heavy shoulder of the jailer. Dal; Dal. The name was echoing so loudly in her mind that it seemed incredible that the men in the room could not hear it. Dal, she wanted to cry out. Dal. I'm here. It's Mahala. I'm here. I've come to get you out. The unspoken words deafened her, dazed her. She could only gaze feverishly into the dark cell, waiting for it to happen.

Mr. Durkee sensed something pressing in her manner. He said hospitably, "You want to have a look at the prisoner? He ain't much to look at, but you're welcome to see him." He moved forward accommodatingly and held his lantern high, so that its pale beams flowed into the little room. As though the sight had terrified him, Cuffee began to moan and pray. "Oh, Mr. Martin, don' put me in no jail cell. Don' shut me up with no nigger stealer. Take me back up no'th with you, an' I'll never run off no more. Take me back up no'th with you . . ." No one paid any attention to him.

Sitting on his straw pallet in the remote corner of the cell was a man. Mahala's eyes fell upon him, in that first moment, without recognition. This is not Dal, she thought stupidly; not Dal. Then the man moved, lifted a shoulder, turned his head slowly to look at his visitors. That face, so white, so very thin, the eyes staring dead black from the pallor of their setting, the lips almost colorless, set in a line of contempt; that figure, wrapped in filthy rags that could not hide the sharpness of the knees and elbows. Dal—Dal, the voice in Mahala's mind was shrieking. You're ill. You're dying. O God, Dal.

Durkee, the jailer, naturally wanted to appear well before his guests. "Git up, you," he said urgently to his prisoner. "Can't you see these gentlemen want to look at you?" He bustled into the room, throwing his light more clearly upon Dallas Ord's bitter face, but it was to be noted that he did not approach his prisoner closely. "We got a companion for you, Mr. Abolitionist," he said, and slapped his thighs with delight. "We got just the very man to keep you company." He had to pause while laughter shook him. "We got a black gentleman to room with you," he said, shouting with laughter. "You're so fond of niggers that we went to all this trouble just to get a black boy to keep you from being lonesome. Come in here, you," he shouted to Cuffee. "Come in and meet your friend from up north. He'll be real pleased to welcome you."

Cuffee, black, mud-smeared, openly terrified, crouched against the wall, rolling his eyes at the white man across the room. He was still moaning. "Don' leave me alone with the white man, Mist' Jailer. He kill me sure." Nobody paid any attention to him.

Young Martin—with an effort, the older men were amused to see—finally plucked up courage to swagger into the room. He walked into the dirty little cell and stood face to face with the man, wrapped in his tattered blanket, staring them down with the bitterness of his contempt. Young Martin did not shrink from his gaze. "So you're the man who steals niggers," he said, with a good attempt at bravado. "I hear you're one of the Northerners I've just left behind me. I come from the North," he said with his boyish boastfulness. "I know the kind of man you are. You like to run with niggers. All right. I've brought you one to run with."

The prisoner gave her back a look from his black eyes, hard, fierce, inscrutable. Finally—they were all, for some reason, waiting for him to speak—his lips lifted in a half-smile. He said in a soft, drawling voice, "Quite a little man, aren't you?" and then they saw that he was shaking with his own private amusement, shaking so that, in his weakness, he was obliged to put out a hand and steady himself against the wall.

Mr. Durkee was scandalized. "Here, you," he shouted loudly. "You keep a civil tongue in your head, or you'll be sorry." He raised an arm threateningly, but he still kept a safe distance from his prisoner. The man Ord gave him one look like a blow in the face. Then, deliberately, he turned his back upon his visitors.

Mr. Merriam felt that this distasteful passage had gone far enough. The young fellow had acquitted himself well. The runaway was safe under lock and key. The affair was over. "If you gentlemen will come with me," he said politely to the waiting posse, "I'd be happy to offer you a little refreshment, after our exertions." There was a general movement toward the door. Young Martin, lingering to give the jailer a handful of money for his trouble, finally rejoined them, and the whole episode made a fine tale of adventure to recount to the ladies at Belle Isle that evening.

Southern ladies were not expected to take either part or interest in political discussions. The ladies of Belle Isle, after they had hovered as hostesses to the road-weary searchers, retired gracefully and let the menfolks talk.

The girl Mahala, behind her boy's disguise, admired their elegance: Mrs. Merriam, small and dainty like a ruffled doll, with fine rings on her fingers and diamond drops in her ears; little Lacey, as pretty as a pink, a flirt at fourteen, smiling at the gentlemen, fluttering her long eyelashes, tossing her yellow curls. Ah, she would break their hearts in another year or so, Mahala thought, smiling at her, bowing over her hand with all the gallantry she could summon to Mr. Martin's aid. If I was really Martin, she thought, springing to hold the door for the ladies to pass through, if I was really the fine lad I seem to be, those blue eyes might catch my fancy. Now I am afraid of them, she thought, closing the door with relief. Women are more likely to guess my secret than these men. I do not know how to flirt with women, she thought as she turned back to the room full of gentlemen. Miss Lacey would know that pretty soon. Her brother, who does not like me, is safer. Young Rufus Merriam is hot and wild; because I am a Northerner he dislikes me, even though I have declared sympathy for his side in this quarrel. But he will not suspect anything else. His mind is too full of his own anger, his own impatience.

It was safe to take a chair beside him, to accept a glass of toddy, to begin to thank everyone for his trouble in finding the slave.

"I'd always heard of southern hospitality," Mr. Martin said, smiling in his boyish way, "but this beats all. There's no way I can repay you gentlemen for what you've done. I've been a trouble to you ever since I came to Darby. You've been more than kind."

That was true, Mahala thought, watching the flushed, smiling faces. If it weren't for Dal, I'd feel like a dog. They've been polite and generous. And before I'm done, I'm going to repay them with an injury. I oughtn't to be sitting here. I oughtn't to eat their salt. But I've got to play my part. I can't fight fair. I've got to trick them and deceive them. It's for Dal, she thought, steeling herself against Mr. Merriam's smile, against the laughter and gay talk, against the warmth and comfort of the room, and the hot drink in her hand. They give me this, but they give Dal rags and a straw pallet and filthy food. And in the end they'd give him a rope, and be glad they'd killed him.

They believe they're right, she thought, still watching Merriam's fine jovial face. They're gentlemen and they're men of honor. They're protecting their property. Dal stole from them, and when they punished him they'd call it justice. They can't see; they can't see a black-skinned being and call him human. They see him as a nigger and a slave forever. And I can't see one and call him a slave. I can't know he's a slave without trying to free him. It's the way we're made; the way we have to think.

Aloud she said, "When I crossed the river, I thought I was done with Abolitionists forever, but the first thing I come here, I see one of them. Have they caused you much trouble?"

Mr. Merriam sighed. "All this antislavery ruction is a trouble to us. We're peaceable men. We want to mind our own business and let other people mind theirs. But these northern fanatics won't let us. They've got the whole country stirred up—whites and blacks. The Negroes down here are getting so that we can't get a day's honest work out of 'em. Crops'll suffer, you mark my words. Property owners have to spend half their time keeping track of their slaves, and, when the Negroes run away, spend plenty of money getting 'em back. You were lucky, Mr. Martin, to find your man. Otherwise, you'd have had to advertise a reward for him, and you'd have been lucky to recover him then."

"What's the South going to do about it?" young Martin wanted to know. What could they do; what could anyone do, North or South, except struggle while politicians wrangled in Washington, and newspapers screamed their different tunes, and the whole country rocked with it.

Mr. Merriam said positively, "The South will have to cut loose from the North. Get free of it. Run its own affairs, steer its own ship, and let the North see that it's an independent state."

There was a general murmur of assent at this speech, and

young Martin asked, wondering, "Do you mean nullification, Mr. Merriam?"

One of the younger men answered for his host. "Yes, by God! The sooner we cut loose from the whole kit and caboodle of 'em, the better off we'll be. Old Calhoun was right."

Mr. Merriam was more moderate. "I don't say that. I think we can work it another way. We're already beginning to do it. We're not buying as much from the North as we did. People are refusing to touch northern goods. We're beginning to make goods for ourselves—cloth and shoes and soap and flour and foodstuffs. We'll get so's we can forbid northern products in southern markets. When we do that, the sane men in the North will begin to see that we mean business."

He's like John Palfrey, Mahala thought, listening. He's probably like all the practical, sound businessmen all over the country. The bankers and storekeepers and factory owners. Traders everywhere. Conservatives, she thought, tasting the word like a bitter drop on her tongue. John is a conservative in the North, as Mr. Merriam is in the South. They don't want trouble. They don't want things stirred up and broken. They want everything to be as it's always been, without change. They're loyal; they love their country. They see that the radicals—all of us who want change—are going to disturb the peace. They see that we want to fight. And they don't think anything is worth the damage that will cause. They say that *they* are the practical ones—as though no practical man would want to free a slave. They see all the money that would be lost, all the trouble and confusion that would come. They dread all change. That's how they're practical. They're honest about it. They're kind men, as well as cruel; they can be polite and generous and brave. They'd fight for what they think, as well as we would. Perhaps John Palfrey would fight me as hard as I would fight him, if he knew what I was doing.

Everyone began talking at once, now. Who'll buy our tobacco? The South'll buy it—or England. There's plenty of market south of the Line, you wait and see. Factories, too. We'll make what we need, and be damned to those skinflints in Massachusetts. Massachusetts, they said with intense bitterness. That's the worst state of them all. They make more money out of spinning slave-grown cotton than we make out of selling it to 'em. And they yell the loudest about slavery. Let 'em see how they like it when we stop buying their cloth and shoes. The poor devils in their factories are worse off than any Negro slave in the whole South. We'll trade with England and Europe, if we want foreign markets. We've bought goods of the North, and loaned 'em money to run their businesses. Now let 'em try to get along without us. Some of 'em are sorry already, one man said with satisfaction. Some of the people who ran stores in New York and Philadelphia were pretty hot against slavery, at first, but now they're changing their tunes. Men who were good Whigs and independents are switching over now, and trying to stop the radicals from threatening the South. They're trying to tell us they're our friends, now, when they see the way things are going. The last election showed that.

Young Rufus Merriam said, "The Whigs are pretty near gone gooses, anyway. The whole party's breaking up—with all these Know-Nothings, and Free-Soilers and Americans, and Anti-Slavery split-offs. If they lose in '52, there won't be enough of 'em left to wad a gun."

A doubter questioned this. "The Democrats ain't too solid, either, I've noticed. There's too many of these by-blows to let any party be what you might call healthy. If it goes on this way much longer, the Democrats may win in '52, and they might even win one time more, but I'll lay you three to one that if all these misbegotten anti-this and anti-that parties ever got together, they'd run even the Democrats out of office."

There was a great pooh-poohing of this idea. "The old-line men of both parties know enough to keep that from happening. Look at Dan Webster," someone said. "Look at how he's come over to us. He's as hot as a Democrat, for the Fugitive Slave Law. They'll be sorry they got Black Dan stirred up. He'll give 'em what for."

Mr. Martin, the only northern man, was, happily, too young to be expected to have an opinion about politics. He was allowed to sit and listen respectfully to the pronouncements of his elders and betters. Hot whisky punch is warming to the organs of eloquence. The talk went on and on.

In the sudden darkness of the cell, two men listened. Footsteps thumped over bare boards as the twenty men stamped out of the jail-house. Voices made a confused babble, the last of them Mr. Durkee's, bidding farewell to his visitors. Then, after a pause while the jailer must have stood in the doorway watching their departure, his heavy tread crossed the outer room once more, a chair scraped over the floor, money chinked softly. He would be sitting now, the listeners thought intently, resting after his exertions and counting the tip young Mr. Martin had given him. Would Durkee settle down, perhaps stay all night, to keep watch over his new charge? Or would the money tempt him to go out? Coins chinked again. Were they being put away for another time? No. Again the slow footsteps crossed the room, hesitated at the doorway, then went more softly down the steps. Mr. Durkee was heading for the tavern. This was the time for work in the dark cell.

Cuffee whispered, "That's Mis' Haley, Mr. Dal. Did you know her in gentleman's clo's? She's fixin' to git you out."

Ord's hand pressed his arm in the darkness. "I knew her," he said in a queer voice. "I'd know her in any clothes. Is she all right?" he asked the Negro urgently. "Is she safe with those people? Are you sure they don't suspect her?"

His trembling voice worried Cuffee. "Yes, sir, Mr. Dal. She's fine. Those gentlemans don't think ary thing about her, excusing she's a rich boy from up no'th, that hates the Nigger Lovers like poison, and wants to buy her a farm and live right here. Mis' Haley got everything fixed. She made me run away and git catched again. She helped 'em to find me, and when they got me, she acted up, mad as a hornet." He laughed softly, as though the whole thing had been a fine joke. "Mis' Haley whupped me good, for those gentlemans to see, and cussed like a nailer. She so mad—" Cuffee listened to Ord's quick breathing in the dark cell— "she so purely mad, she say to put me in here with the Nigger Lover, to teach me a lesson, and those gentlemans was tickled and said that's the very thing." Anxiously he waited for Ord to answer. Something bad ails Mr. Dal, and no mistake, he thought, holding his breath. He ain't laughin' and jokin' like before. He ain't got no spirit. He's low sick, and that's a fact.

Ord said, "I hope to God she gets out all right."

Cuffee decided that they'd better talk about something else. "Us better git to work, Mr. Dal," he said persuasively. "Mis' Haley say don't waste no time. Tonight, us got to git out o' this jail-house."

Dal Ord's voice said, "Did they search you, Cuffee? Were you able to bring anything in?"

Cuffee said, "Yes, sir, Mr. Dal. Mis' Haley helped me stow things for you." He fumbled inside his shirt. Then, cautiously, a match was struck, and in the wavering light the two men looked at each other.

Ord's hand pinched out the flame. "Wait a minute. If they see a light in our window, someone might come in to investigate. I'll hang my blanket over it." Cuffee could hear him moving sure-footed across the room, as though he was used to living in the darkness. When he had finished his arrangements, he came back to Cuffee. "Have you got a candle?"

Once more the locofoco struck, sputtered, made a light. Carefully Cuffee held his candle in the flame until it caught fire. "There, sir, Mr. Dal. Us kin see what we got to do. We got to work fast, Mis' Haley say. She got everything planned for you."

In the tremulous light, Dal Ord's face flamed with hope. "What does she want you to do? What's she planned? God," he said, suddenly shaken beyond his control. "I thought she couldn't get here. I thought she wasn't coming, or had been caught." His eyes blazed down at the dark and humble face. "You're a good man, Cuffee, to take this chance for me."

Cuffee looked at him anxiously. "You's sick, Mr. Dal. Us got to git you out powerful fast. I sure thought Mis' Haley go crazy waiting to git here. You go sit down and let's see what can I do to prize open this jail."

Ord said, "I'm all right. I can help." Then the weakness in his limbs made him a liar. Cuffee's arm helped him to the dirty and disordered pallet.

"You see what I says," Cuffee scolded softly. "You ain' goin' to be no help to me, does you fall out. I got to try this door."

From his bed, Ord was suddenly hopeless. "You can't break the lock. I've tried it, night after night. They've put on a new bar—iron—straight across on the outside. You can't budge it. And the window's barred with iron, too."

The Negro was not discouraged. "Those gentlemans doesn't know it, but I been in this jail-house before. I got in with a passel of niggers that ran away from a coffle, and I got out, slick as owl grease. If'n the door don't open, the window will." Patiently, with his large black hands, he began to test the bars of the window. They were apparently solid, set into a heavy wooden window frame. After considering for a moment, the Negro turned away and went to inspect the small iron stove in the other corner of the cell. It had not been lit for a long time, months or years. Under Cuffee's touch the thing rattled, metal screeched and the old stove tilted drunkenly forward on three legs. Cuffee straightened, with a useful tool in his hand.

"Stove leg as good as a crowbar, pretty near," he said with satisfaction. "Now us'll see how that window bar's settin'."

It was a pleasure to see him work. Dallas Ord, resting on an elbow, watched from his bed as the rusty iron dug into aged wood. The window frame came away in one piece, spike and all, revealing the second line of defense—an iron bar, clamped against the upright bars that guarded the window. Cuffee studied this arrangement thoughtfully. Below the bar, bricks of the wall showed their faded color. Once more, Cuffee returned to the battered stove and dealt with it. This time he went back to the window with an assortment of tools; a stove lid, a part of the fender. The iron bar was well sunk into the brickwork. For a time it resisted all efforts to dislodge it.

Cuffee was not discouraged. "Somebody put this *in*," he said, straining against the pry, "and somebody can git it *out*." The fender was not heavy enough, nor the stove leg. Awkward though it was, the round stove lid did the job. The bolt pulled a little, then a little more. When the final tug came, it let go altogether, and came out with a crunching of brick and metal. The ends of the window bars hung free, as the sill split off altogether, leaving a gap in the brickwork so that cool night air rushed into the little cell like a voice calling from outside.

Dal Ord was on his feet now, working side by side with the Negro, pounding against the old bricks, tearing at the hanging splinters of wood, fighting the wall as though it was an enemy. Cuffee tried to dissuade him. "Won't do us no good to git outen this jail-house if you's so tuckered out you can't run. Mis' Haley skin me for sure if I lets you git sicker'n you already is."

Ord said, "I'm all right. We've got to hurry. Durkee might come back any time now, and if he catches us, we're done."

Cuffee did not appear to hurry, but the bricks began to come away in his hands as though he was shelling peas. The gap widened, became a hole, an opening, a way of escape. Cuffee slid a leg through, bent his back to try the width, then came swiftly back to Dallas Ord.

"It's big enough, Mr. Dal," he said calmly. "Us better be gittin'." His hand supported Ord's body anxiously. "Is you strong enough to make it, Mr. Dal? You got to drop a long ways after you gits through."

Ord shook him off impatiently. "I'll make it."

For all his gentle manner, Cuffee was in charge here. He said, "I'll go first, Mr. Dal. I's studied the ground down there, and I knows how to fall. I kin ketch you, does you fall wrong."

Ord hesitated a moment, then stood back. "Hurry, boy," was all he said. Weakness was flowing over him now, so that the room swam before his vision. He watched the black shape of Cuffee moving carefully through the pale light of the opening. The round head hung, for a moment, bodiless as Cuffee swung over the ledge, then dropped out of sight. From below, the Negro's voice called softly, "All ready, Mr. Dal." With every atom of his strength, Dallas Ord forced his body to obey his will.

The beauty of Cuffee's plan was its simplicity. Where any guess would say that an escaped prisoner would run far and fast, Cuffee went to ground as near the jail as possible. In the brief time he had, he had foreseen everything, thought of everything, provided for everything. Just across the ravine from the jail stood a tobacco shed, a great sprawling building, slat-sided for drying the leaf, and on the far side of this building was a pit made to receive the refuse of the tobacco, the wilted tops, the strippings, any sort of rubbish. Above this pit, a heap of debris rose halfway up the rough side of the shed. Under the heap, in the pit itself, Cuffee had hollowed out a space, propped it with broken boards, hidden his supplies. It was to this refuge that he guided Ord's weakening steps. But not until, at the very wall of the jail-house, he had forced Ord to stop and change his shoes.

"You got to, Mr. Dal," he said urgently. "They'll git the hounds here, first off, and give 'em a smell of your scent. Mis' Haley brought us extra shoes, a-purpose. We got to change."

Ord was in a fever of impatience. "They'll see us here. We've got to get away." But he obeyed, nevertheless. "I can't go far, Cuffee," he said after a few feeble steps. "You'd better leave me. I'll never make it."

Cuffee's arm was supporting him. "Yes, you will, Mr. Dal," he said, over and over. "I got it planned. It ain't far. You'll make it."

Under the pile of tobacco, he wrapped Ord warmly in a blanket and poured brandy down his throat. "Us got to rest," he said, fussing like a mother hen over his charge. "If'n I lets you git sick, Mis' Haley like to kill me. Us got to rest some and git out o' here."

Two days spent under a heap of evil-smelling refuse would not be pleasant in any circumstances; two days of tense waiting, while hounds coursed up and down the ravine a hundred yards away, and mounted men rode and shouted through the woods beyond, were two days of hell. Dallas Ord was a sick man, weak almost to helplessness. It is probable that he would have died if Cuffee had not sustained him. But Cuffee's courage never faltered; he never despaired, never ceased to watch and guard, was never at a loss. Brandy and food from his hidden store gave Ord strength; his certainty gave Ord hope.

"That Mis' Haley voice," he would say, peering from the peephole he had contrived above their refuge. "I kin see her horse. She helpin' the gentlemans hunt for us, and she goin' to make 'em hunt the wrong way. She got 'em all fooled," he'd say, laughing at the joke of it. "She foolin' those gentlemans, fine as cat hair. And when they's tired of huntin' for us, she going to git roarin' drunk and ride off in a big hurry. And after she gits away from 'em, she'll come back and find us."

Ord couldn't believe such luck at first, but when, after the second day, the chase had evidently turned in other directions, he began to hope. He was feeling stronger, he told Cuffee that night. It was time to go. But the Negro still refused.

"Mis' Haley got it all planned. Does we go too quick, we don't meet up with her, like she said. It ain't safe till the third night, Mis' Haley say. Then she goin' to give up lookin' and git out of town. That's when we's got to make tracks."

After the fetid warmth of the rubbish-pile shelter, the spring night was cool when they did start out. Ord was carefully wrapped by Cuffee in a greatcoat and the blanket, folded like a shawl, but the keen air made him shiver, and his legs were as weak as a baby's. Three miles through the dark woods left him exhausted, and he was glad to crawl into a nest of brush when daylight began to paint the sky. Cuffee reconnoitered the ground, then crawled in after him, carefully arranging the twigs to conceal their hiding place.

"Tomorrow night us gits to the place to meet Mis' Haley," he said confidently. "Then us goes to traveling."

When a man is lightheaded with fever, with illness and exhaustion, events slide together, shifting and slipping through his head in a crazy dream. Days and nights flowed past Dallas Ord, daylight and dark; dark and daylight; nights of stumbling through forests, through fields, of creeping along fence-rows, hiding in ditches, crawling into shallow caves, under haystacks. In the sliding dream Ord moved, spoke, struggled, felt himself held and tended beside hasty small fires, drank thirstily when a bowl was held to his lips, slept without changing the dream, and woke to the same dream in the black night when he rose to go on. Somewhere in the dream Cuffee walked beside him, holding him up, helping him to walk, leading and guiding him between the trees of the woods, feeding him, hiding him at dawn.

And the other figure in the dream might have been only a part of the old dream of his days in the jail. Mahala's hands touching him, her voice speaking to him, her pale face appearing before him like that old haunting vision. What she said to him and what he replied were a part of the old dream, too; the dream in which he had passed days and weeks in his cell, when he had talked to an absent Mahala, argued with her, pleaded with her, cried out to her. Where the old dream of captivity ended and the new dream of headlong flight began, Ord could not tell; nor if the one was a dream and the other a reality, nor whether the hand that touched his face now was more real than the one he had imagined so many times.

He was not aware when they were in danger, or how far they came, or when they found help. Once he lay for a day in a Negro cabin; black faces looked down at him in the firelit room, black hands tended him. And though Cuffee was a part of that dream, Mahala seemed forever beyond his vision. Later, there was a nightmare in which he crossed a river. A boat seemed to rock beneath him, water splashed against the sides of the boat, and oars beat a soft rhythm in his ears. Cold followed immediately. Strong arms held him while icy water rose to his waist and his steps were clogged by the current of a stream. After this, he remembered nothing more until he awoke in bed in a smoky room, and Mahala's face bent over him. He thought she was weeping. He thought he heard the murmur of her voice. He closed his eyes and the scene faded. Wheels jolted under him presently, and a horse's hooves clopped on a road. Again he awoke in a bed and found himself in a white room, bright with sunshine. He turned under smooth sheets and saw a gentle face above a Quaker surplice. A voice he knew called quickly, "Come, Mahala! I believe he is awake. I believe he might know thee."

Pain and fever had left him, and the horrible whirling in his mind, the roaring of strange voices in his ears, the shifting, phantasmal shapes before his vision. He lay waiting, breathing light shallow breaths not to shatter this heavenly peace, not daring to believe it was true that he was safe in a clean bed, that he had finally escaped, that Mahala would really come to him. Then he saw her face bending over him, white, haggard, drowned in tears, but with a radiance of joy upon it, and he heard her voice say brokenly, "You're all right, Dal. You're going to get well. You're safe and the fever's gone. You're going to get well, and I can take you home again."

CHAPTER TEN

"I hope everything goes off all right," Noxon said nervously, fidgeting in his chair, blowing a great cloud of smoke from his cheroot, fiddling with the seals on his watch chain.

Major Burnet said robustly, "Of course it will go off all right. We've got the upper hand in this town. We've got the majority of the people on our side. We can see that nothing out of the way happens." He looked around the meeting for agreement. Heads nodded emphatically. Yes, sir, we can see that everything's all right. The Nigger Lovers won't dare to start a ruction if they know we're on deck. They wouldn't be so foolish.

Someone said, "Mr. Webster's too popular for folks to want to insult him."

There was a good deal of argument about this. "Well, he used to be, of course. But lately I've heard folks say he must have lost his senses, to switch around so and side with the Southerners. It don't set good, the way he's been acting for a year now."

Burnet said, laughing, "We ought to like that. He's as good as a Democrat now. Half the Whigs won't hear his name mentioned since he made that speech for the Compromise Bill, but the Democrats—especially down south—have fallen in love with him. I heard he sold more copies of his speech south of the Line than he did up here."

Noxon said sourly, "He's looking at the White House, but he'll never get into it. He ain't one thing or the other, right now. He couldn't run on a Democratic ticket, and the Whigs won't look at him. He's cooked his goose, all right."

Palfrey spoke for the first time. "I don't care about his politics. If he'll talk good and strong against the Abolitionists, he might be able to bring some folks to their senses. That's what we want. This isn't a political meeting. If Webster talks the way he did in Buffalo last week, it'll be an anti-Abolition meeting, and a good one."

The Major said thoughtfully, "That's right. We can use a good rousing speech against 'em. But we've got to be careful, just the same. Folks used to think Dan Webster was just about God, but right now there's a lot of talk about him. All this business about his taking money when he went into office. That don't go down, with a man like Webster. It sounds like graft, and, by Jolly, they say they can prove it. There's going to be a stink about that, before they're through. They're out to get Webster, and no mistake."

"Do you think he took the money?" one of the boys asked, his eyes as big as butter-pats. Dan Webster taking graft; old Dan Webster, the great orator, taking a cut of money like a North Side heeler. You couldn't tell about anybody these days, he said, shaking his head. Old Dan Webster taking graft. Well.

Major Burnet shrugged his shoulders. "They must have some kind of proof, or they wouldn't have dared to accuse him. Dan Webster won't take an insult lying down, you can bet on that. And he hasn't said much to contradict it. It's well known that he's hard up for cash. Always has been. And it costs a lot to be Secretary of State in Washington. He may have thought it was all right to take a little present from his friends. But if it's proved, it ain't going to do him any good with the voters, and that's what he's always had his eye on." This was getting away from the point of the meeting, however. Burnet said briskly, "Well, that's his lookout. We ain't trying to run him for president. All we've got to do is see that he gets a turnout for his speech, and we can do that all right. It's a good time to make a showing, after that Anti-Slavery convention they've just had. Garrison drew a big crowd, and they think they're all hell, right now. We've got to show 'em that Dan Webster can draw a bigger crowd. That's our job."

"Won't it look kind of funny to have Democrats making a fuss over a Whig?" Noxon asked nervously. "We've got to remember the party."

Palfrey finished making notes on a pile of papers, and began to talk. He was looking brighter the last week or so, Major Burnet noticed. He'd been dumpish for a while; moody, gone off the handle easily. It was probably about that girl of his, the Major thought, watching Palfrey's hawk face swoop upon the party chickens. The boys liked Palfrey, Burnet thought, watching closely. They're flattered when he talks to 'em. But they're a little afraid of him, all the same. They know he's got something. Not just brains. They know he's smart, but they know he's harder than they are. He don't give a damn. He'll get what he goes after. He's got an awful drive. Now he was giving them Hail Columbia.

That girl must have got back, the Major thought, his eyes on John Palfrey's lean face. John's come to again. He's got his fighting pants on. He's lively again.

"This isn't just the party, the way we've thought of it before," Palfrey was telling them. "If these crazy fools get control, there won't be any party to fight for. There won't even be any United States, like it was before. They're out to split up the country. Garrison *wants* disunion. He *wants* to split with the South. He *wants* to break up the Constitution. He doesn't care if he wrecks the whole nation, as long as he destroys the slaveowners." His voice was not loud, but it seemed to burn the words into their minds.

Someone asked timidly, "Are you in favor of slavery, John?"

Palfrey whirled to answer. "Good God, no. Not any more than you are, or any sensible man up north. I think it's bad. But I think it's bound to go out by itself, if you wait for it. It can't last, and the Southerners know it as well as we do. It's out of date. It's part of the past, and before all this towrow started, a lot of southern slaveowners said so, and were in favor of freeing their slaves. Now these fanatics are calling 'em names, and naturally they'll defend themselves and defend slavery. But if we let it alone and throttle Garrison and some of his crazy men, the Southerners will do away with it themselves. Our job is to stop the Abolitionists, and let the slaveowners abolish slavery in their own way." His eyes were blue fires in his head. "That's what Webster wants," he said, blazing at them. "He may be after the Presidency, but he's looking at the whole country, too. He knows that if things go on this way, we'll have a break. A break with the South," he said slowly, so that his words dropped separately upon them, like sparks from a bonfire. "A break, and if we won't let 'em break, we'll have a bloody war."

Moses North poked his head around the door of Mahala's green sitting room and looked in. Seeing that Ord was not asleep, but pacing the room like a dog on a treadmill, he pushed the door open and entered. "You want anything?" he asked, as Ord turned toward him. "Mahala's gone out and she asked me to kind of keep an eye on you." He chuckled. "She's been like a hen with one chick, ever since you got here. I don't blame you for getting restless."

Ord said moodily, "She saved my life. She's got a right to boss me if she wants to, I guess." He paced to the window where, beyond the bellying curtain, a spring wind was blowing over the town, carrying its rich mixed scent of damp earth, water, and fresh-cut lumber from a canalboat moored near the hotel. He stared down at the scene, frowning. "I go wild, sitting around here when there's so much to do," he said. "The weather's warming up, and now's the best time for getting slaves out. Too many of 'em die or get sick when it's cold. I know." The frown deepened on his pale face. "I'd have died myself, if it hadn't been for Mahala."

Moses settled himself comfortably in a chair and began to stuff an old churchwarden pipe with coarse tobacco. "More likely you'd have died of hemp poisoning," he said, rumbling with laughter. "Haley said it was a near thing to a hanging, the way those men talked. She said she could never have got you out if it hadn't been for Cuffee. Haley was scared to death, but Cuffee swore all along he could get you out of that jail—and he did. That was real lucky."

Ord came back across the room, threw himself into a chair, then got up again and resumed his restless pacing. "Cuffee's a good nigger," he said, "but he couldn't have done anything if Mahala hadn't planned it and carried it off. I was no use to 'em. I was too sick. I don't even remember half of it." He paused at the farther window and stood with his back turned to Moses North. "I was a danger to them then, and maybe I'm a danger to you now." Suddenly he whirled to face North. "I've told Mahala that I think Palfrey's suspicious of us—of me, particularly. I've thought so for quite a while, and I told Mahala before I went away that he was beginning to suspect us. She won't believe me." He looked at the old man sharply. "Is she in love with Palfrey?" he asked in a level voice. "If she is, she'd better marry him and stay away from us. There's going to be trouble, if we keep on the way we're going. Palfrey's in the house too much. It hampers us, and we can't tell what he may see, if he comes in unexpectedly."

Moses shifted in his chair. "Well, I don't know *as* she is, and I don't know *as* she isn't," he said judicially. "It's hard to tell, with Mahala. But I've always had a notion she was in love with you." He looked at Dallas Ord curiously. "I've never made it my business to find out how you stood, but I've never worried much about Palfrey. It's natural that a young woman likes attention. Palfrey's been company for her, and I guess she does like him some. But I'll tell you this—" he leaned forward and pointed the stem of his long pipe at Ord—"I can tell you that when she heard you were in trouble, she couldn't see Palfrey or anybody else, for dust. You'd have thought the house was on fire, the way she got out of it."

Ord sighed and turned back to his window. In the sunny room the Dutch clock clacked peacefully, the curtains swung in the light airs; outside, a horse trotted smartly over the cobbles, its buggy rattling after it, and a man's voice sang out a long-drawn

"Looow bridge." Ord sighed again. "I ought to be working," he said as he watched the movement in the street below. "I'm getting stronger now. It wouldn't hurt me any. The trouble is, I promised Mahala—"

"Promised Mahala what?" her voice called from the door. The starched flounces of her print dress rustled as she came into the room. "What are you two talking about? What's going on here?" Her eyes flew to Ord's moody face. "The only thing Dal's promised me is to stay here until he's well again. And he's not well yet." She went over and laid her hand on his arm. "You're better, Dal, but you aren't strong enough to travel. You'd only get sick again. And there's plenty to do here. We know Negroes will be coming through again soon. You can help with them." She studied his dark face with anxiety. "I've heard the Patriots are going to have Webster stop off and make a speech here next week. That may mean trouble. He may stir them up so that they go after us harder. You could go to their meetings and find out about it."

Ord was watching her closely now. "Did Palfrey tell you that?" he asked in his light, drawling voice, as though anything John Palfrey said didn't matter.

Mahala flushed. "Yes, he did. And he'd know, if anybody would. He's helping Major Burnet prepare a committee of welcome," she said as though the words were dragged out of her. "Webster's going to speak from Frazee Hall and then there's going to be a dinner for him at the Globe Hotel. John says it will be a big thing. They expect to swing the city away from Abolition. They're all excited about it. John says they're going to make a real effort to stamp out the Underground." She stood facing Dallas Ord, and her speech to him was strained and angry, between defiance of his mockery and anxiety at the news she had to tell.

Ord grinned. "I told you you'd get into trouble if you got to running with the nigger catchers. One of these fine days you'll find yourself riding off in a posse to chase fugitives with the marshals."

"That's a lie," Mahala said furiously. "John Palfrey isn't a marshal. And I have nothing to do with his activities. I don't care what he does. It's none of my affair."

"It would be your affair if he found you hiding a runaway slave," Ord said with sudden bitterness. "What do you think he'd do then? Let you go? Keep your secret and let you go on working, if he knew you were on the Underground?"

"He won't find out," Mahala answered, matching his bitterness with her own. "I'm not a fool. I don't let him come here when we've got anyone going through. John's no danger to us, I've told you a thousand times. You only say so because you don't want me to see him. You don't like him, and so you say he shouldn't come here."

Her father broke into the quarrel with his easy, peacemaking words. "You're getting all worked up about nothing, Haley," he said to her. "Dal don't dislike Palfrey. He thinks he's a smart young man. But that's the very reason why he and I think maybe we'd ought to be kind of careful about him. We can't have him suspicion us. He's got too much influence with Burnet, and there's nothing Burnet wouldn't do to make a big show of catching a bunch of Abolitionists. That's the only reason Dal spoke about it. I'd just been saying the same thing. If they're going to have Webster here and make a big fuss about it, that's just the time they'd like to stage a capture. And that means we've got to be extra careful. Maybe you'd ought to kind of keep John away until that's over with."

Mahala turned away from them both. "I'll do whatever you say, of course," she said formally. "You're in charge of this station. If you want to forbid Mr. Palfrey the house, you can do it."

Dallas Ord made one of his lightning changes of temper. Suddenly he was laughing, all the anger, all the bitterness, gone from his face and from the gay, rallying tone of his voice. In two strides he was beside her, catching her arms behind her back and leaning over her shoulder to sing a foolish child's song to her.

"Haley's mad, and I'm glad,
And I know how to please her.
A bottle of wine to make her shine,
And John to —"

Before he could finish, Mahala had pulled away from him and run out of the room. Ord laughed. "It'll take me two days to make up," he said to Mahala's father. "I ought to know better than rile her up." He smiled at Moses. "Never mind about Palfrey," he said with his old confidence. "I'll take care of it. I'll go down and see Burnet and maybe get into some of his meetings. If we keep an eye on the noble Patriots, we ought to be all right. I'll tell Haley I'm sorry."

Webster's getting old, Palfrey thought, watching discreetly as the great man talked to Mr. Granger. Even if this scandal hadn't broken, and his stand on slavery hadn't turned folks against him, I'll bet he'd never get to the White House. He's had bad luck all along. Clay against him, and Calhoun after him like a tiger. He's tired now. He's old. He looks like a sick man.

The massive head went back. Mr. Webster was laughing at something Granger said. For a moment, the deep lines relaxed, the face was jovial, the hot eyes ceased to burn. "Buffalo rain," the famous voice boomed. "Black cats and nigger babies. I didn't think anyone'd stay to hear me, but when I saw they were bound to remain, I did my best for 'em. But it was wet."

Major Burnet said, "A great speech, sir. A great speech. I haven't always applauded your sentiments"—he waved gracefully—"but when I read about what you'd said in Buffalo, I wanted to shout amen."

Webster said, "It's something new, to have Democrats applauding. I'll have to get used to it." He bit generously into a pork sandwich and said, "You gentlemen'll excuse me if I'm hungry. I had breakfast with Mr. Seward in Auburn, but it seems to have receded into history." He drained his glass of brandy and water and pushed it toward the bottle. "That goes to the spot, gentlemen. Another drop of moral suasion, and I'll be able to convert all your backsliders." A liberal drop was poured. Mr. W. dispatched it with alacrity. "Now tell me something about your situation. I'll talk better if I have the facts."

The facts made him frown; the bushy brows drew forward, the eyes blazed, the large, mobile mouth drew down. "Radical fools and hotheads," he said fiercely. "It's time you did something about it. Your town is known as a laboratory of Abolition, libel and treason. It reeks. The whole country smells it. Even New York City wouldn't let Garrison and his crew hold their Anti-Slavery convention there, so where did they come? Syracuse, just last week. They knew that Syracuse would take 'em in. It's worse than Boston. And that's saying something," Massachusetts' son said bitterly. "It's not a month since they refused to let me speak in Faneuil Hall." He looked around the circle of faces that stared fascinated, respectful, solemn. "I made 'em regret it," he said with satisfaction. "Three days after I published a letter telling 'em what I thought of 'em, the Common Council, who've got some sense, passed a motion requesting me to speak as planned. Of course I refused," he said negligently, "but it did as much good as though I'd spoken. When I left the city a mob of people gathered to see me off, and they made such a fuss I had to say a word to them right there, in front of the hotel. They won't do that again in a hurry." He smiled grimly at his audience.

Mr. Noxon said hastily, "I'm sure you'll find everybody in Syracuse enthusiastic to hear you. It's a big event for our town."

"I hope they'll think so when I've finished with 'em," Webster said with meaning. "And I hope you'll see that what I say is printed the way I say it. They mixed up my Buffalo speech so that the report the New York papers made was just the opposite of what I meant. I think it was done on purpose." The great man leaned forward to speak so that Noxon should not fail to understand. "I said I regretted that slavery existed in the southern states *but* that it was clear Congress had no power over it. And what they printed was that I regretted that slavery existed *and that* Congress had no power over it. That was a deliberate perversion of meaning. A deliberate perversion. It suggests that I deplore Congress's position in the matter, whereas I merely made a statement of fact." He glared at Noxon. "You will be good enough to see that no such—*error*," he underlined the word, "is repeated here."

Major Burnet rescued his henchman. "You may rest easy about that, Mr. Webster," he said in his full, confident voice. "We're heart and soul on your side in this business. All the sound men in Syracuse are against these crazy Abolitionists. There's only a handful of 'em, really, but they make a lot of noise. They carry on so that they get in the papers, and of course when they have men like Garrison and Smith and Weld here, folks assume the whole town is radical. It ain't so, really. We've got a fine town, and most of the citizens are thinking the right way about this slavery business. They know it don't concern them, and they want to keep their noses out of it."

Webster grunted and pushed his glass once more toward the bottle. "You'll know more about that in another hour," he said, and rubbed his hands across his face like a man weary of words.

Palfrey said suddenly, "I think Mr. Webster should know that the feeling here is running very high. The Major's right in saying that the Abolitionists aren't so strong in numbers, but they're growing every day, from what we can see, and they're capable of violence." He looked at the fierce old man and said, "You won't get much applause. You may get hissing. We're going to police the meeting, so I don't think there's any danger of a fight, but it won't be a favorable audience."

Webster stared at him for a moment before he spoke. "I expect that," he said. "I don't care what they do. I'm going to tell 'em what I think about 'em."

Palfrey bowed. "That's what I hoped, sir." His face flushed suddenly with anger. "They're trying to destroy this country. They've got to be brought to their senses. They're endangering the whole nation."

Daniel Webster nodded his head in approval. "Gadarene swine." His great voice tolled. "Gadarene swine. Running violently down a steep place into the sea." He raised the glass to his lips and drank. Then he got heavily to his feet. "We'd better be going, gentlemen. The sooner we start, the sooner it's over. I'm not so young as I was, and this trip's been fatiguing. I'll be glad to get back to Washington."

A crowd standing in the street has to talk, has to gossip and laugh and comment on the speaker if it knows anything about him—or if it doesn't. Market Square was jammed with men and women. It was a new thing to see real ladies out in public to hear a political speech, but Abolitionists would do anything, as one gentleman said, spitting in disgust and watching a haughty dame withdraw her skirts. Antislavery ladies had lost all sense of decency, they were so dead set to do something about the slaves. One man said he admired 'em for it. They couldn't stand to think of black men being beaten to death by cruel masters. It was a cross to 'em to have to act unwomanly, but they were willing to suffer for the cause. The first man snorted loudly at this, and it looked for a minute as though they might have sharp words.

Most of the ladies of fashion had managed to keep out of the worst of the crowd by engaging seats, or at least standing room, on the steps of the Market Hall. That wasn't too good a place to hear from; not unless old Dan Webster had a powerful voice; but they could see him all right, and it wasn't so crowded. The rest of the populace—and it did seem as though half the city had turned out to hear the speech—was jam-packed into the street, on the sidewalks, filling the whole square where Genesee Turnpike crossed Montgomery Street. Frazee Hall was right on the corner, a fine-looking building, people said, gazing respectfully at its four stories of handsome red brick. Neat-looking. Opposite, facing its little square, the primly Doric façade of the Market

Hall in its neat white and green was swarming with people crowding the open windows, packed like sardines on the pillared porch. Webster wouldn't see much better, wherever he went, unless of course it was Washington City.

"He's going to have to crawl through a window, just the same," somebody—probably an Abolitionist, you might know—said, and the crowd laughed. It was true that the small, iron-railed balcony at the second-floor level of Frazee Hall was only to be reached through a window.

"It won't feaze Black Dan," a loyal admirer retorted. "Old Dan's got through a lot of tight places before this."

Dallas Ord piloted Mahala through this crowd, watching it with interest. "About half-and-half," he said softly. "Burnet's got his gang out, and they're looking for trouble. There's enough Abolitionists to give it to 'em, too."

Mahala said, "Let's get near enough to see his face. I don't care about the crowd."

She heard Ord's whispering laugh. "You're a fire-eater, Mis' Haley." His southern drawl was very pronounced. "You're studyin' to get in trouble every day God sends." It seemed to amuse him. Still laughing, he guided her through the press of bodies to a place directly in front of the little iron balcony. Through the window behind it, figures could be seen moving back and forth. The sash of the middle window, giving upon the balcony, was removed, while the crowd clapped, welcoming any sign of action after such a wait. Some wag yelled, "Come on, Dan'l. The lions are waiting for ye," and was hushed by the more decorous in the gathering.

The first person to crawl through the window was not Daniel Webster, however. Frank Granger, familiar to them all, straightened and turned toward the audience. The crowd hummed, clapped faintly, and then subsided, shuffling its feet with impatience. After all, they could hear Frank Granger any time. Major Burnet, climbing more nimbly, was better received. The Salt Pointers began a very respectable claque, which the others took up after a minute, and silenced politely when the Major raised his hand.

"'This great man,'" Mahala whispered angrily to Ord, echoing the honeyed words of the speaker. "Webster's a turncoat, and half the country knows it. A Whig, being praised by a Democrat. I should think he'd die of shame to hear it."

Granger was speaking now, spreading it on thick. This great honor that had come to the city of Syracuse. One of the greatest Americans of all history. A man whose honor and integrity none could doubt. The crowd, once more, murmured. Granger brought his oratory hastily to a close, and bundled through the open window into Frazee Hall, the Major following him. Then, while the throng in the street waited as still as a mouse, a heavy figure appeared in the dark opening, a head and shoulders thrust through into the light, a man drew himself erect on the small iron balcony. He wore a dark-blue coat with brass buttons, and stood bareheaded under the May sun.

"Why, he's old and sick," Mahala cried softly, and Ord turned to watch her face, full of sudden pity and compassion, as though the sight of the old man standing there had moved her against her will. "He's sick," she said again, watching with all her eyes.

Above her the heavy figure, shapeless, stout, and seeming unworthy to support the magnificent domed head, swayed slightly, straightened and steadied as his hands caught at the delicate iron rail of the balcony. Daniel Webster raised his head and looked silently over the multitude gathered to hear him, and the multitude looked back. He saw the press of upturned faces, the dusty coats, the occasional bright splashes of color of the women's dresses; he saw, near at hand, the faces of men staring at him with interest, with admiration, with hostility. Across the square of the Hay Market, he saw those faces repeated until they were a confused blur before his eyes.

"Fellow citizens of Syracuse, Ladies and Gentlemen: I thank you cordially for the pains you have taken to meet together this afternoon, forming so broad an assemblage to welcome me to your growing and important city of Syracuse."

The great voice lifted, ringing and persuasive, floating over the blanket of faces in the Square. No movement; no clapping. This was a pleasant word, coming from Daniel Webster, but these people had heard oratory before. They waited for what was to be said.

The old man grasped the slender iron railing of his balcony more firmly as he leaned forward and spoke. Those who stood near could see now that the smile had left his face, that its lines had deepened, that under his jutting brows the eyes were burning. From his face they guessed that Daniel Webster had made up his mind to let them have it, hot and heavy, hammer and tongs. They had come to hear him talk about slavery; very well, he would talk about it, straight out. As he first uttered the word a tremor visibly ran through the multitude.

"You cannot state more strongly than I feel to be true that this original, ancient, unhappy institution of slavery of the African races in the southern states is forever to be deplored."

The crowd murmured as he said this, muttered in its beard, accusingly. If you deplore it, why did you take up for it? If you deplore it, why did you vote for the Fugitive Slave Law? If you deplore it, why did you come here promising to speak on the proslavery side?

If he could not hear the angry words they murmured, Webster certainly could guess what they were. His voice lashed them. Twenty years before, he told them scornfully, the greatest men of the South had recognized this, and were planning to free their slaves. Washington had planned it, Jefferson and Marshall planned it, the influential men of the present day plan to do it, gradually and sensibly, without upsetting the economic and social arrangements of the nation.

"But there are Abolition Societies," the great voice rang. "There are in this country Abolition Societies who have prejudged the condition of the slave, and have done nothing but mischief. They have riveted the chains of the slave. They have postponed far the period of their redemption." The speaker straightened and stood for a moment silent before them, his shoulders back, his head raised, staring at them in defiance. "This is my judgment. It may not be yours."

The murmuring chorus rose higher now, sharper, louder, fiercer. It was not their judgment, voices said to each other; to Daniel Webster. But not all of the voices said "No" to the speaker. Next to Dallas Ord, a huge salt boiler was saying, "Go it, Dan; go it, Dan," over and over. As he spoke, he looked around him to see if any man dared to argue with him, or to speak against Daniel Webster, his man. The crowd was well mixed, Ord thought, seeing how cleverly Burnet had sifted his men through the audience to hold the radicals in check. There won't be a demonstration, whatever Webster says, he thought. Burnet's taken care of that. But this won't make any votes for Webster, and it won't keep the Abolitionists from fighting him.

"Those men who voted to admit Texas," Webster was saying. "Where are they now? They are Free-Soilers of the first water," he said, so drolly that the crowd began to laugh and a few to clap their hands. The old man knew how to play his audience. "They are Free-Soilers, and they loudly denounce Mr. Webster," Daniel Webster said, smiling grimly at them. "I believe he *has* been denounced here," he said blandly. "Is this not Syracuse?"

The ripple of laughter, the spattering of applause, broke out now with a will. Both sides could afford to clap this sally. Mr. Webster said, as smooth as silk, "I believe they hold conventions here," and made the laughter swell in the packed Square. "I believe they denounce Webster as the fit associate of Benedict Arnold," he said satirically, and the crowd howled with amusement.

"He's a wonder," Mahala said softly to Dal Ord. "Lucifer descending from Heaven. He can do anything with people. He can talk the birds out of the trees. We ought to have arranged to stop him. He can turn everyone against us." She had forgotten now that she had pitied the sick old man. Here before her was great power, great danger to the cause.

Ord said, "Don't worry. He may persuade some of the folks who are on the fence, but he won't touch any of our men. It's too late to change 'em. It's too late for Daniel Webster, too. He's betting on the wrong horse this time, and he's going to lose."

But how he could charm; how he could persuade, Mahala thought, as the magnificent voice rolled on, reasoning, accusing, denouncing. No wonder these foolish salt boilers were shouting for him; ready with their great fists to fight for him if any rebel should bat an eye. No wonder the solid citizens of the town were crying, "Hear, Hear," when a point was made. Daniel Webster, Black Dan, the Thunderer, the great senator from Massachusetts, the great Secretary of State. The man who'd gone up against Calhoun and Hayne and Clay. Those he praised felt warm and flattered and proud. Those he blamed could only hold on to their hatred and glare back at him. And if it had been a debate, they could not, for all their hatred and their convictions, have found words bright and powerful enough to have conquered the words Daniel Webster could speak. They could only wait until he had finished, and then set about to oppose him.

He was talking now about the Fugitive Slave Law, and Mahala held her breath to listen. Surely they would shout against Webster now, she thought. Surely this law, which had split the city in two and brought over to the Abolition camp a hundred men never before opposed to slavery, was a brand that would set them burning against Webster, who had framed it.

"I do not say the law is perfect. But it is constitutional. What then?" The question was so sudden that it made them jump. "Is it not to be obeyed? Are not those who are sworn to obey the Constitution to enforce this law? Is it not a matter of conscience?" The terrible voice thundered, accusing them—*"Of conscience?"*

"But what do we hear?" Webster leaned forward so that he seemed to hover over them, like an accusing spirit. "We hear of persons assembling in Massachusetts and New York, who set themselves over the Constitution, above the law, and above the decisions of the highest tribunals, and say that this law shall not be carried into effect. You have heard it here, have you not?" he shouted at them, and flung out a hand to point at the guilty men. "Has it not been said in the County of Onondaga?"

The crowd broke bounds now. "Yes! Yes!" burst from it, and the men who answered were half of them applauding, half of them furious with anger. Yes, they said it, the Patriots cried to Daniel Webster. Yes, the dirty Nigger Lovers said it, bad cess to them and be damned to them for trying to run honest Irish workmen out of their jobs to give to their black men. Yes, we said it, the Abolitionists answered him. We'll say it again and again until we've freed the slaves, and all your fine words won't stop us.

Webster listened to the voices replying and then spoke again. "And have not these men who said it pledged their lives and their fortunes, their sacred honor, to defeat the execution of this law?" He paused and let the crowd roar its answer. "For *what?*" he cried out, whipping their fury higher. "For *what?*" Gripping the rail of the little balcony, he leaned forward to answer his own question. "For the violation of the law, for the committing of treason to the country. For it is treason, and it is nothing else!" His voice soared over the wild shouting in the Square.

"No! No! It is time to put an end to this imposition upon good men and women, upon good citizens. It is treason—treason—*treason*—and nothing else!"

The crowd was crazy now, with excitement, with rage, with gratification. Major Burnet's Salt Pointers were whooping it up, yelling and shouting and clapping, stamping their feet and moving through the crowd to see if any of the damned Woolly Heads wanted to start a fight; ready to break a jaw or black an eye, if anyone so much as looked cross-eyed at Dan'l Webster. Here and there a moment's scuffling broke out, but the Abolitionists weren't going to fight, or at least not with these hoodlums. They were yelling against Daniel Webster, booing him and catcalling, if they were common people; saying, "No!" loudly, if they were men of dignity and position. They wouldn't give the Patriots the satisfaction of brawling under the eye of the great Webster. Let the old man make a fool of himself, they said contemptuously to each other. He thinks he's such great shakes, he thinks he's hell on wheels. But he'll find he's mistaken. We'll show him later, they said, looking sidewise at each other. He'll see, someday.

The old man was pouring the vials of his wrath upon them, now, suddenly as angry as they were. "Who are these men? I am assured that some of them are clergymen, and I am sorry to say some are lawyers; and who the rest are God only knows." He looked around him like a hanging judge.

"They say the law will not be executed here. Let them take care, for those are bold assertions." Once more he gripped the iron railing and leaned forward to drop his words like molten lead upon the assailers of a fortress. "Depend upon it, the law *will* be executed, in its spirit and in its letter."

A great shout arose like a battle cry from the hosts below him. "It will be executed here in Syracuse," said Daniel Webster, towering over them. "It will be executed in the midst of the next Anti-Slavery Convention, if the occasion shall arise. Then we shall see," he cried like a challenge, "then we shall see what becomes of their lives and their sacred honor!"

The old man stood before them for a long minute, still grasping the low railing of the balcony, still glaring at them like a fierce old tiger behind the low bars of its cage. Then, as though he'd had enough of them and their iniquities, he turned suddenly and climbed back through the window and out of their sight. The great speech was over. There had been no fight. There had been some applause, but no real demonstration, for or against him. He had shot his bolt, the Abolitionists said, pushing their way out of the crowd. He'd said his say. He'd threatened them, had he? Very well, perhaps he might see, some time or other, how they'd answer him.

The Patriots lallygagged around for a while, waiting to see if there was going to be any kind of ruction; saying that, by jeepers, the old boy had been too much for the white-livered Nigger Lovers. He'd swamped 'em. He'd swizzled 'em. He was as good as a Democrat, they said, talking out of the corners of their mouths and spitting so ferociously that Abolitionist ladies had to pick up their skirts and skedaddle. Old Dan was all right, and he'd done the Major proud.

When Mr. Webster came down with the Major's party, all smiling now, all trying to talk to the great man, all telling him what a fine speech it was, what a power of good he'd done in Syracuse, the North Enders clapped again and raised a ragged cheer as the carriage moved away. Later, at Mr. Winston's Globe Hotel on Salina Street, a large company, as the *Star* reported next day, sat down to a sumptuous banquet at which the famous guest spoke again, this time with great charm and good temper. Everything was got up in fine style, the paper said, and the entertainment was enlivened with selections played by Kellogg's Brass Band.

Mr. W., looking weary and old, was finally bundled on to the cars later that night, to continue his trip. He was extremely fatigued. His son Fletcher had sickened and been obliged to go home ahead of him, and the trip was not easy. Speeches everywhere, meeting people, rising at dawn to get through the engagements of the day, traveling on trains and boats over the interminable countryside. His mind, he wrote to a friend, was as dry as a remainder biscuit after a voyage. He hoped he had done some good and would be remembered in Syracuse, that Abolition Hole.

CHAPTER ELEVEN

"Everybody says she's *wonderful,* father," Francelia said passionately. "We've *got* to hear her. I don't care how much it costs."

Amidon Palfrey looked at his wife. "There's going to be a great crush getting tickets," he said, jingling the money in his pockets. "I've heard folks talking about it. If it's like other towns, they'll bid anything for them. Ten times what they're worth."

Mrs. Amidon sided with the girls. "Everyone's going," she said, as though that settled it. "We can't have the girls miss Jenny Lind. Tom doesn't have to go. That'll be one saving. But the rest of us ought to. Folks will think it's funny if we aren't there."

Mr. Palfrey heard footsteps on the stairs. "Maybe John will get the tickets for us." He turned to regard John's elegant person clothed in a new gray coat and fawn-colored nankeen pantaloons. A fine-looking boy, he thought heavily, but he's impatient with the family nowadays. He said, "We're talking about seats for this concert, John. I hear there's going to be a great rush for them. I thought perhaps you'd buy for all of us."

John paused in the doorway. "I'll be glad to, father. But you'd better tell me how much you're willing to pay. I'm told there's going to be hot bidding for them."

His mother said, "We want good seats, John. Get five together, right down in front. Tom's not going." She smiled hopefully at her son, and there was a little hush as the thought in all their minds flowed into the air like smoke. What about That Girl? four of them were thinking, so that the words seemed to fill the room. What about That Girl?

John said coolly, "Perhaps I'd better get four for you people and get mine separately. I'm escorting Miss North."

His manner, the words he spoke, seemed to explode inside Amidon Palfrey's head, leaving a cloud of anger behind them. He said in a choked voice, "Never mind, then. You needn't bother. I'll get them myself. You have no time or consideration for your family any more."

John came reluctantly into the room. "That isn't so, father. I'm glad to get the tickets for you. But I thought it only fair to tell you that I was taking Miss North. You've made it plain how you feel toward her, and it wouldn't be comfortable for anyone if we sat together."

Mrs. Palfrey was weeping as usual. "I don't see why you can't let such people alone and go with your own family," she said into her handkerchief.

Amidon Palfrey stood up. "I said I'd get the tickets myself." His voice shook with anger. "I'll ask no favors of a son who has no regard for his family's wishes. You may take anyone you please. I'll look after your mother and sisters."

There was clearly no use in prolonging this quarrel. John Palfrey said, "I'm sorry, father. You're bound to misunderstand me." He turned quickly and went out the door. Inside the room, they sat listening to the sound of the front door's closing, to the rapid beat of footsteps going down the walk. Mr. Palfrey said, "Don't cry any more, mother. I'll take care of everything. There's nothing we can do about John."

Francelia Palfrey returned to her original subject. "I don't care who John takes," she said smartly. "We can't go on moping about John all the time. And maybe that girl isn't so awful, anyway. Amelia said she met her with John at the Cramers' party Friday night, and she said she acted just like anybody. John's so popular that some folks are taking up with his girl, just to have him around. We might as well get used to it."

Her mother said tearfully, "I'll never get used to having a barmaid in the family," and sobbed aloud at the prospect.

Amidon Palfrey got to his feet. "I may as well go," he said to his wife. "I'll get tickets because I promised the girls I would, but I shan't take any pleasure in it."

Francelia capered to the door after him. "I'm going with you," she said eagerly. "I want to see what happens."

The Empire House had been known under a dozen names, ever since it was the first rude tavern Bogardus built on the old Genesee Turnpike, when the town was called Bogardus' Corners, and Cossitt's Corners before it was called Milan and Corinth and finally Syracuse. Now, thirty years later, the old tavern, Bogardus' Tavern, the Mansion House, Rust's Hotel, whichever of its names you cared to use, was long gone. In its place, right in the middle of town, still sitting astride Genesee Street, fronting one way on Clinton Square and the other on North Salina Street, was the well-known Empire House, or as people usually said, Voorhees' House, because Voorhees had recently bought it and fixed it up superfine.

He was a smart man, was Voorhees; a go-ahead, a gumptious man. Getting the sale of tickets for this Jenny Lind concert was just like his smart ways. Such things brought business, made a stir. And, certainly, enough people were crowding around the Empire House today, pushing and shoving, elbowing each other for fair to get a good place near the doors. As the morning wore on, the crowd had pushed well out into the street, so that horse traffic had to edge around it to get by, and, what with their impatience and the pressure of the bodies behind them, it looked as though somebody might get hurt before they ever heard the Swedish Nightingale sing at all.

As the crowd grew, it became impossible to get into any of the handsome stores that inhabited the façade of the hotel. By noon, when the sale of tickets began, storekeepers had been obliged to close and lock their doors against the violence of the mob, and when the fighting actually started, they were ready behind barricades to protect their property. With a crush like that, they felt sensibly enough, you could never tell what might happen.

And still the people kept coming, men and women from all over town and half the surrounding countryside. There were persons of consequence from the fashionable parts of the city, businessmen and salt boilers, rough Irishmen from Salt Point, German barrelmakers from Salina, schoolteachers from the Academy, prosperous farmers from Pompey and Manlius and Fayetteville and Camillus, aristocrats from Onondaga Valley and Skaneateles, politicians and their henchmen, storekeepers and canallers and train conductors. And all of them pushing and shoving and cursing, Mr. Palfrey thought, bracing his elbows against the broad back in front of him as the pressure from behind increased.

Poor Francelia, at his side, was fairly being crushed between two huge Dutchmen from Wolf Street, and her father, hemmed in as he was, could do nothing to protect her. He had begged her to leave an hour before, when retreat was still possible, but she had refused to budge, and now there she was, pressed flat like a herring in a box, and no way of getting out. John was here somewhere, Mr. Palfrey knew, but it was impossible to find him in this melee. Nothing, no one, not even Mr. Phineas Barnum's "Angel," was worth this much trouble, old Mr. Palfrey thought, puffing angrily.

The crowd was beginning to stamp now and shout for Voorhees.

"Open up the doors!"

"Get a move on; get a move on!"

"Hi! Joe, push on the door!"

At this, the whole crowd surged forward, so that poor Francelia cried out for mercy, and some rough fellow in the front ranks yelled, "Jesus Christ and General Jackson!" in a voice which none of the ladies could avoid hearing.

Poor Mr. Palfrey was distracted. "Push your way out, Francelia," he implored her frantically. "You'll be injured, and I can't move to help you."

Francelia, wedged between her two gigantic barrelmakers, could only moan.

But all this was not a drop in the bucket compared to the struggle that began the instant the doors to the ticket office were really opened. Mr. Voorhees, for all his cleverness, had made no preparation for such a horde as now besieged his establishment. He had rigged up one table with one man to sell the tickets and make change for the customers, and when the crowd commenced to shove and push and jam into the tiny space, the unfortunate ticket seller could barely move to wait on anyone, and that made him all the slower, and made the waiting crowd all the wilder. He begged in vain that the customers wait their turns in an orderly manner, but no one paid any attention to him at all.

Indeed, a struggle for the positions near the door now developed into a real fight; men wrestled and struck at each other as well as they could in such a confined position. One blow led to another, men shouted and swore, ladies screamed. When the first female actually fainted, a slight lull occurred, and her neighbors gave over brawling until the poor thing could be handed out, from one man to another, to safety at the edge of the crowd. After that another lady fainted promptly, but she was not so fortunate. No one offered to carry her away, and her husband was obliged to support her lifeless form as well as he could until she came to.

As for the tickets themselves, although the price was supposed to be fixed at four dollars for the pit and two dollars for the gallery, as soon as the first man had succeeded in getting his tickets and returning to the crowd outside, he was beset by a dozen offers for them, and the price began to soar. Six dollars; ten dollars; fifteen dollars. The first man took the fifteen and thought he'd made a good bargain, but as the afternoon dragged on, and the crowd increased, even that extravagant price was low. Single tickets would bring ten dollars apiece; a pair of tickets was worth thirty dollars, forty, at the last a cool fifty. Men bawled their bids from every part of the crowd, fought like nailers when someone else grabbed the tickets away from them.

Mr. Palfrey, hopelessly pushed to one side of the door, able to see the entrance but not make his way to it, gave up and began to bid with the others. It was worth anything to get out of this ruction. Once he caught a glimpse of his son, across the heads of a dozen men between them. He shouted like a good one, and it seemed to him that John must have heard, but the crowd closed in again after that, and he gave up hope of rescue. Francelia was weeping now, but there was nothing he could do to comfort her. Let this be a lesson to her, he said to himself furiously, not to insist upon rushing after every excitement she could hear about.

Another pair of tickets was being offered now. Mr. Palfrey shouted, "Forty dollars."

"Fifty dollars!" A dozen voices drowned him out.

Moses North, looking over the heads of the crowd, said mildly, "Quite a sight. And all to hear some foreign female sing a few songs. It ain't worth it," he said judicially, "but it's a pretty good fight. If you was feeling right up to snuff, Dal, we might have a real good time."

Dal Ord laughed. "Don't let me hinder you," he said, grinning at the old man's regretful tone. "If you feel like breaking a few heads, don't wait for me. I might feel inspired, myself."

"I promised Mahala I'd keep you out of trouble," Moses said doubtfully, but it was evident that he was tempted. "A couple of good men could clear a path to that door, if they took a little trouble," he said and irresistibly moved forward.

Mahala's promise might possibly have been kept if a woman had not screamed just then. It was Francelia, with what appeared to be her last breath. Her two Germans had abandoned her and pushed forward into the scrum, and now, jostled intolerably, she was calling upon Providence to save her. Moses North waited no longer. His great shoulder was a ram against opposing backs and shoulders, his arms moved like flails. Dal Ord came after him in a flash. His slender figure pierced the wall of crowded bodies, slipping through where a larger man would have failed.

"A lady's hurt!" Moses' voice rose into a bellow that drowned the bidders' shouts. "Make way. I'm coming through."

Men turned to curse, blows landed on the swinging arms. A movement was beginning to come from the opposing side, pressing against the two rescuers like a toppling wall. Moses paid no attention to anyone until he heard John Palfrey's voice shouting at him.

"North—Moses North! Let me get through to you. It's my sister—" His voice was choked off suddenly, and it was evident that he was fighting.

Moses was the first to reach the girl and pick her up bodily, but John Palfrey was beside him in a minute, clutching his sister's arm, talking to her hoarsely. He was disheveled, his fair hair ruffled, his immaculate new coat torn in a half dozen places, a cut bleeding a little on the side of his jaw.

Francelia gasped, "Get father. He's here somewhere," and then her head fell back limply against Moses North's broad chest.

The huge man said soothingly, "I'll get her out, John. You and Dal go look for your father. This ain't any place for an old man." He turned carefully and, with his burden, began to push his way out.

Whatever he might feel about Dal Ord at another time, John was glad of him now. Ord was slender, but he was made of steel. Together they moved against the struggling, shouting mass of creatures before them. Everyone was excited now; everyone, more or less, was fighting. As the two moved slowly forward, fists working, shoulders hunched against blows, they saw Amidon Palfrey battered and pummeled as he was, shoved against the wall of the hotel. A great struggle was going on around him, and, as the two younger men came near, a final push flung a young fellow beside Mr. Palfrey straight up, shoulder high, and hurled him against the glass panels of a shop door. The glass shattered like ripping silk and fell into the crowd, and as the man dropped he began to scream, horribly, inhumanly, as a horse screams when it is shot.

Who might go next into that broken glass, no one could say. Palfrey made for his father, reached him and made his own body a barrier against the mob. Then he called to his companion. "Ord! Help me to get him out."

Ord's voice at his elbow said calmly, "Just a minute. This man's hurt." Craning to look, Palfrey saw Ord lift the boy who had been cut. "Gentlemen, if you please," he said to the brawling mob beside him. "This boy has been cut. Please help him to get out." His voice, as usual, was low, courteous, but for some reason the men beside him heard it and obeyed. Palfrey saw them stare for a moment at the slim, dark man holding the lad in his arms. Then, without protest, they began to lift the fainting body shoulder high, head high; to pass it over the solid mass of men packed around the door of the hotel. Ord watched them, said, "Thank you, gentlemen," and took out his handkerchief to wipe away the blood from his hands. "I believe the boy has cut an artery," he said coolly. "He'd better get to a doctor as soon as possible."

With the two young men to bulwark him on either side, Amidon Palfrey managed to get out of the crowd in fairly good order, but he was plainly shaken by the experience.

"I must get Francelia," he said over and over, clinging to his son's arm. "Some man picked her up and carried her out. I don't know what's happened to her."

John guided him across the street. "She's all right, father. Mr. North carried her out. He's taken her over to his hotel. She'll be perfectly safe."

His father stared. "She oughtn't to be in a canal tavern." His voice was uncertain.

John Palfrey said grimly, "She's lucky to be there. If Mr. North hadn't rescued her, she'd be in that crowd right now." His father did not mention the matter again.

He found his daughter resting on a sofa in Mahala's green parlor, sniffing gingerly at a bottle of smelling salts, while a tall, red-haired woman in a blue dress bathed her wrists with eau de cologne. The room was cool, shaded against the afternoon sun, so that it looked to his weary gaze like a cave of refreshment. Without intending to, he sank into a soft chair, accepted the glass of brandy that Moses North brought him. Everything was so confused today, he thought, feeling the liquor hot on his tongue. Not as young as I was, he thought, sipping again, letting the fiery stuff restore him. Not up to a fight any more.

He looked around the room. A nice place, he had to admit. Not what he'd expect in such a tavern. Decent, respectable. He looked at his son and the knowledge came to him, with a little shock of surprise, that John was familiar with this place, with these people. To see him standing there, leaning against a tall chair back, chatting with the enormous Mr. North as though he'd known him all his life, gave Amidon Palfrey a strange feeling.

These are the people John's fought me about all winter, he thought, looking from one to another; this is where he's been coming, night after night, while his mother and I wondered where he was; that red-haired woman is the girl he's been running with, for all we could say to stop him. And today, the old man thought, looking down at the half-emptied glass in his hand, today this Moses North carried Francelia out of the crowd like a babe in arms, and now the red-haired girl was bringing Francelia around with her own smelling salts, while Amidon Palfrey drank Moses North's best brandy.

There had been another man who had helped them, a dark fellow he'd seen around somewhere. The face was familiar, and the soft southern voice. That was the clue; he'd seen that chap at one of Burnet's meetings. He'd made a speech, Mr. Palfrey remembered. A Southerner. Perhaps he and John were working together against the Abolitionists; perhaps that's how John had met these people.

There was nothing he could do now except express his gratitude, Amidon Palfrey saw. He finished the brandy, put down the glass and got to his feet. "If Francelia's better, I'd like to take her home," he said, looking toward the sofa. "Her mother will be worried about her." He turned to Moses North's great bulk and spoke with surprising humility. "I have to thank you, Mr. North, for rescuing my daughter. I couldn't move, myself, in that crowd, and she was in great distress. You've been very kind."

North took his hand and shook it genially. "You needn't think about that, Mr. Palfrey," he said as though it had been nothing at all. "I thought she looked kind of unhappy, and so I just tucked her under my arm and came home." His laughter filled the room.

John Palfrey said, "It sounds easy when you say it, but Ord and I had all we could do to get through that jam. I've never seen anything to beat it. If it's like that on the night of the concert, they'd better call out the police."

Mahala, turning toward them from her patient, showed Mr. Palfrey her smile. "We'll have to get father to escort us, or we'll never get out alive."

Her father said, "No, ma'am. If you young folks are foolish enough to get into another muss, you'll have to fight your own way out. I don't mind a common riot or such a thing, but I ain't going to any concert." He looked over at Miss Francelia, sitting up now on her sofa, listening to this talk with wide eyes. "That is," he said gallantly, "unless Miss Francelia'll go with me. She and I get along first rate, don't we?" His face crinkled all over with his smile.

Francelia Palfrey cried with utter devotion, "I'd go *anywhere* with you!" and everybody laughed.

The talk, the laughter, might have gone on for hours, Mr. Palfrey thought, watching the young people. But considering what had happened, he couldn't be curt with his host. After a bit he was able to catch John's eye and tell him to go fetch the carriage. "Your mother will be distracted," he warned his son, and wondered how he was going to explain matters to her. There was no doubt that it was going to be very difficult.

It was going to be difficult because, although Amidon Palfrey had certainly thanked Mr. North and his daughter profusely for their attentions during and after the ticket riot, the matter could not, conceivably, end there. After a man has, at the risk of injury, saved you and your daughter from a frenzied mob, and later taken you both into his house and ministered to you, you cannot possibly cut him—or *his* daughter—dead the next time you see them. You cannot even speak against him to your nearest and dearest in the agitated bosom of your own family. You cannot condemn your son—or your daughter—for making friends with the daughter of such a man. This, at least, was what Amidon Palfrey reluctantly felt. His guns had been spiked, he thought, watching his wife's tears flow. He could not actually commend his son for falling in love with Moses North's daughter, but neither could he wholly blame him.

"Don't feel so bad, mother," he said as consolingly as possible. "It may not be so terrible. She looks like a nice, decent girl."

Mrs. Palfrey, struggling through her tears to make ready for the Swedish Nightingale, refused to be comforted. "It's bad enough to have you and John so smitten with a common tavernkeeper's girl, but now Francelia's got to go chasing after her, too. I declare," she said hopelessly, "I don't see what's got *into* everybody. Just because some old man helps you get out of a crowd where you never ought to have *gone*"—she looked accusingly at her husband—"why, you all seem to think it's something great, and you're all possessed to take up for the people that helped you. You could have *paid* him," she said bitterly to Mr. Palfrey. "That would have settled everything and left no afterclap."

You couldn't reason with a woman, Mr. Palfrey thought wearily, struggling into his best frock coat. You shouldn't argue. Some things a woman never would admit, and you might as well stop trying to make her.

Later that evening he was obliged to stand by his guns, spiked or not. They had scarcely taken their places on the hard wooden pews of the new Baptist Church when they saw John come in, escorting Mahala North. Amidon Palfrey heard his wife gasp and felt her hand on his arm. "There they are," she hissed in his ear.

"Over there, with Annabelle Moss and Oren Bensted." Then her grip tightened on her husband's arm. "And Francelia," she fairly wailed. "Francelia and Joe Redfield."

Mr. Palfrey took the situation in hand. "Be quiet, Emma," he said sternly. "You cannot make a scene here. People will be looking at you. You've got to pretend you know all about it and don't mind. Smile," he said, and it was an order. "Bow to them and smile."

Weakly, Mrs. Palfrey did as he said.

Across the hall, John returned the bow rather stiffly, and Francelia waved her hand as though there was nothing the matter. The tall girl on John Palfrey's arm moved forward like a swan on a lake, her wide skirts of India muslin drifting around her like white plumage, her neck arched proudly, her short, coppery curls glowing like flame. Along the rows of chairs, heads turned to look at her; behind a dozen hands, comments were whispered. Mahala noticed nothing of this. Once she turned and smiled briefly at something John Palfrey said. She had dignity, old Amidon thought, admiring her against his will; she had courage, too, to face this crowd. Emma might go farther and fare worse, if she was looking for a daughter-in-law.

But now the house quieted, the house lights went out, the footlights beamed yellow, and out upon the stage Miss Jenny Lind, Mr. Barnum's prize, New York's darling, the toast of the country, the idol, the adored, came forward and began to sing. Her voice, as clear and pure as fountain water, rose effortless, and filled the church. Amidon Palfrey settled back against the slats of his hard seat and was at peace.

Outside, in a crowd almost as large as the other but better behaved, Moses North and Dal Ord stood and listened. Oppressive heat, on this July night, had forced the managers of the place to open every window. The heavenly voice flowed out to the silent throng. Like a bird note, like the song of a wood thrush, it fell upon the quiet air, died away.

Moses North joined in the frenzied applause, begging for more.

"It don't seem human that anyone can make a noise like that," he said in wonder. "I ain't surprised that the whole country's gone crazy about her."

Dal Ord, standing on the church porch, was staring in through the open window, so absorbed that he did not hear what his companion said. Moses asked, "What's the matter with you? I said I didn't wonder they were all so crazy about her."

Through the window Ord could see past the rows of seats to where a pair of heads, one copper, one gold, leaned together. After a moment he said, as though he was not really conscious of his own words, "No. I don't wonder they're so crazy about her."

CHAPTER TWELVE

"There's other ways we can send 'em," Moses North said, spreading the map out on the table before him. On his great nose, a pair of steel-rimmed spectacles perched like windows, hiding the bright blue of his eyes. "I don't see what's to hinder our sending 'em along to Lockport, just the way we did the last bunch. They got through as slick as a whistle."

Mahala leaned forward, her two hands clenched into fists before her on the table. "I'm worried," she said slowly, staring at the pale markings on the map. "I don't like it. Those last Negroes got through, but I think something leaked, just the same. I think somebody knows something about it. I think they're going to be waiting for us, if we try it again that way." She looked up at her father. "I wish Dal was here," she said, her voice suddenly sharp with fear. "I don't like to have him traveling with them. If they get caught, he'll be taken too. I wish he'd come on ahead. Then we could discuss the best thing to do."

Her father refused to be alarmed. "I think you're making a mare's-nest of this when you don't need to. Did John say anything for certain about their watching the trains?"

Mahala shook her head. "No. Nothing definite. I feel that he doesn't like to talk to me about the Patriots now. He used to tell me everything they were doing, but lately he doesn't say much. If I ask questions, he looks at me queerly. I feel sometimes that he's suspicious of me." Her face darkened as she said, "He ought to be. I'm betraying everything he does say. He'd never speak to me again, if he knew. It makes me *hate* this," she cried in a sudden fury. "I wish we'd never come here. I wish I'd never met John. I can't bear this lying and cheating. I'd rather go back to Ohio where we worked with our own people."

"It's hard," Moses North said quietly. "You knew it was going to be hard when you chose to work with us. But there's no reason why you have to go on, if it's bothering you. You can go back to Ohio. Or you can marry John Palfrey, if you want to, and work for the other side. Dal and I can get along."

For a moment his daughter covered her face with her hands. "I'm sorry, father," she said wearily. "You know I don't mean it. I don't want to quit. I don't want to go back—and I'm not going to marry John. It wouldn't be fair to him, in the first place. And I could never feel as he does about slavery. I'd always have to work against it, wherever I was."

"Are you in love with Palfrey?" It was the first time Moses North had ever asked the direct question. Now, all the laughter, all the geniality and lightness had gone out of his face. He was a stern old man, looking with blue eyes that could burn into his daughter's face.

Mahala did not reply for a time, but sat staring at her clenched fists. "I don't know," she said at last. "Sometimes I think I am, when I'm with him; sometimes I don't know. At first, I knew I couldn't marry him, partly because his family and everyone he knew would hate me and make John unhappy on account of me. But lately they've been nicer. People speak to me and ask me to parties with John. Even his mother spoke to me the other night—" She broke off to stare, unseeing, before her. "I don't really care about that. Whether they like me or not. It's only for John."

Her father said again, implacably, "Are you in love with John Palfrey? I've got a right to know—and so has Dal."

Mahala moved in her seat as though a pain had shot through her. From her drawn face and the way her hands flew to her breast you would have said that some nerve had suddenly seared her, like a burning wire, or that some mysterious muscle in her heart had suddenly contracted and sent a wave of anguish through her body. She said with difficulty, "Dal doesn't want me any more. He did once, and I've waited for him to forgive me and want me again. But now he only wants to laugh at me. He's stopped loving me. John is the one that loves me."

For the third time Moses North said, "Are you in love with John?"

With a violent motion, Mahala pushed back her chair, rose and whirled away from the table. "I don't know," she cried in an extremity of pain. "I don't know. It doesn't matter. I'll go on working," she answered her father. "You needn't be afraid I'll quit. I'll help get these fugitives through." Tears were streaming down her face now, and her voice was no more than a whisper. "I promised Martin—and I promised Dal," she said in a voice so low that her father could barely hear it.

Moses North went to her and took her two thin hands in his immense palms. "I won't ask you again, girl," he said, his voice as tender as a woman's. Gently he drew Mahala toward him and held her sheltered in his arms against every pain she might feel. "Don't worry," he said softly. "You'll do whatever you think's right, and I'll be pleased, whatever it is. You'll know what you want when the time comes," he said with absolute certainty. "You'll see what to do. There's always a knowledge, down at the very bottom of your mind, that knows what to do. If you listen to that, you won't go wrong."

After a moment, sighing like a tree in a wind, Mahala drew away and went back to the table. Leaning forward, she studied the map once more. "We've got to figure something out, in case of trouble," she said. "The train will be in at noon, and we've got to hurry."

Her father looked at her, considering, then sat down and began to talk briskly about the problem. "They're mulattoes, about a dozen of 'em, Dal says in his letter." He frowned over the scrawled note. "He says, 'Am bringing stock by rail, arriving at noon, Wednesday, 1 doz. fleeces gray wool, as per last order. Goods in superfine condition, dyed, dressed and ready for immediate reshipment. Please arrange to meet with me at that time and settle the business.'" He looked up, grinning. "Ain't that like Dal, to think somebody might open his letter and get on to what he was doing? That boy don't trust anybody at all."

Mahala said moodily, "He's got reason not to," but her father paid no attention and went on with his planning.

"Maybe we'd better not go to the depot, in case some of Burnet's men should be nosing around. If we're here, ready for him, it will be just as good. If everything's safe, we can send 'em on the evening train to Lockport, or maybe it would be better, this time, to have 'em get off at Rochester, and let Fred Douglass send 'em up to Charlotte and over the lake. We don't want to send the pitcher to the well once too often."

"I think it may have gone too often already," Mahala said, running her finger along the inked routes on the map, tracing the red lines that twisted up from Elmira on the south, through Binghamton and Lebanon and Canastota and Peterboro; on from Peterboro to Syracuse and Oneida Lake, north through Baldwinsville and Fulton and Oswego. West from Syracuse to Skaneateles and Auburn and Port Byron and Weedsport and Ira and Fair Haven. Up from Owego in the south, skirting Cayuga Lake, through Ithaca, then west to Rochester; or turning east for a bit and running just beyond Syracuse to Auburn and so to Fair Haven on the lake. Or the long route, north from Ithaca, pausing at Peterboro, and ending finally at Ogdensburg in the north, a longer way but safer for that reason, and to be used when pursuit was hot.

Under her remembering eye, each of these lines meant a special occasion; she saw not simple country towns, not merely roads or railroad lines or boats, but a chain of stations. She saw farmhouses, where a secret room was carved out of a haystack, where

Negroes lay in attics or cellars, listening to the sound of a marshal's voice, trembling until he had gone away.

She remembered men with faces like the Judgment Day, looking at danger and saying, "Yes. I'll take those Negroes through." She thought of women, under the very eyes of a slave catcher, carrying a basket piled high with freshly ironed clothes across a kitchen where armed men were talking, and up the back stairs to the attic. There, the blue print ruffles would be whisked off, the bottom of the basket would be full of food, bread and meat for the terrified black men who waited for them. It wasn't a thing you could leave, she was thinking. Not even if you wanted to. If you ever belonged to the Railroad, you'd always belong to it. You'd always have to do your part, bear the danger, take the chances, meet the difficulties. If you'd ever touched it, if you'd ever helped one patient, trembling Negro to get away, you were in it forever. You had it in your blood. She had it in hers.

"What's the quickest way we could get them out of the city, if we had to?" she asked, frowning. There was no reason for her to be so apprehensive, but fear nagged at her unceasingly. Something had gone wrong. The worry on John Palfrey's face told her so, although he said nothing. Someone was waiting for them, threatening.

"Well, if we can't use the cars, we'll have to use horses," North said thoughtfully. "And it's not easy to get rigs enough for a dozen at short notice. If we'd planned it in time, we could have arranged beforehand with some of the farm stations near town. They could have driven in, casually, and sort of been on hand when we needed 'em. Now we'd have to hump ourselves to get enough."

Mahala looked up sharply. "Isn't Hiley Purvee in the bar? I thought I saw him when I came in. If he is, he could take a message to Mr. Smith to send us some help. He's the fastest man we've got." She looked at her father through narrowed lids. "Call him in here and let's talk to him."

Old Moses said admiringly, "You're smart's a whip, Haley.

That's a good idea. I'll bring him right in and we can kind of get our feet under us, just in case something does go wrong."

On the train, chuffing along out of Kirkville, a conductor passed down the car and slipped a piece of paper into Dallas Ord's hand. Ord closed his fingers on it and turned away to converse with the elegantly gowned lady at his side. He was traveling in toney company, the other passengers noticed; all the ladies—there were seven of them—rigged out in fancy clothes, the latest style, with long veils over their bonnets, and lilac gloves on their hands. They must be actors, or fast-living women, the farmers' wives thought, trying not to be envious; they were painted and enameled like stage actors, with their powdery white skins and painted lips and cheeks. Good women didn't dress so. The gentlemen of the party were quieter, more decent-looking.

After a moment, when everybody was laughing at something he'd said, Ord glanced at the slip in his hand. In crabbed writing the message read: "Be ready to jump before we get to the depot. They wired to Chittenango that marshals have hired a special engine to chase you. Get your goods off quick." It was signed "A Friend." For a moment he frowned, staring at the note. Then his habitual lazy smile returned. Still with his easy, negligent air, he tore the note into small pieces and leaned forward to toss them from the open window of the car.

Beyond the swaying train, the countryside showed a late, overblown lushness; not the exuberance of spring burgeoning, with its yellow-greens and yellows, but a darker color, a heavy, almost a blackish, green that was too ripe, past its prime, unvirginal, and yet sumptuous, too, in its own way. The trees—elms and sugar maples, mostly—were heavy dark-green plumes against the August noon. Beside meandering brooks, willow trees were silvered with dust. At the edge of swampy lowlands, wild grape climbed over half a hundred young elderberry bushes and chokecherry trees, covering them like a cloak so that only scalloped grape leaves and the meager bunches of its unripe fruit could be seen.

Goldenrod and pale-purple asters were beginning to bloom in the fields along the roadside. Orchards, as they slipped past the car windows, were bending with fruit, some of it already beginning to show cheeks of pink and red, weighting the boughs so that their tips hung low enough to touch the tufty grass that grew beneath them. Autumn was coming, all these signs said, but it was not here yet. Summer scents were still in the air, summer heat poured from a sky like blue glass, summer sounds rose where boys, bare as they were born, splashed and yelled in the swimming hole of a little creek.

Presently, the first outdwellings of the town appeared. Tumbledown sheds, houses straggling in some sort of order like a street, a lumberyard where men and horses were working, and then, at last, the Grand Canal, not very wide or impressive, after all, but evidently busy. Two barges passed, heavy with salt barrels going east to New York or Albany; then a pair of express packets, racing. By this time, the train was running straight up a street of the city of Syracuse, going slowly now, tolling its bell, tooting its whistle at intervals, and, as it approached the depot, a watchman issued from a house, and walked solemnly ahead of the puffing engine, ringing a large dinner bell to warn the populace.

It was at this point that the handsome party belonging to Mr. Dallas Ord—or at least traveling with him—rose, without haste, and made its way to the end of the car. The train was crawling now, no faster than the bellman could walk, and these impatient passengers, who apparently could not wait to reach the station, surprised everyone in the car by jumping off and hurrying out of sight down a side street. All, that is, except Mr. Ord, who perhaps had nothing to do with them after all, since he kept his seat and watched this peculiar performance with no more interest than the other ladies and gentlemen near him.

Someone said, "They're jumping out, by golly!" and everyone turned to see what Mr. Ord would do about it.

He smiled, as though the whole thing was a good joke,

shrugged his shoulders and said, "They must be strangers to the town. Perhaps they didn't know the train stopped here."

The man who had first spoken said, "Ain't they your friends? I thought they was with you."

Mr. Ord said politely, "Only train acquaintances," and the matter was dropped.

This was not the end of the excitement, however. In a minute, before the hasty visitors were fairly out of sight, an engine whistled violently down the line. Another train on the same track, the passengers exclaimed, craning to look back. Coming right after us, lickety-brindle. Will they hit us? the ladies cried in terror. Will there be an accident? These cars, one lady wailed to her husband. I *told* you we'd ought to come with our own horses. Trains are always having accidents. Now we'll be killed.

The engine behind pulled down its speed, fortunately, and there was no accident, although it did keep its great black nose fairly touching the last car of the Syracuse Express until the two of them, like a tandem of horses, poked into the dark cave of the depot.

Then what a to-do arose! A parcel of men jumped from the cab of the rear engine and ran forward to the train, rushing up to the doors where the passengers were alighting, pushing past people, staring rudely into everyone's face, stamping through the empty cars, looking everywhere for something, and cursing when they didn't find it. Was it an escaped criminal they were looking for? Or fugitive slaves? None of them on this train, misters. We're all there is. Other passengers? Well, the conductor admitted, scratching his head, there *were* a couple of others, but they must have got off ahead of time and gone home. Some blowhard in the crowd had to say, "There was a bunch of folks jumped off before the train stopped. Maybe they're the ones you're looking for."

The marshals were onto this like a flash. "Jumped off? Ran away? Where'd they go?" they shouted to the man who knew so much. "Were they niggers?"

The fellow was probably sorry he'd spoken. He said sulkily, "I don't know where they went. I never saw 'em before, since I was born. And they weren't niggers, either. They was as white as you be."

The marshals snorted and turned to Dallas Ord, who had picked up his carpetbag and was preparing to leave. "Hey, you. What's your name?"

Ord said with exquisite courtesy, "My name is Dallas Ord, sir. May I ask what business it is of yours?"

The man was affronted. "I'm a United States marshal, that's what my business is, and you'd better answer my questions if you don't want to go to jail for obstructing justice."

Ord shrugged his shoulders. "Ask them, then," he said, and stood looking bored while the marshal fumed.

"I have information that you smuggle slaves," he said, looking at Ord without conviction. "I'm told you've brought a party of fugitive slaves into this state. I demand that you give 'em up."

Ord said sweetly, "Any fugitive slaves that you find in my possession you're welcome to. You're at liberty to search me."

The marshal glared at him. "You'd better be careful what you say," but there was really nothing he could do. He held Ord until the train had been ransacked, and then tried to make him admit something about the people who had jumped off the car. Ord, smiling pleasantly, admitted that some people *had* jumped off, but regretted that he had no other knowledge of them.

"You were seen sitting with them and talking to them on the train," the marshal said, threatening.

"Yes," Ord agreed, "I talked to quite a few people on the way from New York. That's not unusual. But who they were or where they went, it grieves me that I am in no position to say."

He admitted under questioning that he was going to stay at a hotel, the Old Liberty Tavern, and would be there for a day or so, presumably, although he could never tell how his plans might change. Did he know any people in Syracuse? Ord considered. Well, aside from the people at the hotel—where he'd stayed before—he had met Major Burnet and Mr. John Palfrey at various times. They might be willing to give him a character.

At this the marshal stared, and presently the interrogation ended and Mr. Ord was permitted to go on his way.

"It's damned funny," the marshal said to his deputy. "We was told to look for this man Ord. They said in Albany that he might be a runner. And we find him spang on the train the nigs were supposed to have taken. And some folks jump off in a hurry and run away. But this Ord says he don't know nothing about 'em, and there's no way to prove he did. And the folks he says he knows here are Major Burnet and his chief helper! It's damned funny, that's all I say."

His deputy was tired. "Well, *I* say let's get us a snifter," he suggested pitifully. "I'm drier'n a covered bridge."

The pursuit of the fugitives was unanimously postponed to a later hour.

The little room at the back of the cellar of Old Lib was stuffy on this hot afternoon, but it was well-hidden. Outside its door, a pile of rubbish, broken boxes, old chairs, riffraff of every description, seemed to fill the whole space, masking the entrance to this secret chamber so that no searcher would have thought of looking there for a slave hole. Inside the room, a candle's light threw leaping shadows on the rough-cast stone walls. The occupants of the room sat in a circle around the box on which the candle stood. They sat motionless, tense, listening when a footfall sounded overhead, their dark eyes rolling sidewise at each other, at the door that led outside, at the tiny window high up on the wall that brought them sounds from the street.

For a long time no one came, no steps approached them, no hand fumbled in the rubbish that hid them. Five men and six women, beautifully appareled, sat in the room. The ladies were gowned in sarcenet, bombazine, *barège*, watered silk; wore bonnets with feathers and flowers; wore long gauze veils, veils of *blonde;* wore ruffles of lace at their necks, kid gloves on their hands. The men wore spotless nankeen, light worsted pantaloons with swallowtail coats, red waistcoats, stovepipe hats; wore gloves, snowy neckcloths, cravats, linen shirts; carried money to jingle in their pockets.

Heavy tread made the boards creak over their heads, and every eye turned upward, staring desperately at the darkened rafters. Someone was hurrying across the back kitchen. The cook? Mr. North? Loose boards groaned again as the footsteps returned. In the room below, a woman in sea-green satin broché stirred carefully, not to damage her finery, and whispered, "Maybe they's just hurryin' around to take care of Marcy. She was low sick."

Her companions, sitting as stiff and still as statues, like great dolls in their fancy clothes, not daring to move, hardly daring to stir their painted faces lest the color of them should change, looked at each other, their eyes alive and frightened in their heads. A woman murmured, "Sure was," and after that there was no more to be said. Above them, footsteps came and went, the floor boards creaked, afternoon light slanted, warm and yellow, through the dusty windowpane.

Business in the bar of Old Lib was brisker than usual that afternoon. Farmers were coming in from the country today, hitching their horses to the posts in front of the tavern, tramping into the barroom with a sigh of pleasure to get out of the heat, leaning their elbows on the polished counter, calling for something to wet their whistles. After that they would, as often as not, ask the Negro boy tending bar where Moses North was. Moses was a popular man in the town already, and folks liked to pass the time of day with him.

These farmers, in their linen dusters or even in their common work clothes, would amble through into the little room that Moses called his office. A rumble of talk would come from the room for a time; perhaps another man would enter, carefully closing the door behind him before he said a word, and the talk would go on. Later the farmer would emerge, wiping his mouth with the back of his hand, and swagger off down the street as though he was ready to buy out the town. In the hot sunshine, his docile horses stood through the long afternoon, switching their tails at the flies, stamping their feet, shifting under their harness, watching the stream of customers that came and went at Old Lib.

The whole town was lively today. Something was going on. The word flew around town in a twinkling. Something's happening. Major Burnet's called his men out. The Salt Pointers are ready for a fight. Knots of men on street corners stopped to gossip about it. Is he after the Nigger Lovers? Is he on the trail of those varmints? What's he going to do? The regular assembly on the veranda of the Syracuse House was very grave. Time he did *something*, they said, looking at each other significantly. The way things have been going around here! What things? somebody wanted to know. Well, you know how it is. These Abolitionists are getting too all-fired cocky. They think they own this town. Meetings and everything. But have they *reely* run some niggers through? the questioner pressed them. Well—no one knew, for certain, the wiseacres said, wagging their beards. But all this stir must mean something. Probably the Major or some of his boys had found out something. Maybe they'd decided to clean up the place.

In Tammany Hall, Mr. Kirk said that he hoped they'd catch the miscreant, if there was one—he looked sly, as though he knew something about it—and get it over with. It wasn't good for trade to have folks riled up all the time.

"Hell," somebody said, grinning at the busy street, "don't seem to be doin' much harm, if today's a sample. If it's a nigger they're chasing, I hope the poor damn fool gets away," he said, spitting neatly at the cuspidor. "You don't catch me doing their dirty work for the South. They can chase their own niggers. I told Burnet so, too."

Little boys flocked after a company of Burnet's men swaggering into the depot. The bell was ringing for the late afternoon train, and a marshal and his deputy were examining the passengers as they bought their tickets. White man; white woman; white boy; all white. Not a Negro in the place. The marshal proceeded to search the cars to make sure that no one was concealed under the seats, behind the doors, even in the engine. The conductor objected to this, but was overruled. The engineer stood with a sledge hammer, watching for someone to enter his machine. "They'll have to have an order from the Master Mechanic, if they want to get on this cab." The marshal scowled at him but desisted. There was no place to hide a fugitive there, in any case, unless it was under the water tank. The baggage car was the logical place for contraband, but they had already searched that and found nothing.

Meeting briefly to compare notes in Major Burnet's office, John Palfrey met what he had been waiting for.

"They aren't at the depot. They aren't at Dr. May's or Loguen's. We know that. We've watched the houses all day and all last night. If the folks that jumped off the train are the ones we're after, they're right here in town somewhere, and we can find 'em. They got off at about Lock Street, the conductor said. That means they could have run across the Canal easy, and be hiding in one of those dumps on the other side. We've got to search 'em. If we wait till dark, they'll get away sure."

Palfrey said grimly, "We've got a job on our hands. All along, from Whitehall up the Hill, are nigger houses. Dozens of 'em. These fugitives might be in any of 'em."

Major Burnet looked at him regretfully. "I hate to do this, John, but you can see we've got to. It's ten to one they wouldn't take a chance on running as far as Whitehall or the Hill. They'd be foolish to. They were all dressed up, the folks on the train said, and they'd stand out like a sore thumb amongst those ordinary niggers. They're trying to get through as whites, and so they'll stay with white folks. That's just plain common sense."

Palfrey looked straight at him. "What do you suggest?" His voice was perfectly level.

Burnet said uncomfortably, "Damn it, John, we've got to search the hotels along the Canal. Old Lib." He stirred under Palfrey's gaze. "I know you like those people, John. Maybe they're all right. But the word came to keep an eye on Ord, and he's told the marshal that he's going to stay at Old Lib. We know he's a friend of North's."

Palfrey turned away abruptly. "I'm not denying it. I do hate to have friends of mine disturbed. The way they were before," he added, looking bitterly at Deputy Guppy. "It's insulting to decent people to have an officer coming into their private apartments. They didn't find any fugitive then, and they won't this time, but I can't stop your searching." He reached for his hat and walked rapidly to the door. "I *can* go along and see that they don't insult my friends," he said. The door banged behind him.

The Major sighed. "I hate to have to do this," he said again, following his men down the stairs.

Mr. Noxon understood him. "It's hard on John having us suspect his best girl's father," he agreed, hurrying to keep pace with the Major. "But he's seen it coming, you can bet on that. He's been as glum as an owl every time we talked about it."

Old Lib met the Major's party with open hospitality. Moses North greeted them in the bar, offered drinks, was refused curtly by the Major.

"We've got a search warrant, Mr. North. We've received information that fugitive Negroes may be hiding in your hotel. We're going to search it."

Moses said genially, "Well, it's a likely-looking place, and I don't blame you, but you searched it once and I kind of hoped that'd do for the season. But if you think we've got black boys hiding under our beds you'd better take another look. I won't object any, if you don't annoy folks. I don't want to spoil trade." He grinned at John Palfrey and said with great good nature, "Well, John, how does it seem to be hot on the trail?"

Palfrey flushed. "I've assured Major Burnet that he's been misinformed, but I agree that every hotel must be searched, as a matter of form." His face was grim.

"Surely, surely," Moses North agreed with sympathy. "It ain't pleasant, but it's a duty," and his giant's laughter filled the room.

Burnet said stiffly, "Let's get going. We haven't got any time to waste." He moved forward into the passage, his little army of searchers tramping after him. At their rear, old North followed, his great voice booming down the passage so that everyone in the house must have known they were coming.

"Straight ahead, gentlemen; first door on the right is my daughter's sitting room. She don't often entertain niggers there, but you might find one. Who knows?" He laughed again, as though the whole expedition amused him. "You'll find a friend there, though, I shouldn't wonder. Mr. Dallas Ord came in this noon, and maybe he'll join the hunt. He's from the South, and he ought to be real handy at hunting stray niggers."

At the door Major Burnet said sharply, "We've had a warning that your friend Mr. Ord is running slaves for the Abolitionists. We've been told he isn't a Southerner at all."

Moses said, "Well, now, his family'd be surprised to hear that. They seemed to think he was born right in Virginia. But maybe they're wrong."

Sunlight, filtering through green curtains, flowed into the passage, and Dallas Ord stood in the open doorway bowing like a Frenchman, his face bright with mischief.

"Welcome, Patriots. Did I hear someone say that I was wanted?"

John Palfrey took three steps and confronted the slight dark man. "We want to see you, Ord," he said, his voice as cold as stone. "It's on your account we're disturbing Mr. North and his family. We've had word from Albany that you—or a man answering to your description—brought a party of fugitives here this noon. What have you got to say?" In his hostile face his eyes burned hot and angry, as threatening as weapons trained upon Dallas Ord.

Ord gave him back a look like a blow. "I hope you can back

up a charge like that, Palfrey," he said contemptuously. "Those are fighting words."

Palfrey said instantly, "I'll be glad to. We had a telegram from Albany saying that a man like you in appearance was traveling by train, today, with a party of ten or twelve escaped slaves. This party was traced as far as Albany, where the man Myers, who is known to be a slave runner, bought them tickets and saw them onto the train, bound west. That party did not leave the train at any point east of Syracuse, therefore they must have reached this city. You were seen by a number of witnesses traveling in company with—or at least in conversation with—a party of men and women. When the train got into town, all the other members of the party jumped off the train before it reached the depot. They were seen hurrying through the streets, probably going north from Lock Street. You came through to the station to throw off pursuit, and then you also came north, as far as this hotel. What explanation have you?"

Ord gave him a slow smile, so arrogant, so insulting that it brought the blood into Palfrey's face. Still smiling, cool, satirical, Ord said, "Dear me!" The gentle voice, the mild exclamation underlined his insult. He said, shaking his head, "That's very bad. What can I possibly say? I think you'd better search me, to see if I've got those niggers concealed. I certainly came in this noon from Albany on the train, and I certainly did talk to some people on the train, and they certainly did leave the train before I did." He laughed softly in Palfrey's angry face. "The only difficulty is that the people I talked to certainly looked like white folks, as far as I could tell. And if I'd been shepherding 'em up here past the dragons of the law, I should think I'd have stayed with 'em. But that's all I can say. I'm willing to submit to a search."

Palfrey swung around furiously to Burnet. "We won't get anything out of him, of course," he said. "We may as well begin to search the house."

"Before you go," Ord said sweetly, "I don't need to remind you that I'm only a guest in this tavern, and that its owners are Mr.

North and his daughter, who weren't mentioned in your telegram."

"You needn't remind me," Palfrey said between his teeth. "I'm not likely to forget that these innocent people are going to be annoyed because of you."

"You have my sincere regrets," Ord said with deep irony. He moved to the door with his curiously catlike grace, held it open and waved the party through. "After you, gentlemen. I shall be delighted to assist in the search."

The first floor revealed nothing: kitchen, dining room, pantries and woodshed, barroom, public rooms, North's little office, all bare and innocent. Cellars next. Two dozen feet tramped past the irate Mrs. Butterworth, tracking dirt, as she said loudly to the quivering Minerva, all over her clean floors. The cellar was not so clean. The earth floor was littered and thick with dust and debris. What pale light trickled in through the high windows showed a confusion of rubbish, old boxes, piles of wood, a bank of sand with a few of last year's turnips withering upon it, a roomful of discarded furniture, every sort of flotsam and jetsam from the stream of the tavern's past life, with dust thick and stifling over all. The searchers scratched around in the disorder, turned over musty boxes, sounded the walls, peered into corners. Really, the place was a sin and a shame, as Mr. North confessed, apologizing for his residence.

"We've been so busy getting the place going that we haven't had time for fancy housekeeping," he said regretfully. "My daughter'd have a conniption fit if she knew you gentlemen were looking at this mess. She'd be mortified to death. We'll have to get after it and clean it up."

But for all their searching, there was not a frightened Negro crouching in a corner, not a slave woman hiding under a box or doubled up in an old trunk. There was no sign of anyone in any part of the cellar, so far as Burnet's searchers could see, and after a dusty half hour they tramped back upstairs, under the fierce eye of Mrs. Butterworth, and began to search the bedrooms.

The back wing, as Mr. William Guppy could have told them, was dank and unused, without a closet or a cubbyhole to hide anyone. Must, mildew, dust; rickety furniture, grimy windows. The party passed from room to room, rapping on walls, peering under beds, opening cupboards, finding nothing, no one. There remained, then, only the front part of the house, the few rooms now let to transients, the rooms of the owners of the establishment.

Major Burnet, hot and dusty from the search, said sharply to North, "We'll have to see your rooms, North. We've got to satisfy ourselves that there's no one here." He turned to John Palfrey just behind him. "You take half the men and do this side of the hall, and I'll do the other."

Before John could answer—or protest, if he was thinking of such a thing—Moses North said with a slight hesitation, "I kind of hate to have you go into my daughter's room right now. She's got a friend staying with her that's been taken sick. It wouldn't be good for her to have a lot of folks rooting around in there, if she's feeling bad."

The Major pulled up short. "We can't help that," he said, with less than his usual amiability. "We don't know that you haven't got a fugitive hidden in there, instead of a sick girl. We've got to see every room."

Before Moses North could reply, Palfrey began to speak. "Let me go in there alone," he said to the frowning Major. "It'll be better for the sick person, and I can search as well as a whole party. I'll meet you downstairs and report."

One of the searchers started to say, "But, Major—"

Ord's voice broke in, silky, insulting, "Perhaps the Major doesn't trust his lieutenant. Perhaps he feels that since Mr. Palfrey knows Miss North, he might betray the cause for her sake."

Palfrey cried, "Why, damn you—"

Burnet cut him off. "I have perfect confidence in my staff. If Mr. Palfrey will be good enough to make the search in Miss North's room, we will wait for him in the bar. Good day, gentlemen." He turned on his heel and marched down the hall, his cohorts after him.

Ord bowed to John Palfrey. "My apologies, sir," he said, and to Palfrey's surprise turned also and followed Moses North toward the stairs.

To knock on the door was only decent, but it was a relief to Palfrey when Mahala's light step answered it after only a moment's pause. The doorknob turned under her hand, the door opened a crack and he heard her whisper, "What is it?"

His own voice sounded strange in his ears when he said, "It's John Palfrey, Mahala. I've been ordered to search this room." How could he say such a thing to her? How could he do this thing before her watching eyes? How could he accuse her? But if he found nothing, no one, there would be no accusation. A hollow, somewhere under his heart, rang with these questions. How; how?

He heard Mahala say, "Come in, if you must. I have a sick woman here, in bed. She oughtn't to be disturbed." The door opened wider, and Palfrey saw Mahala standing before him, tall, straight, wearing a white dress that seemed no whiter than the face that looked back at him with reproach, with appeal, with pride. Strangely, she had bound her head with a blue scarf so that her hair was wholly covered, and this drapery gave her a foreign air, like an Eastern woman who might have been wearing a veil. Behind her, the bedroom was closely curtained to a dim twilight, and even the curtains of the high, testered bed were drawn, concealing the sick woman who lay there. Everything in the room was white, so that the bed loomed like a white hill, like a white tent, and the covered chairs and tables stood like drifts of snow in the gloom.

Palfrey drew a breath and stepped inside the room. Before Mahala's eyes he could not repress another word of apology for what he was doing; for what he might have to do. "I'm sorry, Mahala. I have to do it. The marshals have had a warning that some fugitives have come this way. They think they might be hidden in this house." He did not ask her if this was true.

Mahala said, "Look, then," and drew back so that he might search the room. She made it neither easier nor harder for him. She did not remind him that he had been angry when her room was searched before. Neither did she show him the faintest shade of sympathy for what he must be feeling. She did not join the search or help him, or speak a word while he stepped awkwardly about the room, walking around the furniture as though a black man might be crouched behind every chair, peering into corners where only a fool would have hidden, fumbling in the clothespress for a body lurking behind the hanging garments. Not until he approached the bed itself did she stir, and then it was only to sigh, as though she could hold her breath no longer, and now must release it and stand before him fairly panting, like a runner exhausted after a race.

Palfrey said, "I've got to see your sick woman, Mahala," and waited beside the curtained bed with his head bowed, not looking at her while she drew the stuff aside.

Against the white pillows was the face of one who had died in grief. Below high cheekbones the cheeks fell into delicate hollows, the lovely line of the young mouth was a line of sorrow. Long black lashes rested against skin the color of old ivory, and the smooth brow was the pale color of ripe wheat. Sorrow and suffering were written on the quiet face, and patience and meekness and resignation. The dead woman had been beautiful, but now, as she lay before them, there was a strangeness about her, something grotesque, something not right. Palfrey, staring down at her, fastened his eyes upon the wave of brilliant hair that showed beneath the edge of her bedcap. Brilliant hair, red, shining like copper threads. No, he thought painfully. That is not right on this woman. No other woman in the world has hair like that. No other woman but Mahala. Not this pitiful dead woman. Not anyone.

He raised his eyes to Mahala, saw her standing there in her

pale-blue turban, heard the breath sigh softly between her parted lips; saw her hands clasped before her so tightly that the knuckles were white. She's frightened, the heavy voice in his mind cried in agony. How can I do this to her? He said in a whisper, "You shouldn't have put that hair on her, Mahala. I'd always know it was yours." That was all he could say.

For an instant he heard her breath catch in her throat. That was the only sound. She made no outcry, and her only movement was a slackening of her body as though the hope, the necessity, that had kept her taut and upright through this ordeal had left her, and now she was barely strong enough to stand erect without it. When she spoke, her voice was only a breath.

"What are you going to do?"

"What are you going to do?" The words echoed over and over in Palfrey's mind, ringing as though his brain was an empty room, finding no answer, raising no response. What can I do? he thought, watching Mahala, searching her face for the answer. He saw her lift her hand uncertainly, groping for the support of the bedpost. Then, without thought, without answering the question, he moved forward and caught her in his arms.

Protect her; take her away; get her out of this. There was the answer to everything. Take her away from these people who put her in jeopardy. Snatch her away from danger and risk. She's got to come with me. She can't stay here any longer. She's mine, he thought, holding her against his breast, feeling the sharp struggle of her sobbing breath, tasting salt tears on his lips. I'll never let them have her again. I don't care what happens. I don't care what she's done. They'll never have her again. I'll take her away from them.

She was saying something, over and over, as she rested in his arms. "I don't know what to do. I don't know what to do."

Palfrey said, his lips against her face, "You'll do nothing. I'm going to take you away from them. You're mine. You're coming with me."

Then he felt her move, start, draw away from him. "No—how

can I go? You know what I'm doing. You know why that woman is on my bed." She was staring at him now, and in her face hope was struggling painfully with dread.

Palfrey said fiercely, "You never ought to have done it. You'll never touch it again. I'll take you away from this."

Slowly Mahala drew away from him until she stood entirely apart, not touching him, but gazing into his face as though she could see through the mask of his features into the mind behind them. She spoke deliberately, giving judgment. "You could never understand. You could never forgive. You could never let me do what I have to do. Not even if you love me."

Palfrey cried out in anger. "I do love you. You know that. But I can't let you do this thing. You see what the danger is. Your father should have protected you from it. Ord has got you into this."

Mahala raised her hand. "No one could protect me from it. I did it because I wanted to. And I'm in no more danger than they are," she said, suddenly burning. "They take all the risks. They are willing to die for it. And *I'm* willing to die for it," she cried, flaming at him. "My brother did die for it—and I would." For a moment the two stood facing each other, eyes fastened upon each other's faces, locked, like an embrace, into a kind of clenched struggle, neither giving way, neither yielding.

At last Mahala said, "You see what I am. Now call in your marshals. I'm willing to go with them."

The marshals, Palfrey thought, as though all that—the search, the warrant, the fugitives, the men waiting for him below—were a part of something that had happened so long ago he had utterly forgotten them. With an effort he brought them back into his mind. He would have to do something. He would have to decide.

He said deliberately, "I'll never give you up, and I will take you away from them. I'll tell your father and Dallas Ord that they have no right to let you run this risk. Never again. Because we're going to stop this business, Mahala," he said, biting off the words. "They won't take you this time, but the next time I might not be able to stop them. And every time your father or Ord brings through a fugitive, we're going to fight them. Someday we'll catch them. But we'll never catch *you*." He took her hands for just one moment and held them while he finished speaking, "We won't have to catch you, because you won't be here. You won't be running slaves. You'll be with me."

He did not wait for Mahala to answer, but turned quickly and went out of the room. Mahala heard his footsteps as he ran down the stairs. Wearily, heavily, she moved after him to the door, opened it and went down the hallway to the head of the stairs. Voices, small at that distance, floated up to her, scraps of a question, fragments of an answer.

Palfrey's voice, sharp and quick. "No fugitives there—we'd better go along."

The United States marshal's voice, louder, blustering ". . . took you a long time . . ."

Major Burnet's voice, smooth. "You're sure . . . everything safe to leave . . ."

All the voices blurred for a moment, and Moses North said something she could not catch.

Then John again, his tone strained ". . . better see about the sick woman . . . a dangerous condition . . . Mahala seems badly exhausted herself."

Dallas Ord's voice, too low to hear, made a break in the crosshatch of sound. What had he said? Mahala wondered anxiously. If he insulted Palfrey, now after what had been done, what might come of it?

The voices went on for a few moments, weaving together, breaking off, beginning again. Finally there were abrupt farewells. Heavy feet marched to the door. The door slammed.

They're gone, Mahala thought, suddenly so weak that she was obliged to cling to the stairpost. They're gone. John's let us go. He's lied for us. For me. He's done this for me. But how he hated to do it. She made her way slowly back to that silent room. It was as terrible for him as it was for me. He violated himself when he lied for me just now. He betrayed himself, as much as he betrayed Burnet. He did it because he believes he can persuade me, she thought in great pain. He wants me to come over to his side. He thinks that if I love him I will come.

She was standing in the middle of the floor, lost in these thoughts, when her father and Dallas Ord came quietly into the room behind her. As they came near she looked up at them, not knowing what to say. They would be pleased with what had happened, she thought bitterly. They would feel triumphant, as she had felt many times before when she had outwitted the enemy.

Ord walked to the bed and looked down at the face of the dead woman. He said nothing for a time. Then he turned to Mahala.

"Palfrey knew, of course." It was not a question.

Mahala replied without inflection, "Yes. He knew. But he lied for us. I'm ashamed." Her voice was carefully level. "I wish he hadn't done it."

Ord looked away from her. "I know," he answered, as though he had heard not only her words but all the thoughts that had been in her mind. "It's my fault. I should have taken care of it myself."

Moses North went toward the door. "I'm going to get Loguen to take care of Marcy's body. He can see to that. And then Dal and I'd better start getting those other folks away. The carriages are all waiting and ready, and now that Burnet's men have gone, we hadn't ought to have any trouble. The stations along the line are expecting 'em."

The door closed behind him quietly. His heavy tread sounded, one-two, one-two, as he went down the stairs. The room was as silent as a desert. The man and woman stood without speaking, without looking at each other.

"I'm a fool," Ord said slowly. "I knew this might happen. Palfrey's suspected us for a long time. I told you that. Now we've put a weapon in his hands. And he'll use it." Ord looked at Mahala with smoldering eyes. "We're through here," he said, glancing around the pleasant room. A smile touched his lips briefly. "Trains won't run from the Old Lib any more. We'll have to move."

A flush rose in Mahala's face. "But he didn't use the weapon," she said in a strangled voice. "He didn't tell. He didn't arrest me. He lied for me. He used the weapon against himself. Oh," she cried in agony, "I made him do it. It's my fault—my fault. He must hate me. I'm ashamed. I'd rather he'd arrested me than to have done this. He'll hate himself—and hate me."

Ord's face darkened. "Does it matter that he hates you?" he asked, looking at her so fiercely that she turned away from his gaze. "He's our enemy, Mahala. You know that. You've said so from the first. He's in love with you, but he's still your enemy. You've got to fight him. It doesn't matter how he feels now. The truth is that he's got a gun pointed at you, and you've got to surrender—or get away from him. All three of us have. We've got to run away. Disappear. Close up the Old Lib and make other plans for a station." His eyes never left her face as he said this. After a moment he added slowly, "You've got to go—unless you want to surrender and marry John Palfrey. Do you owe him as much as that?"

Mahala was suddenly trembling with anger. "I owe him everything. More than I can repay, whatever I do. I've broken his honor. I've made him betray his own cause. Because he loves me." She broke off for a moment, panting. "You never think of anything but our work," she said furiously. "It doesn't matter to you how people feel—how I feel. If *you* loved me, you'd never put me before your work. You'd never lie to save me, if a single slave would be lost because you lied. Why shouldn't I owe John a debt? Why shouldn't I want to repay it? He's given up what he believes, for my sake. Why shouldn't I give up what I believe, for his?"

Ord's face was grim. "Because you can't," he said harshly. "You can't, and Palfrey can't—and I can't. We aren't made that way. I'd never ask you to try. If you marry Palfrey and think he'll change—or you'll change—you'll be fooled. It won't work, Mahala—because it isn't true. Palfrey's a man. He's strong. He saved you this time, because he thinks he can take you away from us, and he thinks that after he's married you you'll change and believe what he believes. And you think so too, perhaps. Or you think you'll change into another kind of person. But you won't. And he won't. It won't work, Mahala," he said again. "You're fighting me now because you know—against your own will—that what I say is true. You're trying to escape. But you can't ever get away."

"I *can* get away." Mahala faced him with a desperate defiance. "You've held me all this time. You've said you loved me, but you've starved me. Now you can't hold me, if I want to go. I'm tired of waiting. I'm tired of working."

Ord did not answer for a time, but stood looking at her, his eyes dark with pain. At last he said, "I've never held you, and I won't hold you now. I love you and I know you. If I've starved you, I've starved myself worse. You know the reason for that," he said with sudden bitterness. "You wanted it so."

"No—" Mahala cut in fiercely. "I begged you to come back, but you never would. You left me alone. You didn't want me. You only wanted to work. You didn't care when John fell in love with me. You don't care about it now. You only care because it interferes with our work. That's all you really love now," she cried out at him. "You've forgotten that I'm a woman. I'm really Martin, to you!" She laughed angrily. "John knows that I'm a woman." Her face flushed as she uttered his name. "John loves me—not my work."

Ord said slowly, "When you're hurt and angry, you try to kill both of us. None of this is true—any more than what you said when Martin died was true. Someday you'll wake up and know I'm right. You'll remember that you and I are one person. Nothing can divide us. We belong together. If Palfrey took you away from me, he couldn't keep you. You'd have to come back." His eyes were fierce upon her. "I can't lose what's mine. You'll only lose yourself for a while, if you do this thing. But I can't stop you. Go and marry John Palfrey," he said, as light as a breath. "Go to him." His eyes burned upon her face. "You can go to him freely. I won't stand in your way. Because you'll come back to me." Without waiting for an answer, Ord turned swiftly and went out of the room.

Alone, Mahala stood looking after him. Anger, fear, pain and a profound surprise were written upon her face. "Dal," she cried out once, and then was silent.

"He's gone," she said aloud, staring at the empty doorway. "He's left me. He won't come back."

CHAPTER THIRTEEN

"You haven't got any proof that Palfrey let those niggers through," Major Burnet said, frowning over his segar. "All you can say is that he did search one room in that hotel, alone. That don't say that he found anything. I don't believe he did. They'd have been fools to have counted on our not looking there for 'em."

Perley Deacon hunched his shoulders forward and said, "It don't prove he *didn't* find 'em, either. It's damned funny to me that after all the warning we got about those slaves coming through, and being told about Ord and everything, we never got so much as a sniff of 'em. We searched every hotel on the North Side, let alone just the canal, and we never saw a thing. The only place we didn't all see was that girl's room, and I bet it was so full of niggers you couldn't move."

"But why would John Palfrey turn his coat like that?" the Major retorted. "We've known John all his life and we know that he's been heart and soul in our movement, right from the start. It's not like him to do such a thing. Look what he's said in meetings about the Abolitionists. If he feels like that about 'em, why would he want to go and help 'em, when we're after 'em? He was as hot on the trail as any of us when we were searching yesterday."

Perley grunted. "He may still be hot against most Abolitionists, but if he was to find that his best girl was in with 'em, and going to be arrested for smuggling slaves, you can bet he'd side with her. It's not in nature that he'd tell us the truth. I say you can't

Take Yo[ur]
Supplen[...]

WASHINGTON [...]
By The Man at t[...]
($2.50) ... A [...]
up of the head[...]
who dominate the [...]
written by an [...]
server who know[...]
Doran publication[...]

THE BAY. By [...]
($2.50) ... T[he...]
man's stubborn pi[...]
of happiness—a [...]
novel of modern [...]
with Dickensian [...]
Lippincott public[ation...]

HOME FRONT [...]
Carl Sandburg. [...]
collection of the [...]
prose and poetry, [...]
can, stirred to pass[...]
events of recent y[...]
Brace publication. [...]

ROGUE'S LEG[ACY...]
ette Deutsch. ([...]
lon, throughout [...]
life, was censured [...]
day he is acclaim[ed...]
The engrossing b[...]
mented genius. A [...]
publication.

*Titles thus mark[ed...]

THE RETURN. By Margaret Rhodes Peattie. ($2.00) ... Scene—a small Vermont town; characters—everyone from Senator Jones to baby Jessup; time—that glorious day when the boys come home from the war. A heart-warming novel of a not too distant future. A *Morrow* publication. 1218

BRIGHT BANNERS. By Elizabeth Seifert. ($2.50) ... Liz Arnette seemed too young and beautiful to be teaching college students wartime adjustments, but the faculty had a surprise in store, particularly one handsome professor whom she cured permanently of being a woman-hater. An engaging, modern romance. A *Dodd Mead* publication. 1219

VICTORY THROUGH AIR POWER. By Major Alexander de Seversky. ($2.50) ... An acknowledged expert on the strategy of aerial warfare tells how America can subdue her enemies. A *Simon & Schuster* publication. *1220

ONE WORLD. By Wendell L. Willkie. ... The inspiring record of Mr. Willkie's famous world tour and his personal interviews with United Nations leaders. ... **TARGET: GERMANY.** ... The Army Air Forces' official story of [the] 8th Bomber Command's [first] year over Europe. Thrilli[ng] graphic illustrations. Both *Simon & Schuster* publications. *1225

PEOPLE OF MY OW[N By]
Edith Pargeter. ($2.50 [...)]
The story of a vivacious [...]
family who found throug[h...]
experience that home is wh[ere the]
heart is. A *Reynal & H[itchcock]*
publication.

FISHERMEN AT WA[R. By]
Leo Walmsley. ($2.5[0) ...]
Thrilling true stories of th[e...]
exploits of northern fisherm[en who]
are adding a colorful ch[apter to]
Britain's saga of the sea. A [*Double*]
day, Doran publication.

JOURNEY THROUGH [...]
By Larry Barretto. [($2.50)]
... A timely novel about [a pas]
sionate Indian Summer [in a]
couple's married life and i[ts effect]
on their son. A *Farrar & [Rinehart]*
publication.

SHEEHAN'S MILL. B[y John]
Reese. ($2.50) ... A b[ig]
novel of the nineties, woven [around]
the flamboyant career of L[...,]
a rambunctious Irish-Amer[ican. A]
Doubleday, Doran publicati[on.]

**TWO TIMELY BOO[KS]
BOTH for only $1.[...]**

*Titles thus marked not available through the Dollar Book Club to Members in Ca[nada]

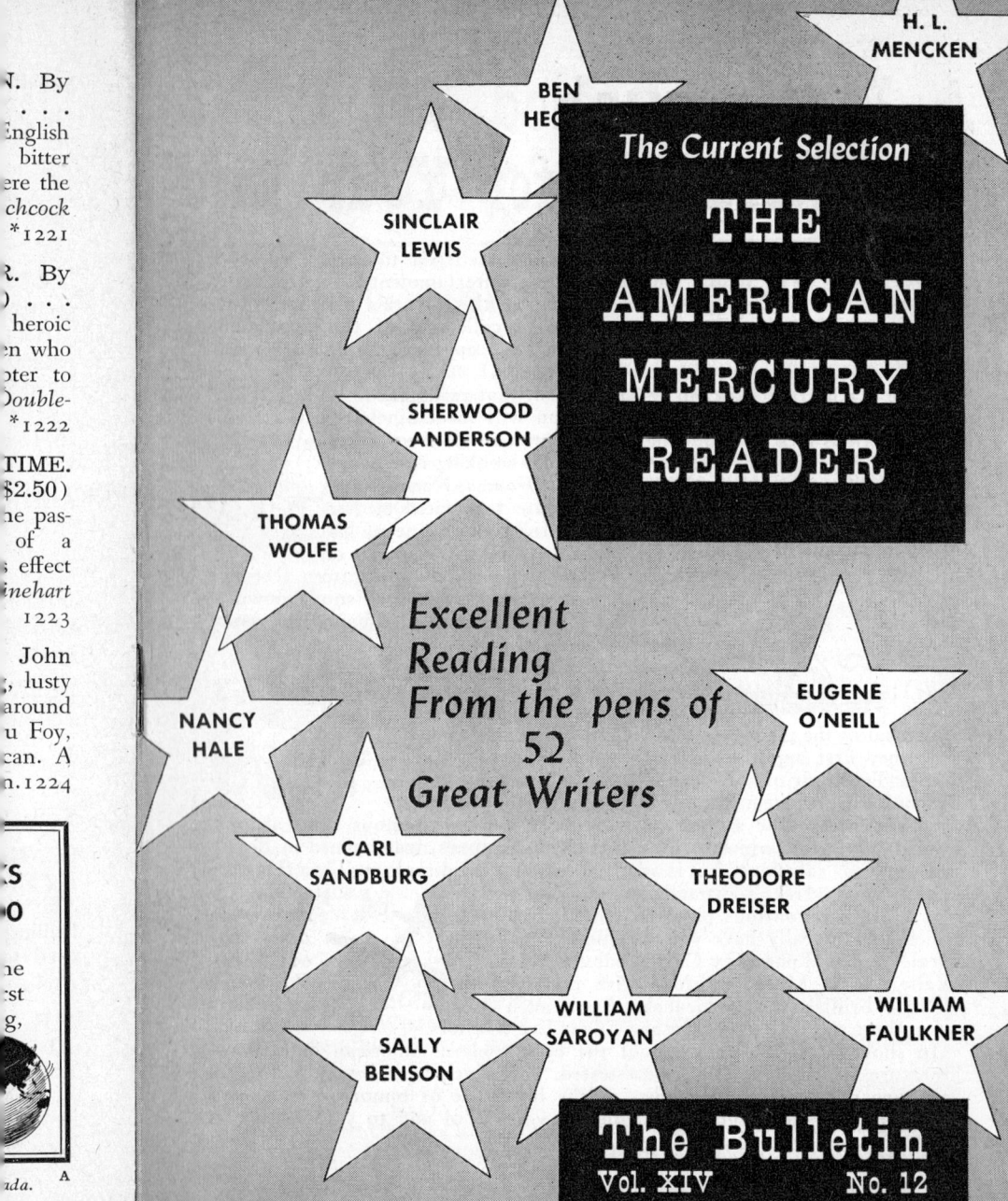

trust him, as far as those hotel people are concerned. John's a good boy, but you can't expect him to arrest his own sweetheart."

Major Burnet shrugged his shoulders. "Well, what do you want me to do? Throw him out of the party? Expel him from the Patriots? I say, ask him to prove his innocence. It doesn't seem fair to convict a man without giving him a chance to defend himself."

There was a general murmur around the room at this. The men of the inner committee were divided in opinion. Perley Deacon was strongly for excommunication. The Major, who carried more weight, of course, was inclined to ask for an explanation, and, if it was satisfactory, to forget the matter. The others were uncertain. It was a bad time to have this happen, somebody said. Just when we're getting started good. Just when we're getting active. Now, if we make a plan and it goes wrong, it'll be blamed on John Palfrey. And if it is true that he's ratted on his party, then he's a real danger to us.

"We've got work to do," Mr. Noxon said, catching the spirit of the meeting. "The Nigger Lovers are getting so high there's no talking to 'em. We've got to think of something that'll take 'em down. Show 'em we mean business. We thought we were going to catch 'em this time, but we slipped up somewhere. We can't fail again. Mr. Webster told the people of Syracuse that they were going to be come up with if they kept on their crazy ways, and it's up to us to see that they are. I don't know about John Palfrey. Maybe he peached on us, and maybe he didn't. But that's not the point. With him or without him, we've got to hump ourselves and catch those Abolitionists where the hair's short. And we've got to do it pretty soon, or we'll be a joke to the whole town."

"We're watching the trains and the canalboats now," a committeeman said doubtfully. "I don't know what more we can do. If the Woolly Heads would start a riot or something like that, we could come down on 'em like a thousand of brick. But they're too clever for that. All they need to do is sit quiet and smuggle their niggers out of town, and they think they're smart as all hell. And if we can't catch 'em, it looks like they are."

"We'd have caught 'em this time, if it wasn't for John Palfrey," Perley Deacon said, harping on his single string. "He's the one—"

"What about John Palfrey?" The door had opened unheard in the clamor of tongues, and Palfrey's tall figure stood before them. As he came slowly into the room, they saw that he was angry. His face was set like flint, and the lines around his mouth were marked in white against the darker color of his face. Under drawn brows, his eyes were the cold blue of an electric spark.

"What about John Palfrey?" he asked again, staring at them without a flicker of his eyes, without moving a muscle of his face. "I heard you say that you'd have done something—if it hadn't been for John Palfrey." The blue gaze traveled over them like the eye of a hawk, circling, hovering, ready to swoop. "What would you have done if it wasn't for me? And how did I prevent you? I'd like to know," he said very quietly. "It's something I'd like to hear."

Major Burnet said nothing, but turned deliberately and looked at Perley Deacon. As he turned, every eye in the room turned upon the man. It was his time to speak. Hair in his eyes, shoulders hunched like an obstinate old buffalo at bay, Deacon spoke.

"I said it." There was a little pause after his words. Every man looked at him and then looked back at John Palfrey to see how he would take it. After a moment Deacon's heavy voice went on, slowly, obstinately, not to be stampeded, not to be frightened. "I said, and I'll say again, that I think, after what happened yesterday, you're a dangerous man to have on this committee. What we say here is important. It's secret, or it's no good at all. If one of us here is going to protect his friends when we're after 'em, he hadn't ought to be on this committee."

Palfrey did not move except to say, still in his quiet, ominous voice, "You believe I prevented you from finding those slaves yesterday?"

For the first time, Deacon hesitated. "Well—I can't prove you did. And you can't prove you didn't. That leaves it a draw. And if it's a draw, there'll be a lot of folks who'll wonder about it. That's what I say."

Palfrey's gaze held. "I see," he said. "But if I could prove to you that I was a loyal member of this group, you'd be willing to trust me again." It was hardly a question.

At this, Major Burnet broke in. "That's how it is, John. I've told 'em that I haven't the slightest doubt about you. I know that you're heart and soul in this movement. That you're out to scotch these Abolitionists every way you can. And I tell 'em that right now we need your brains to help us plan something smart. We can't do without you."

Palfrey moved, came forward and stood facing the circle of men around the table. He said slowly, as though he was working out a problem as he spoke, "I've got a plan. If you're willing to hear it, perhaps that will convince you that I'm with you, whatever happens." There was a general stirring at these words; men muttered to each other, nodded their heads. It was clear that they all needed his plan, wanted to hear it. Only Perley Deacon held out.

"What about yesterday?" he demanded.

"I'll say this about yesterday," John Palfrey said, speaking directly to him. "I can say, on my word of honor, that there was not a living soul in that room besides Mahala North—and her friend who'd been sick. I can't prove it now. If you'd wanted to look in there at the time, you'd have seen. Now it's too late to prove anything. But if you want to take my word for it, that's the truth. I saw no party of fugitives, heard nothing about them, and have no idea where they went or how they got through. You'll have to make up your minds whether you want to believe me."

A chorus of "Yes" settled this argument. Proof was out of the question. Yesterday was past. But if any man could work out a plan to succeed tomorrow, that was all the proof they needed of his loyalty.

John Palfrey waited until there was no doubt left anywhere in the room but that they wanted him; until even Perley Deacon, reluctantly, added his amen. Then, without haste, he moved forward and took a chair in the circle. "I'd like to hear what you've been proposing," he said.

"That's just it," Noxon said plaintively. "We haven't really been proposing anything. We've been saying we *ought* to propose something. We're going to be a joke around this town, after all we've said, if we don't do something pretty soon. We had a lot of meetings and made a lot of speeches, and folks know that we've been chasing some slaves. But we don't ever have anything to show for it. What we want is a plan. You said you'd thought of something."

"I have," Palfrey said, frowning at his hands on the table before him. "I've been thinking of what Webster said in his speech. He said that the law would be executed here, in its spirit and in its letter. He said it would be executed in the midst of the next Anti-Slavery Convention, if the occasion should arise." He paused and looked around the circle of faces. "That's what I've been thinking of. 'If the occasion should arise.'" His face was lighted now; warm, challenging.

Perley Deacon said, "I don't call that much of a plan," but Major Burnet cut him off.

"What do you mean exactly, John?" he asked, watching Palfrey's face like a man who expects to see gold nuggets shine through the mud in his placer pan. "What occasion are you thinking about?"

Palfrey turned to him, talking with his old enthusiasm. "We can make the occasion. We can make it arise. We can make Webster's words come true. That would make the people think. Make them remember. Webster prophesied it—and now it comes true. That would be all the more impressive. He said that the law would be carried out, *in the midst of the next Anti-Slavery Convention*. That's our time! That's our plan! The Abolitionists have done all the planning, so far. Now we'll plan something. And we'll carry it out. We'll demonstrate for 'em. We'll show them exactly what we mean when we say we're going to execute the law." His words were coming fast, persuasive. The men around the bare office table leaned forward to hear him.

"They're going to have a convention next month. I've heard some of them talk about it. They're going to have a lot of their big men here, the way they did this spring. And right while they're in session, we'll challenge them. They've boasted for years that Syracuse is wide open to runaway slaves. Look at the number of them living here openly. Working right in our shops. Even owning houses and paying taxes, just as though they were free men, and had a right to be here. Loguen, the preacher, is a runaway slave and he boasts about it. He knows that nobody will touch him. He's a friend of Dr. May's and a lot of the most influential men in town. And maybe he's too strong to touch. But there are a lot of other Negroes here that can be taken. We ought to make an example of someone. Take some escaped Negro, trace him and find out whom he belongs to and who claims him. Then have the marshal arrest him, give him a legal trial according to the new law, and send him back south. Nothing would convince the slave runners that this is a law-abiding, constitutional town like a demonstration. We've shaken our fists a lot, but we've never hit anybody. Now we could show them that Syracuse intends to obey the law, and we'd show that by obeying the law. And if we did it just the way Webster promised, they'd never forget it."

Noxon looked doubtful. "That's kind of drastic," he said. "We might have a riot, if the Abolitionists got roused up. They'd all be together, spoiling for a fight, I shouldn't wonder. They might stir up a real ruction."

Major Burnet said contemptuously, "Since when have we been afraid of anything those psalm singers could do? Suppose they did start a fight. We've got enough men to stop them pretty quick. I say that might be a good plan. We'd have to study it a lot and be sure there wasn't any hitch in it. But I believe you've got a good idea there. What do the rest of you boys say?"

The rest of the boys said yes, with a thundering shout. This was more like it. This was action, doing something instead of sitting around on their bottoms talking about what they'd like to do. Show those blue-nosed Abolitionists that they couldn't go around breaking the law without paying for it. Show them that Syracuse wasn't a healthy place for stolen goods. Show the niggers down south that the Syracuse station on the Underground Railroad had been closed, someone said, drolly; show them that the train had jumped the track at Syracuse. After that, there wouldn't be so much talk about Syracuse as an Abolition Hole.

Major Burnet let the enthusiasm ripple for a while, let the men talk, exciting each other with their own threats, working up their spirits to the proper pitch. Even Perley Deacon had to admit that the plan had something in it. It might work, and if it worked, it would be a good thing for them. The others had no doubt at all. Yesterday's fiasco was forgotten. Doubt John Palfrey? After such a plan as that? Not much, they said, slapping him on the back, clustering around him. If those Woolly Heads were going to be caught, Palfrey was the boy to catch 'em, they said affectionately. They'd never thought much of Deacon's ideas, anyway, they said, spitting liberally on the floor. Perley was naturally a suspicious cuss. But Johnny was all right. They'd like to buy him a drink, they said, swarming around him. After a talk like that, he'd earned one, and forthwith they all trooped to McGuffey's Bar and called for a round of what killed the cat.

There was a queer look on Moses North's face, Palfrey thought, meeting him in the doorway of the Old Lib that night. Not his usual large geniality, not the same easy, happy manner, not his great laugh ringing down the passageway as he ushered Palfrey into Mahala's sitting room. Tonight he was not exactly ill at ease. No; he was always an easy man, sure of himself, calm. But he looked at Palfrey with a new speculation in his eyes, as though he was measuring him, considering him, wondering about him in a new way.

Palfrey's own manner was curt. It irks a proud, high-tempered man to be fooled by anyone; to be fooled by his friends is not forgivable in most cases. Giving myself away time after time, Palfrey thought, following North down the dark hall. Telling them things I'd have cut my tongue out rather than say to an Abolitionist. Protecting them from search because I thought they were innocent.

But did you always think so? a voice in his mind asked. Did you, these last weeks, really believe them innocent? You doubted, even then, the accusing voice said. You wondered about them; about North, about Ord. Even about Mahala. Why did you demand to search her room alone, if you were sure of her? Was it altogether your consideration of her privacy? How can you blame these people, after all? They came here with a purpose of their own. They did not seek you out. They tried to avoid you at first. A hundred times Mahala has tried to warn you that you should not pursue her. She could not tell you her secret and betray her cause, but she tried to keep you away. You would not listen to her. Even after you began to doubt, you would not leave her alone. You can be angry with what a man thinks, but you cannot blame him for fighting for what he believes, even if you hate it.

Moses North left Palfrey at the door, and inside the room he found Mahala sitting in her usual chair by the light, sewing on her mourning picture. The tomb, the weeping willows, were nearly finished now. Three figures, in solid black, drooped in attitudes of sorrow beside the pinkish marble. A name had been inscribed in minute letters in a scroll at the top of the picture. Mahala looked up from it as Palfrey entered, raising a white face in which her eyes burned like fires.

Under the streaming light of the lamp, her bright hair curled softly over her head in little feathers of red-gold. For a moment she did not seem to know what to do or say. Her needle flashed in a single point of light suspended over the canvas; her lips parted, but she did not speak. Then, as though she had been frightened, she stood so quickly that her work dropped to the floor. Her hands made a small gesture, drawing apart, the fingers spread, then slowly closing as she watched John Palfrey cross the room toward her.

Palfrey did not stop until he stood directly before her and took her hands in both of his. He said, "I've come to get you, Mahala. I told you I was coming. I won't wait any longer. You're going to marry me and come away from this place."

Still she did not speak or move, but stood before him, looking up into his face as though that was all she could ever do. Palfrey said softly, "I've got to have you, Mahala. I can't go on without you."

Suddenly, as though she had just come wide awake, her hands twisted in his. "How can I?" she asked in a kind of desperation. "How can I go with you, now that you know? How can you ask me?" Her eyes searched his face for an answer to this question. "You know that I'm an Abolitionist, and you hate Abolition. You know that I've been running slaves. You know that I don't think the way you think. How can you want me?"

Palfrey said, "I don't care what you think. I don't care what you've been doing. It doesn't matter at all. All I care about is having you and keeping you safe. I'll never let you be in danger again."

Mahala drew away from him, and Palfrey saw in her face the same look of agony and indecision that he had seen the day before when she had cried out, "I don't know what to do." He was suddenly afraid. "Why does it hurt you so?" His voice stabbed her. "Is it because of Ord? Is it because you don't want to leave him?"

"You don't know about him," she said. "You don't know about me. You can't see why I'm afraid. You wouldn't understand."

Palfrey said violently, "Tell me, then. If you love him, go with him. I'd understand that."

Mahala lifted her head and some of her old fire and recklessness seemed to return to her. "Dallas Ord has gone away," she said in a strange voice. "He said he gave me to you freely." There was a fierce little smile on her lips as she spoke. "He's gone back to do the thing you're fighting against. You needn't think about Dallas Ord again. He's gone."

Palfrey said, as though she hadn't spoken, "Are you in love with Dallas Ord?"

"I was," Mahala answered, and it was like a cry. "I was going to marry him, long ago. But then I hurt him, and told him he'd betrayed me. I was out of my head when I said it." Her voice was bitter. "He's gone," she said again, not looking at Palfrey. "He's gone away. I'll never see him again."

For a moment, anger burned like a fire in John Palfrey's mind, so that through the smoke of it he could barely see Mahala as she stood there before him. Then, dimly, he saw that she was weeping, hopelessly and inconsolably, standing alone before him with her hands raised to cover her face, and her body shaken with sobs. Weeping for Ord; weeping for himself; it didn't really matter. Between them, they'd injured her, wounded her to death; forgetting in the heat of the fight that it was she they were fighting for. Palfrey said, "O God, Mahala," and took her in his arms, lifting her face to kiss it, holding her body against his, bending over her, making her a part of him, kissing her until he felt her responding to him.

"I don't care about anything," he said when he could speak. "I don't care who you've loved. You love me now. You've got to love me. You've got to come with me. You've got to belong to me." What he said was wild, foolish, broken, without sense, but it did not matter. All that mattered was the stirring of her mouth under his, the pressure of her lifted arms around his neck, her hair brushing like silk against his cheek.

I've won, he thought in the blur of his mind. I've got her. She's mine. No more talk, no more arguing. I don't care about anything. I don't want to know what she thinks or what she believes. All I care about is this.

An hour later, Moses North said mildly that he thought night was a kind of funny time to get married. "Most folks plan to wait for daytime, to get ready and get a good start. You know what you want to do," he said, looking at his daughter. "If Mahala's sure this is what she wants, I won't say a word. Midnight or morning, I'll give you my blessing. But I wouldn't want you to go off half-cocked."

Standing in the circle of Palfrey's arm, Mahala said, "Whenever John wants it. I'll do what he says." A youngness had come over her, a girlishness, as though she had put off the strength and valor she had worn like an armor. Now she was any girl, any woman, standing in the embrace of a man who loved her; who would command her and direct her. I wouldn't know her, Moses North thought, looking at her flushed cheeks, at her eyes as bright as fever. She's like her mother, he thought heavily. I never knew she was like her mother before. She's always been like me; like a son to me; like Martin. Now she's changed and she belongs to somebody else.

John Palfrey said, "I don't want to wait. I've waited for her too long already. I'm afraid if I let her wait till morning, she'll change her mind." He was smiling. He too, Moses thought, looked younger, hot, impatient, ardent. They make a handsome couple, he thought reluctantly, watching them together. They'll mate with each other like a pair of eagles. They ought to have fine children. Aloud he said, "Well, you do as you're a mind to. I'll go along with you or not, just as you say. You're the ones to decide."

"Tonight," John said, and the look he gave Mahala was something Moses North couldn't bear to watch. "Tonight. We'll go now."

Telling Emma would be an ordeal. With his hand on the doorknob, Amidon Palfrey braced himself for it. Emma would certainly cry and carry on, but she would have to get over it. It was too late, in any case, and beyond that, Mr. Palfrey was conscious that he was glad of it. John's a man, his father thought with pride. He's got what he went after, whatever anyone thought. He'd always do that; get what he went after or die trying. He stood by his guns, John did, ever since he was a shaver. You couldn't turn him, if he'd made up his mind. When he was a boy, you could whip him and he wouldn't say a word, wouldn't cry or try to get out of it. He'd take what was coming, but he'd have his own way even if he knew for certain that he'd get licked for it. Now his mother would have to give up trying to run him and make the best she could of her new daughter-in-law.

He opened the door and said to Mrs. Palfrey's back, "Emma, I want to talk to you."

His wife switched around from her mirror, plaiting the gray braid of her hair down across her shoulder. She said quickly, "What's the matter?" Her eyes flew from her husband to the door and then back to him. She knows it's something wrong with the children, Mr. Palfrey thought. She looks just as she used to when they were babies and one of 'em started crying. It's hard to be a mother. Harder now they're grown up than when they were little and had the colic.

He said, "John's downstairs. He's come to tell us that he got married last night. He married Mahala North. They stayed at the Syracuse House because he didn't know whether you'd want them here."

Emma Palfrey said, "Married? Married to that girl?" On her face was a look pitiful and bewildered, as though she had been struck a dazing blow from behind that made her reel and totter forward to catch at her husband's hand for support. "John's *married?*" she repeated, and gave a little cry that wrung Amidon Palfrey's heart.

"But we've got to accept it, Emma," he said, when the worst was over. "We can't fight against it. It's done. He's married. It's too late. And if we make a fuss now, John will simply stay away from us. We'll lose him altogether, if we don't welcome his wife. You've got to see it that way."

Emma Palfrey moaned. "But she's not fit for him," she said hopelessly. "She's not good enough for John. We oughtn't to let our girls associate with such a woman."

Amidon Palfrey stopped that. "Never let me hear you say anything like that again," he said sternly. "I told you weeks ago that I'd met this girl and her father, and they were respectable people. John will never forgive you, and I wouldn't blame him, if he knew you said such a thing. This girl is just as decent as Francelia and Emily, and it won't do them any harm to be with her. She's a fine-looking, smart girl, and I'm going to tell John that we want them to be happy."

Mrs. Palfrey said, with a last spurt of rebellion, "You men don't think about anything but whether the girl's handsome. This girl's got you bewitched. She may be respectable, but she looks fast, just the same."

Her husband said, "That'll do, Emma. I don't want to hear any more about that. If you don't want to see John again, I'll tell him so, and he'll go. If you're going to be kind and sensible, you can wipe your eyes and go downstairs and give them your blessing. I'm going to give him mine right now." And with that he turned and marched out of the room.

Poor Mrs. Palfrey couldn't help it if John did know she'd been crying. Her round face was pink and her eyes swollen when she went downstairs to him. But she did make a brave attempt to bear up. She kissed her son and then burst into tears on his shoulder.

"I'm not blaming you, John," she said through her tears. "I know you couldn't help it. And I'll try to like your wife, if only you won't stay away from us. I can't bear that."

John was like a little boy. "Please. Please don't do that. I'm so happy that I want you to be happy too," he said ingenuously, trying to dry her tears with his own handkerchief. "You'll love Mahala, when you know her. She's the most wonderful girl in the world. I want my whole family to love her. I've never been so happy in my life."

Apartments in the Syracuse House were not exactly palatial, but they were the best the city had to offer, barring residence in a private house. John Palfrey regretted it. "This isn't nearly good enough for you, my darling," he said fondly to his bride. "It's only for a little while, though. We'll buy a house in some good neighborhood, as soon as we can find one. Or we'll build, if you'd rather." Nothing was good enough for her, he thought, drawing her down into his arms, burying his face in her hair. No one could be worthy of her. He, himself, was not worthy. But I've got her, he thought, and felt pride and possessiveness fume in his brain like strong liquor. "You belong to me," he said, as his arms tightened around her. "You're mine. No one can ever take you away."

Cradled in his arms, Mahala looked around the room. The plush chairs, the long rep curtains, the heavy carved walnut furniture were unspeakably beautiful to her. "I love this room," she said passionately. "I won't let you make fun of it. It's ours, John," she said, laughing at her own foolishness. "It's part of our loving each other. If we build a dozen houses, I'd never feel about them the way I do about this room, because I've been so happy here."

There is a classic pattern for the speech of love.

"Say that you love me."

"I love you—I love you."

"Will you always love me?"

"Always. Forever."

"Are you happy?"

"I'm in Heaven . . ."

I'm in Heaven, Mahala thought, burning under his kisses. This is it. This is everything I wanted it to be. I was right to marry John, she said to herself, wildly triumphant. I married him because I couldn't resist him; because I was so much in love with him. But I was afraid, even then, that I might have been wrong. Now I know, she thought, pressing her hands against his temples, holding them there, to feel the very shape of his bones, to acquaint her fingers with the very structure of his being. Now I know I was right. Flesh of my flesh, she thought, drowning in pleasure at his touch. This is what I wanted, after all. This is right. This is everything.

Rapture has no words. Palfrey said brokenly, "I love you—I'll love you forever. My wife—" He could not speak further.

Mahala thought dimly, This is a dream. This can't be true. This is a dream.

CHAPTER FOURTEEN

"I'M GLAD the weather's cleared off," Mrs. Palfrey said, pulling on her gloves in the front hall. "I wouldn't have gone a step if it had kept on raining like it did yesterday. If there's anything I abominate," she said rapidly, chattering as though she couldn't bear to stop for a minute; as though there mustn't be a moment's pause when she was trying to entertain her strange new daughter-in-law. "If there's anything I despise aboveground, it's traipsing around to fairs and sociables in the rain. I just won't do it, that's all. I've told Mr. Palfrey so. Some folks may be so crazy to see Tom Thumb, or whatever, that they're willing to wade in mud. But you don't catch me doing it. I'll go tomorrow, I said to Mr. Palfrey, *if* it clears off. If it doesn't, you'll just have to take the children yourself, if they're bound to go. But you needn't think I'm going, because I'm not."

Mahala, staring through the fancy colored glass in the Palfreys' front door, saw trees first purple, then crimson, then blue. How anyone could tell what the weather was like before they'd opened the door remained a secret. "It was a beautiful day," she said, as though the day had been over the minute she stepped into Mrs. Palfrey's handsome residence. "Warm and sunny. There ought to be a lot of people at the Fair."

Mrs. Palfrey said, "Yes, I expect so," and then called, "Emileeee," in a genteel scream. "Those girls," she said indulgently to Mahala. "Always primping. It's as much as your life's worth to get them started anywhere. Emileeee! Celia! Hurry. Your father's waiting in the carriage."

Francelia said pertly, "Don't wait for us, ma. We aren't ready and it won't do you any good to yell. You and Mahala go out and sit with father, and we'll be down in a minute."

Her mother sighed. "Those girls," she said, shaking her head. "I don't know what young folks are coming to. Headstrong and disrespectful. I hate to think what my mother'd have said to me if I'd kept her waiting this way." But she was smiling as she spoke.

Celia was her darling, Mahala thought, smiling in reply. Celia was a darling anyhow, with her hot temper and her quick tongue and her violent likes and dislikes. Ever since summer and the day of the Jenny Lind riot, Celia had been Mahala's passionate champion. But even with Celia's warm advocacy and Mr. Palfrey's careful kindness, this was not an easy family to join, Mahala thought, following Mrs. Palfrey through the door and down the steps. That first meeting, when all of them had been so stiff, so frozen with embarrassment and nervousness, when Mother Palfrey had evidently been weeping and was likely to weep again at any moment, when John had been so torn between love and a proud defensiveness that he was ready to walk out with his wife at the faintest shade in a voice, the swiftest glance from an eye.

Well, that was one ordeal over, Mahala thought, tripping down the flagstone path to the street, in the wake of her mother-in-law's garnet silk flounces. That was one stile she wouldn't have to climb again. They'd seen her; they'd met her; they'd accepted her, after a fashion. They had come to call on John's new wife at the Syracuse House where the young Palfreys now lived. John and his wife had called more frequently at the family home on Fayette Park. Now, on this first of October—burning blue in the sky, burning red and gold on the trees; last night's frost tingling in the air like hard cider on the tongue—young Mrs. John Palfrey was stepping into the family carryall. She was taking her place demurely behind the broad backs of her new relatives, about to drive out to the Onondaga County Agricultural Fair to view the exhibits.

This isn't I, Mahala thought, staring at Mrs. Palfrey's neatly braided chignon. This isn't Mahala North. This is somebody else; someone I don't even know. I don't know this Mahala any more than the Palfreys do. I don't know what she's like, what she might do. They're afraid of me because they don't know what I might do, but I don't know either. John doesn't know. No one knows whether this polite person who dresses up and goes to ride is good or bad, wild or sober. My father knows, she thought with a sudden pang. He knows—and Dal would know.

But Dal's gone, she said to herself violently. Dal's gone and I'll never see him again. And father doesn't care what I do, as long as I'm happy. And I *am* happy, she told herself, as though the fact needed to be stated. John; think of John. I'm in love with John, and he's in love with me. I must be happy. I must be good. There's nothing to be afraid of.

The front door, with its jewel-colored glass, opened wide now, and the two girls came out with a great flurry of floating ribbons and shawls, with flowers and feathers nodding on their new bonnets, every curl elegantly in place, their faces flushed with running, their blue eyes—so like John's—beaming. They skipped into the back of the carriage, crowding in beside their new sister, laughing and chattering, as eager as kittens. The Fair, they said, talking against each other in such a rush that Mahala could hardly catch a word of it. The Fair. It was going to be marvelous, thrilling. Everyone was going to be there, everyone they knew in town, and of course thousands of country people who didn't count at all. First they must stop at the Hanover Arcade and see the exhibits. That was what everyone did. After that, they must drive out to the Fair Grounds—which were really Mr. Bastable's farm, loaned for the occasion—and see the horses and animals.

From the front seat, their mother tried to calm them down. "Girls! Girls! You must be more quiet and ladylike. What will Mahala think of you, if you act like this?"

Celia could never be put down. "Mahala's as bad as we are. We're *all* excited. It's the first thing that's happened here in *ages,*" she cried, reproaching her family. "It's so *slow* here. Nothing *ever* happens. We're all simply *dying* for some excitement. Aren't we, Mahala?" she appealed to her new idol. "Mahala's probably just as bored as we are, only she's too polite to say so. Don't you love excitement, Mahala?"

Mrs. Palfrey answered her. "Mercy sakes, what a thing to say! Of course Mahala isn't bored. She's a married woman and she's got better things to think about than excitement, I should hope. You girls are too young to know anything about it."

I'm a married woman, Mahala thought, sitting back between the two girls, while the carriage rolled over the new plank paving of Warren Street. I'm a married woman. I've got better things to think about. And Celia says that nothing exciting ever happens here. If I had been a polite young lady before I married John, I should have been bored, too. But I had excitement enough, she thought grimly. Enough and to spare. Fear and worry and suspense and pain. I was not a polite young female. I was a man. I was Martin. I had work to do. I did anything, everything, because I believed in it. Now, what do I believe in? Have I forgotten what I used to feel? Am I a different person because I am John's wife? Do I think what John thinks, because I'm married to him? Am I peaceful now? Has Martin's ghost vanished?

The Arcade was crowded with visitors. Carriages were lined up on both sides of the street before it; men and women and children were streaming over from the depot where the train had just come in from Utica. The stage from Salina was unloading passengers on the other side of the street, and ladies in Quaker gray and close bonnets were alighting from a farm wagon next to it. Everyone was pushing inside the Arcade to see the exhibits. You could hear the buzz of talk before you got to the doors; everyone talking at the top of his lungs, to be heard above the crowd. A good-natured crowd, even on the streets, everyone dressed up to the nines, showing off a little, strutting a little, ready for a good time.

Farther up the street, near the Syracuse House, already the learned judges of the court were piling into buggies and canopy-tops to ride up North Salina Street to the Courthouse, where the court was in session. With them were all the lawyers and politicians in creation, talking nineteen to the dozen, whispering together, slapping each other on the back, shaking hands as though they hadn't met for forty years. They looked knowing and wise and clever, standing on the hotel veranda jabbering away with their hands clasped under their coattails or their thumbs stuck in their vest armholes; rocking on their heels, pursing their lips, nodding their heads, wagging their beards. All that was very fine and impressive on a day when a great throng was in town to see the sights. The farmers might go home and tell their neighbors, "I saw Lawyer Clover on the porch of the Syracuse House, and he was talking with all the high muckamucks, as cool as you please, and the big bugs were listening to him, I can tell you."

That was a sight for the country bumpkins to see, and there were a lot of them there, right enough, whether they noticed Lawyer Clover or not. There was a God's plenty for them to see on a day like this, and they were all ready to see it, whatever it was. If you have got up at four o'clock, fed your stock, done your chores, scrubbed up, eaten your breakfast, and driven ten miles into the city, you feel ready for whatever may come along. They pushed into the Hanover Arcade and elbowed their way up to the counters and tables and booths where the exhibits were, their eyes sticking out like sixty. Beside them, ruddy and brown as they were, neat as wax in their good black suits, in their best bonnets and bombazines, the fashionables from the city looked almost too genteel to breathe.

But they, too, stared at the heaped fruits. There were apples: Greenings, Pippins, Russets, Northern Spies, Pound Sweets, Strawberry, Early Jo, Snow Apples, Seek-no-further, Winesap, Baldwin, Weathy, Delicious, Jonathan. There were quinces: the Orange, the Champion, the Rea. There were grapes: Concord, Niagara, Delaware, Isabella. In baskets, in heaps, mounds and piles of gold and yellow and red and purple and green; polished, shining, lucent. Like jewels from the Orient and gold from Ophir, they were spread before the gazers, and their scent rose in a delicate and enticing perfume that filled the air of the hall.

Besides these, there were vegetables: corn, golden and white; summer squash and crook-necked and gnarled green Hubbards; pumpkins big enough for coaches; cabbages silver-green and purple; carrots and turnips and beets and potatoes. There were sheaves and baskets of grain: wheat and oats and barley and buckwheat. In one corner were the dairy foods: cheese in huge fifty-pound hoops, covered with white cheesecloth, boxed in thin new wood; butter in tubs and firkins, in molds and pats, as yellow as cowslips, as sweet-smelling as sunshine. And at the end of the room, where the fine ladies and the farmers' wives could oh and ah over them, were flowers of every kind that could be grown, and some, the farmers said, scoffing, that couldn't. "Over two hundred kinds," a farmer would say to his wife. But she would have no eyes for most of them. "Look at those *day*lias, Jonas," she would say, whispering as though she was in church. "They're a good six inches acrost. They're three times as big as mine. What do you calculate they put onto 'em to make 'em so big?"

Mrs. Palfrey was a good housewife and she was willing to spend some time looking at the harvest fruits, but the girls dragged her off before she'd more than glanced around, to see the needlework. The lace, they cried in ecstasy; the crochet, the knitting, the embroidery! "Look at this counterpane! See this bedspread! Come look at this little love of a bonnet! Mother—the shell flowers, the wax fruit, the fancy piece made of human hair!"

After an hour, Mr. Palfrey had had enough of the crowd. "It's half past eleven," he said, dragging out his fine turnip watch. "We'll miss the display of animals if we dawdle here any more. Mr. Bastable's got some superfine horses this year."

Reluctantly, his ladies were dragged away from the needlework, the hand painting, the woolwork, the fish-scale flowers. It was dreadful to go, Francelia pleaded with her father, forgetting altogether that she had longed to see the lovely horses.

"What a pity that John couldn't be with us," Mrs. Palfrey said, glancing at John's wife to see if she was remembering him. "John would have loved to see the horses particularly."

"Poor John's so busy," his wife replied, shaking her head sadly. "He's always so busy. And just lately he's been up to his ears in work."

"Is something special going on?" Mr. Palfrey wanted to know. "Something Major Burnet's doing, perhaps? It'd be a good time to make a show against those crazy Abolitionists right now, when they're having their convention or whatever they call it."

Mrs. Palfrey said, "It's too bad they have to make a fuss today, when everybody's out for a good time. I hope they don't do anything rough. I always worry so about John."

Mahala tried to be calm. "He didn't speak of any demonstration against the convention. I don't see why he'd want to annoy the Abolitionists. They've got a right to hold an orderly meeting, I should think."

Her father-in-law said indulgently, "It's a matter of politics, my dear. Women don't understand such things. John feels it's his duty to take a firm stand."

We won't talk about it, Mahala thought wearily. We won't speak of such things. Ladies don't talk about politics. Ladies don't know about conventions. The little white wooden Congregational Church seemed to be full, as they passed it. Quite a good crowd attending the convention of the Liberal party. Mr. Palfrey glanced toward the opened doors and said, "Poor old Ga't Smith. He's been a good man, until he got this Anti-Slavery bee in his bonnet. Now he's trying to make folks think he's got a party behind him. He couldn't carry enough votes to be elected dogcatcher."

The horses trotted smartly down Genesee Street, over the old Turnpike road. Past Fayette Park, past Orange Street and Almond Street and Lemon Street, and so to Chestnut, and there was the

Orphanage, tall and narrow-shouldered, with its cupola, very fine, and just behind it a tremendous gathering of rigs hitched along the roadway that led to Mr. Bastable's farm. There were tents, there were paddocks filled with horses and cattle, pens where bulls stamped and bellowed, enclosures crowded with sheep and swine, creatures of every kind that lived on a farm, all sleek and handsome, fat and well-groomed, waiting for the judges to look at them and give them the grand prize.

Mr. Palfrey sighed with content to be among a man's concerns again. "This is something like," he said, pulling the team in, hitching it to a post in the shade. "Now you'll see something worth seeing."

Mrs. Palfrey sighed to think of all the traipsing around, but the girls had forgotten their pain at leaving the Arcade, and were in a fever to see every animal on the grounds, and Mahala, feeling the sunshine warm on her shoulders, was suddenly gay and happy. Why should I worry? Why should I feel guilty to take pleasure as other people do? I have a right to be here. There is nothing to be afraid of.

Oh, the horses, Celia was crying now, as she had cried out over the fancywork. Oh, the darling fat things. The colt, mother; look at that colt with the furry tail and such a fat back. Belgians, her father corrected her. Very fine draft horses, powerful and kind. Their coats were the color of stirred maple sugar, Celia said, adoring the golden creatures. Their necks were as thick and arched as the zebras in a Noah's Ark. Why couldn't we have that kind of horses to draw the carriage? I like them better than our horses.

But before her father could instruct her, a sound brought all talk to a halt. A bell was ringing back in the city. Dong! dong! dong! Then again, urgently, dong! dong! dong! The notes rang clear as honey on the autumn air. Dong! dong! dong!

A fire? people asked each other, turning their heads, listening. Is that a fire in town? No, someone near the Palfreys said, starting to run. That's the Congregational Church bell. That's the signal. More men began to run, leaving their womenfolk behind, rushing over to the road, unhitching their horses, grabbing for their whips. It's the signal, the signal.

In their pens, the animals stood listening, too, and now they were alone with no one to admire them, for all the men began to hurry out of the Fair Grounds, running, pushing each other, dashing for their horses to get back into town.

Mr. Palfrey said, "The signal? What do they mean? Why should the bell ring?" But as he spoke he, too, turned away from the handsome Belgians and began to move toward the road. "Come, mother. If something's happened, we'd better get back to town. I want to know what this means."

Over their heads, the bell repeated and repeated its warning. Dong! dong! dong! The signal, Mahala thought, and felt a trembling go through her like a ripple over water. The Vigilantes. Something's happened. They've taken a fugitive. John *was* planning a demonstration. That's why he's been so strange these last days. He wouldn't talk to me. He wouldn't tell me what he was doing. And I knew there was something in the wind. I knew it all this time. That's why I've been afraid. I knew something was going to happen. What shall I do? she thought in a panic. What shall I do? How can I do anything, now that I am John's wife? But how can I do nothing? Where is my father? she thought in great fear. I must see my father. I must see John.

Going back in the carriage was like being in a road race. Every sort of rig—buggies and Democrat wagons and surreys and lumber wagons—ran neck and neck up the old Turnpike. A man, standing up on a buckboard with his whip working like a flail, tore past Mr. Palfrey's sedate pair as though they had been standing still. Dust rose in a cloud, so that Mrs. Palfrey choked and begged her husband to slow down, to get out of the crowd; but he would not listen to her. Even he was beginning to catch the excitement, and Ben and Bess, the sober bays, felt a whip they had almost forgotten. "I can't help it, mother," he said, giving

Ben a good lick. "Something's gone wrong. I've got to get back in a hurry."

Men and women were streaming out of the Congregational Church on East Genesee Street, running toward the Canal, and the stream of vehicles was rushing in the same direction, all of them pouring out into the broad space of Clinton Square as though a dam had burst, as though a freshet had broken and was pouring the whole populace of the city helter-skelter into a single lake. And as men ran, as horses galloped, over their heads the bells spoke, deep-voiced, insistent, warning, tolling out their three notes—clang! clang! clang! until they rang in every ear, beat in every pulse. Come! come! come! the bells said, ringing all over the city now, from steeple after steeple. Help! help! help! the bells said to all the men and women in the city. Danger! the bells said, danger! danger!

Mr. Morrel's cooper's shop was a peaceful place on that Wednesday morning, the first day of October. A sunny morning, after three days' rain and wind; equinoctials, people said, struggling with umbrellas, splashing through puddles on the uneven pavements of the city. But today the weather had cleared, just right for the County Fair and the Liberal Party Convention, and it was a pretty morning even for a man going to his work. Soon after eleven o'clock most of the workmen—white men they were, Germans and Irish, mostly, and good enough fellows when they weren't full of rotgut from Robbers' Row—had gone off home for their dinners. Windows were open, blowing a soft south wind into the shop, blowing in the sweet and acrid smell of burning leaves to mingle with the odor of freshly sawn timber in the workroom. Hammer strokes sounded pleasantly in the quiet place where a Negro man was still working at a barrel, pounding neatly and surely, humming to himself a little as he worked. His back was toward the door of the shop.

What happened next was a kind of nightmare to the man Jerry, working alone on Mr. Morrel's barrels. The skies fell upon him.

Violence, hands laid upon him unawares, men erupting into the room all in a minute, leaping upon him from behind, pinioning his arms, dragging him about, shouting at him; and before he knew what was happening, shackles had snapped over his wrists, and he was helpless before them all.

"What is it?" he asked as soon as he could get his breath. "What's the matter, Mr. Allen? What I done now?"

Allen was some sort of policeman, and Russell Lowell was another. Jerry knew that, and so did all the other Negroes in the town. There was trouble sometimes among the colored folks, a razor used too freely, a man beating his wife a little too loudly. White or colored, people had to have trouble sometimes, and Jerry had seen the inside of a jail before. But why did they jump at him? he wanted to know. Why did they come so quietly and pounce on him? Why did they shackle him, like a slave in a coffle? he thought in fear. Why were all these other men standing around looking at him, threatening?

Mr. Allen said more calmly, "It's a complaint, Jerry. Your woman's been making a fuss again. You've got to go and see the Squire."

"You been stealing," one of the other men said, grinning at him. "Just a little charge of theft against Jerry Henry. You'd better tell it to the Judge."

Why should they laugh at that? the Negro wondered, moving toward the door with his captors all around him. What did I steal? What they got against me this time?

"I ain't stole," he said as well as he could, stumbling along between his guards. "I ain't stole nothin', Mr. Allen. I can't tell the Judge nothin' because I ain't done nothin' to tell. I don' know how come you arrest me this time."

Allen said gruffly, "You'll know soon enough. We ain't got time to jaw now. You'll have to answer the charges in court."

Outside the shop a buggy was waiting, and behind it a surrey, with the side curtains buttoned tight. Mr. Allen made for the wagon, pulling Jerry along beside him. "In here," he said, shoving his prisoner into the musty depths of the back seat. "Sit still and keep quiet, if you don't want to get into more trouble than you already got. If you try to shout or make a fuss, we'll have to gag you."

How come they think he goin' to holler? What good for him to make a fuss? How come him throwed in a dark carriage and drove off, lickety-split, with three white men right with him and two more in the buggy ahead? Fear was beginning to make such a din in the Negro's mind that he couldn't hear his own thoughts. What is it? What's happening to me? What shall I do?

The carriage turned down North Salina Street. A dray, piled six tiers high with new barrels, passed them, ambling off to the saltworks. A farmer's wagon, with the farmer and his wife all spruced up for the Fair, trotted past. As they rattled over the bridge, a packet boat was warping into the landing in the packet basin, and women in bright dresses sat in chairs on the cabin roof to watch. The surrey turned west on Water Street, clattered over the cobbles and swung around sharply to a stop before the Townsend Block in Clinton Square.

Sunlight was so bright in his eyes, after the gloom of the closed wagon, that the Negro stumbled as he got out, would have fallen except for Allen's grip on his arm. In the momentary confusion, a man near by turned to look. Fetters on a Negro's wrist. That was all he saw, really. He might or might not know the Negro; there hadn't been time for a clear look. But he certainly did know Allen and Constable Lowell, who each had the colored man by an arm. And it was also clear that they were hustling him along, fairly dragging him to the door that opened on the stairs to Commissioner Sabine's new office. That was enough. The man ran three steps and shouted after the party.

"What's happening, Allen? Why have you got that Negro ironed?" His voice echoed and resounded up the stairs. No answer. Heavy footsteps clattered on the bare boards, and a man's voice cried out in terror, "Mr. Wheaton! Mr. Wheaton!"

Wheaton turned back to the street and found that an easy

crowd had gathered to see what the commotion was about. He didn't hesitate.

"They've got a Negro up there. They've arrested him. They're going to railroad him south, by this new Fugitive Slave Law. Are we going to let them do it?" His voice was high with anger.

A half dozen voices in the crowd yelled, "No, no!"

Wheaton didn't wait. "You men stay here and don't let 'em take him away. I'm going to warn the convention." In a minute he was running down the street toward the Congregational Church.

Men in the little gathering stared after him in wonder. It wasn't often you saw a dignified citizen like Mr. Wheaton running hotfoot through the streets, like a boy. Lucky for that nigger Wheaton was on the spot, someone said. Lucky for him that Wheaton's store burned down and he had to come and boss the new building. That fire was lucky, after all. It's an ill wind, somebody else said, and there was a general laugh. But about that nigger, it was a shame. Let the South catch its own slaves, they said, scowling, muttering to each other. We won't catch 'em. If any nigger's got enough gumption to get all the way to Syracuse from down south, he ought to go free. Damn the Fugitive Slave Law, the crowd said, pressing closer to the door of Mr. Commissioner Sabine's office. They may have got him in, but they won't get him out.

"It's simple," Lear said, lounging back in his chair, taking a long draw on his segar, turning to smile at Major Burnet and Mr. John Palfrey. "The Commissioner's hearing won't be any trouble. It's a formality, really. I've attended several. The whole trick is to have your papers right in the first place. That's what's delayed me so long." He winked broadly at the Major. "Mustn't go off half-cocked on a thing like this. Wait until everything's ready, and the whole business will go as slick as grease."

The Major said urbanely, "We are anxious to provide you with every facility at our command, Mr. Lear. We represent an organization pledged to carry out the law."

Lear grinned. "Yes, sir. I've heard about the Patriots. I hear you've had some trouble with the Nigger Lovers here. This little affair ought to remind 'em that the government means what it says." He looked quickly at Mr. Palfrey. "I understand that you're interested in this organization, too, sir," he said smoothly. "The property owners of the South will be grateful to you."

John Palfrey moved restlessly in his seat. "We don't want gratitude," he said rather ungraciously. "We want to prevent trouble while there's still time. The country's in a critical state right now." Before Mr. Lear could answer, Palfrey switched around to frown at the Commissioner's men, who were still fussing over preliminaries. "I wish they'd get started. It was a good time to make the arrest, just before dinner when most of the folks will be working or at the Fair or the convention. If we delay too long, someone will find out about it and spread the word around, and then we'll have a real row on our hands."

Lear asked lazily, "Can't an outfit like yours handle a few Woolly Heads? I can't imagine there'd be much danger, even if they do find out."

The Major disagreed with this. "More trouble than you'd think. We've seen them in action before. They're reckless men, Mr. Lear. Fanatics. They'd go to any lengths to take the slave away."

Lear still couldn't believe it. "You've got the man safe under police protection. I can't see what the Abolitionists could do about it. They'd hardly mob the Commissioner's office. The most they could do would be to try to defend the nigger legally, and that won't work. The law refuses to hear any evidence from a slave. He has no rights. Your antislavery friends can't do anything but talk, and that won't prevent my taking the darky away from them."

From the street below, the sound of loud talking, shouts, catcalls, drifted up the open stairway. Carriages rattled past in the street, a canalboat horn blew mournfully. And then, suddenly, a church bell began to toll, three strong notes, repeated again and again.

Commissioner Sabine, new and nervous in his new office, started when he heard it. "What's that? The bell—the Congregational Church. That's their signal. Someone's told them."

He was badly rattled, there was no doubt about it. It had been a mistake, perhaps, to let this case come before a new man, John Palfrey thought. Sabine had been suspected of antislavery leanings, but when he'd accepted the position they had assumed he was sound. Now, from the color of his face, it looked as though he was afraid. That might make it ticklish. A thing like this ought to be run by a strong hand, by a man who would put it through and get it over. It wasn't pleasant for anyone, John thought, trying not to look at the Negro's face, trying not to hear him moan. No one likes to frighten a man, even a colored man. No one likes to send any human creature back to slavery. But that wasn't the question. The question was whether you cared more about keeping the Union together than you did about any one person's—or any thousand persons'—private feelings. The Union was what mattered, John Palfrey thought, wishing with all his heart that the poor devil would stop crying; the Union, the United States of America, the whole country. We've got to do this. It's the only way. The people who think you can have it both ways are fools.

He said aloud, "What's holding Sabine up? Why can't we begin? It's risky to wait so long. If that bell means that the convention has been warned, they're likely to be down here raising Cain in a few minutes."

The noise in the street was increasing now, the sound of voices had swelled to a roar, the sound of running feet seemed to come from everywhere. At the foot of the stairs men were talking.

A strong voice said, "Bates will keep on ringing the bell. Wheaton's gone to get Lawyer Gibbs and maybe someone else. They'll be here in a minute."

A second voice answered calmly, "We may as well go up, Mr.

Smith. The Negro will be badly frightened. It might quiet him to see you beside him."

In a minute, before anyone could shut the door, the first of them had pushed into the room, crowding up the stairs, swarming into the Commissioner's office. There were dozens of them, it seemed, until the room was unbearably crowded, and Mr. Sabine's voice, pleading with them to go away, to be quiet, to be calm, was wholly drowned out by the babble of tongues. John Palfrey, on his feet now, was ready to go into action; but aside from the crowding and the talking, there was nothing violent about these men. They wouldn't be violent, Palfrey thought, recognizing man after man, friends, acquaintances, well-known and respected persons. They weren't here to fight physically, but to fight legally. Dr. May, with his saint's face, Gerrit Smith with his wilderness of white beard like an Old Testament patriarch, Mr. Sedgwick, Dr. Clary, Dr. Hoyt; man after man, the pillars of the town, the good citizens.

As Palfrey watched, Gerrit Smith and Dr. May moved to the side of the terrified Negro. They were talking to him now, and no one was preventing them. John Palfrey wouldn't prevent them either, he thought grimly. If they'll only stop that coon from bawling, I'll thank them, instead. I can't stand hearing him much longer. But how anyone—let alone Sabine, who was as nervous as a witch—could hope to conduct a hearing in a mob like that was a mystery. The room was as full as it could pack, and the crowd on the stairs was a solid mass of bodies as far as he could see it. There was the smallest possible space free around the Commissioner's desk, and the claimant's lawyer, Mr. James Lawrence, was squeezed against the wall beyond it. Now, out of the pushing crowd on the stairs, a couple of figures were coming through. Mr. Wheaton and a stranger, they were, and they went directly to Mr. Sabine and began a low conversation with him. Someone the Abolitionists had got in to defend the Negro, probably. He'd have his trouble for his pains. With this new law, there wasn't a Chinaman's chance to get the man off.

Lear was looking cockier than ever, Palfrey thought, watching the man without love. He's a bully and a ruffian. I hate to turn the Negro over to him, but there's no other way. Lear won't own him, luckily; he'll have to take him back to his original owner. But Lear likes this sort of thing. You can see it in his face. I'm sorry we have to deal with him. The more people looking on, the better he likes it. He's glad the crowd came, because now everyone can see him parade his power. That's why he was so glad to wait for today, instead of presenting his papers two weeks ago.

Sabine's the one who might crack. He's an Abolitionist at heart, and it's a wonder he took the job, knowing what was coming. He's known for three weeks. Did he tell anyone? Is that why they've come so quickly? John wondered, staring at Sabine's suffering face. Did he save his reputation with the Vigilantes by tipping them the wink so they could fight us? It won't do him any good, he thought, looking at Lear's satisfied smile. Lear won't give up, and he's got a complete case against the Negro. Sabine's sworn to uphold the law, and he'll have to do it.

The lawyer, if that is what he was, had taken a seat next to Jerry and was trying hopelessly to make the terrified creature answer questions for him. The poor fellow could only groan and cry and take on. It was no use. Dr. May, murmuring to him occasionally, got only tears for an answer, and old Ga't Smith could be heard trying to comfort the man. Finally, when the rumpus had died down a shade, the Commissioner began his hearing. Mr. Lear, as claimant, made a statement.

"I represent an ancient people," he said, as though he was making a speech.

The strange lawyer seated next to the prisoner drawled, "The claimant is only required to state his authority. It isn't necessary to give a history of his life."

Lear stared him down. "That's what I'm doing," he said haughtily. "My name is James Lear. My home is Newark, Marion County, Missouri. I've known that nigger ever since I first met old John McReynolds, his first master, back in 1820. I knew Jerry's mother before him. She's still the property of McReynolds, if she's living. Now young Mr. McReynolds wants his man back, and I've got the papers to prove ownership, and to give the date and circumstances of his disappearance. I demand that this fugitive slave be remanded into my custody, for return to his rightful owner, and I present these documents to substantiate my claim." He handed up his sheaf of papers with a fine flourish, and Sabine took them as though they were burning hot.

Mr. Leonard Gibbs—his name ran in an audible whisper around the room as he rose ponderously to speak—said in a rich, orator's voice, "I have a request to make of the Court. The Court undoubtedly knows, as I do, that in this country it is customary to consider accused persons innocent, until or unless they shall have been proved guilty."

Every eye in the room flew to the iron shackles on Jerry's wrists, saw him hold his hands out, bound together as they were, saw the tears on his dark face. A murmur, a sort of warning rumble rose from the crowd, a single angry sound as though it had but one throat and spoke with one voice. It did not utter any words that could be understood, but there was no way to misunderstand what that sound meant. We are angry; we are waiting. Let this man go, or it will be the worse for you. John Palfrey, staring at the ringleaders, wondered for the first time whether there was going to be serious trouble.

"The hands of the accused bear shackles," Mr. Gibbs said, his voice quivering with emotion. "I ask, as a matter of right, that they be stricken off. Furthermore," he said, swelling with wrath, "I observe that the claimant's agent appears in the Court armed with a revolver, visible in his pocket."

Once more the crowd peered, saw the bulge under Lear's coat. Yes, it was a gun, all right, the murmur rose. He's got a gun. He's ready to kill the poor cuss. Make him take it off, the crowd rumbled from its deep throat. Take the weapon away from him.

Mr. Gibbs made the protest ring. "This is a gross insult to the Court and to the people. I demand that the irons be removed from the prisoner. I demand that the weapon be removed from the claimant, before this hearing proceeds further."

While the wrangle went on to no conclusion, Palfrey watched Gerrit Smith's hoary face. A big man; an imposing mind, hot and dominating; there was a recklessness in the old man, fire, the imperious eye. Gibbs was losing his point; would certainly lose his case later, and his case was Gerrit Smith's case. But that would not beat Gerrit Smith. Nothing would beat him. He would win or he would die for it. That was written on his face. Now, how would he take this thing? Would he give up, when Sabine gave his decision, or would he turn his reckless eye on the mob and lead it against any odds? You could not tell, with Gerrit Smith. Dr. May was a man of peace. He might fight, in an extremity, but it would be against his nature, and he would stay his hand to the last moment. But Gerrit Smith was a horse of another color; a war horse, Palfrey thought, narrowing his eyes to study the old man.

The room was growing intolerably hot. What it must be, standing packed into that crowd, was a caution. And the people were growing restless, too. They murmured, they moved and shifted. A voice near the front ranks called fiercely, "You can see how it's going to be. There's no use waiting any longer!"

Commissioner Sabine rapped violently with his gavel. "I will have order in this Court."

But who was going to bring order? The handful of constables and marshals straightened themselves, glared at the crowd. They were outnumbered twenty to one. But for the moment, authority held. The hearing was allowed to proceed.

Mr. Palfrey was obliged to pull in the excited bays as soon as they reached Clinton Square. The whole space of the wide Square was crowded; with carriages and wagons along the curbs, with a moving, shouting mass of people on the open pavement. The main body of the crowd was assembled in front of the Townsend Block, a large, gray stone edifice extending along more than half the length of the block on the south side of the Square. Here, before an open doorway, the mob stood and waited, but not quietly. They pushed, they shoved their way, they yelled and shouted. The horses would have gone crazy if they'd moved a step nearer, and Mrs. Palfrey was already near to fainting with the excitement and shock.

"Take us home right this minute, Amidon Palfrey," she implored her husband. "I won't stay here. We might get killed in this crowd. The horses will begin to act up, and we shall all be thrown out."

Mr. Palfrey said, "Now, mother, hold on a minute. I've got to find out what's up. John's probably in this somewhere," he was inspired to add. "I want to know that he's all right."

His wife moaned, "He's probably fighting. You'll never find him in this mob."

The girls were thrilled by the whole affair. "Let's ask someone what it's about," they clamored, agog with curiosity. "Something terrible must have happened. We've got to know what it is."

This was the first sensible suggestion Mr. Palfrey had heard. He called to a passer-by, "What's going on here? What's all this ruction about?"

The man waved his arms. "It's about a runaway slave. The marshals captured one and they've taken him up to Sabine's office to arrest him. They're going to send him back south." He looked at Mr. Palfrey sharply. "They're going to ship him home—if they can," he said with sudden fury. "They're going to try to run this new law through, and it looks like somebody else is going to stop 'em." The man's face seemed to light up as he spoke, and when he came to the last words he was smiling with fierceness and joy. "There's quite a lot of folks," he said, smiling like a wolf at Mr. Palfrey, "that don't like it. Maybe they'll do something about it," and with that he began to run toward the stamping crowd.

Mrs. Palfrey said, "Mercy on us. Papa—I believe I'm going to faint." But before she could do it she cried out, "Goodness, Mahala, you mustn't get out. You'll get killed in this crowd. Get back in," she screamed weakly. "Papa! Mahala—"

Mahala was out of the carriage now, with barely a word to explain her action. "I've got to go," she said in a voice they had never heard before. "I've got to find John. I've got to go."

Before her new relatives could stop her, she was running across the Square, and, as they watched, the crowd opened to receive her and they saw her no more.

Mr. Palfrey said, "Well, I'm damned," and sat staring after her, the reins loose in his hands.

This time Mrs. Palfrey really did faint, and the girls were obliged to work over her lifeless form all the way home.

CHAPTER FIFTEEN

AT A DISTANCE, any crowd looks like a solid, compact mass of bodies, but actually it is a moving thing, perpetually shifting and changing, opening up here, closing in there, pressing forward, shoving backward, milling about, moving upon itself like a swarm of bees hovering above the limb of an apple tree. And the sound it makes, the mingling of hundreds of voices speaking together, is like the humming of that other swarm. Mahala reached the gathering of men before the bleak building, and as she came up to it, those on the outer fringe turned to look at her, surprised to see a woman running so wildly toward them. Turning, they moved out a little from the body of the crowd, and, moving, they made a way for the runner.

Once inside the crowd, however, it was not easy to progress. Frantically Mahala pushed against the wall of men, pleaded with them to let her through. "Please let me pass. I've got to get through. I've got to find someone."

Nothing could be more shocking than the presence of a woman in such a place; and a lady, never. This person, the men thought, looking at Mahala's wind-blown hair—she had lost her bonnet—at her disheveled dress, at her desperate face, was a queer customer. What did she want in a ruction like this? She was probably scared that her husband would get hurt, the more charitable said, grinning. He'd be mad enough to beat her, as like as not, for making such a holy show of herself. And anyway, a woman had no business in such a mob. She'd get hurt and blame everybody but herself for it. A few tenderhearted males, pitying her distress, moved aside to let her pass, but the crowd itself, pressing harder than ever around the doorway, would not budge.

A man beside Mahala said kindly, "You better slow down, sister. It ain't no good trying to get through this jam. You'll just fash yourself for nothing. These men mean business. They ain't goin' to stir away from that door until they get the nigger out."

Mahala tried to catch her breath. "I've got to get through," she said again, and the man laughed.

"You'll have to climb over their heads, then," he said. "What you in such a chowder about, anyway? Don't you know this ain't a safe place for a female? You'll get hurt, if you're not careful."

"I've got to find somebody," Mahala said, peering everywhere. "My father—my husband—"

The man said soothingly, "Don't you worry about them. They'll be all right. They've got a job to do, and they won't like to have you come interferin' with 'em."

Mahala dropped her eyes. "What's their job?" she asked as casually as possible. "I heard the bells ringing."

The man grinned. "I guess you did. Every church bell in town was goin' it, hammer and tongs. All except the Episcopal, of course. They wouldn't pay any heed to a nigger getting caught. They believe in law and order," he said comically. "Fugitive Slave Law and order. And some other folks here in town ain't so sure they want that kind of law."

Mahala looked at the man. He was large, jovial, kindly. She said, "I know that. Are you going to deliver this fugitive?" There was nothing soft or womanly about the way she said it.

The man stared. "You bet we are," he said in a surprised voice.

"Have you got a plan? Do you know how you're going to do it? Have you made any preparations for getting this man away from the police? Do you know how you'll get him out of town?"

She's a tartar, the man thought, looking at her with new interest. She acts like a sergeant major talking to a private. He said, "Well, I ain't heard about any plan. I guess the men here think it'll be enough if they can get the nigger loose from Hank Allen.

When they've got him free will be time enough to think about a plan."

This strange woman said sharply, "You may find you're mistaken about that. The police aren't fools. They must know how this crowd feels. After the hearing, if you haven't decided what you'll do, they'll take the Negro and put him in jail and let you whistle for him." She saw bewilderment in the man's mild face and said impatiently, "I know what I'm talking about. You'll fail, if you go at it this way. I've got to find some of the leaders. Have you seen Moses North? He keeps the Old Lib Tavern. A large man, very tall, with reddish hair."

Her new friend said humbly, "You must be on the Underground. No, I can't say as I've seen anybody like that. He may be upstairs in Sabine's office. There's a mort of folks up there."

Mahala frowned. "Are any of the Patriots there?" she asked. "Major Burnet? Noxon? Palfrey?" There was the slightest hesitation before this last name.

The man could tell her that. "Yes, ma'am. I heard somebody say that they've got a regular posse of 'em up there, to help the marshals guard the prisoner. Burnet's there, for sure, and the others will probably be there too, if *he* is."

Mahala started to say, "Is Loguen there?" when a yell burst from the crowd. There was a sudden stir in the jam on the stairway. Something was happening above. Several men on the lower steps were pushed violently backwards into the street. Shouts, yells, questions, curses. A huge man with a mane of red-roan hair loomed above the crowd for an instant.

"Look out below," he shouted.

The Honorable Mr. Gibbs of Washington County was plainly talking against time. That much was evident to everybody in Mr. Sabine's office, Patriots and Vigilantes alike. What he was waiting for, what he hoped to gain by this delay was not so clear. Dr. May and Mr. Gerrit Smith were seen talking to Jerry, at frequent intervals, and the Negro still moaned and wept and held his fettered hands out before him. The crowd of unidentified onlookers was certainly growing impatient with all this palaver, and their rebellious murmuring made a constant undertone below the measured phrases of Mr. Gibbs. If he was stalling until their tempers broke, he was likely to succeed. They were tired of talk, they were tired of waiting. There was the nigger; why not take him out? Mr. Salmon of Fulton, in the front rank of the crowd, made audible remarks on the subject, so that no one could avoid hearing what the crowd wanted. Get him out. Take him away from them. You'll never put this Fugitive Slave Law across Syracuse, not if you talk a thousand years.

Mr. Gibbs was orating about Missouri. It was a question, he said, whether slavery was lawful in Missouri, and if it was not lawful in that state, how could the prisoner be claimed as a slave at all, let alone as a fugitive slave? He went on about it for a long time, involving himself in the dubious politics of the matter until the crowd began to stamp its myriad feet. Mr. Gibbs cast them an unreadable glance. Furthermore, he said, eying the ringleaders, even if he was to grant that slavery was to be considered lawful in Missouri, should not a judicial officer of that state, rather than Mr. Lear who had no official standing, testify as to the legality of the claimant's papers?

Mr. Sabine hesitated; Mr. Lawrence, the lawyer for Lear, argued hotly, produced evidence, showed papers, beat down every objection. The law was the law. The Fugitive Slave Law had been duly passed by the Congress of the United States. It was incumbent upon the Commissioner, as a federal official, to carry out that law. He seemed to have the case in his pocket, for all Mr. Gibbs's oratory, and the crowd, muttering in its beard, believed that it must take the case into its own hands.

The noise, the pressure of the crowd, the heat in the room, were unbearable, Commissioner Sabine thought. There was no use trying to get any sense out of anybody in such a hullabaloo. He said so, in his agitated way, and announced that he would adjourn the hearing until two-thirty that afternoon, when the proceedings would reconvene in a larger room. The office of the Police Court, in the Raynor Building across the Square, would provide more adequate quarters. The prisoner was remanded to the custody of the police until the later hearing. Mr. Commissioner Sabine rose with dignity, buttoned his frock coat—the room was really oppressively warm for October—and was about to move toward the stairs when the lid blew off the whole explosive situation.

A man—young Merrick, perhaps—standing at Jerry's elbow, whispered something to the poor creature. Jerry started, looked wildly around, at the Commissioner who tried not to see him, at Lear and his party who were being lordly in their own corner, at Mr. Smith with his prophet's beard, at the crowd, stamping and talking in a solid mass by the stairs. Merrick said a word and then, suddenly, before anyone could make a move or raise a hand, the Negro was on his feet, was running toward the crowd that opened to receive him. In a flash he was at the door, pushed and pulled and shoved by a dozen hands as he went. He was through the door, and a stout old gentleman had slammed the door shut and set his shoulders against it before the marshals could stop him. It was all done in the twinkling of an eye. At one moment the slave was before them, terrified, his eyes rolling wildly, hesitating for the fraction of a second on his feet before he began to run. Then, before they could move to stop him, he was swallowed up by the crowd, he was a part of it, moving through it like an eel, slipping between the packed bodies, darting to the door, and was gone.

Old Mr. Merrick, the father of the young man who had urged Jerry, could not hope to keep his position against the closed door, of course. As soon as Allen and Lowell reached him, he was obliged to move, and the policemen were able to go after their prisoner. But the instant's delay had been useful. The crowd on the stairs, without actively obstructing an officer in the execution of his duty, was still able to impede him. By the time the two policemen had reached the top of the stairs, Jerry had hurtled to the bottom; when they had thrust their way to the street, with the crowd shouting and yelling, getting in their path, running every which way, as frantic as a flock of sheep with a dog after them, they could see the Negro running wildly along Water Street to the east.

They took after him, with a pack of friends and enemies in their wake, running, cursing at whoever got in their way, shouting as they ran across Salina Street, past the Syracuse House and the crowd of men standing on its veranda, following the fleeing figure along East Genesee Street and then north to Lock Street toward the Canal.

"Stop him!" they shouted, sprinting after the Negro. "Grab him! Don't let him get across the bridge!" There were a hundred places where a Negro might hide, if he ever reached the maze of shanties and tenements of the North Side.

Marshal Allen was not much of a runner, and after all a marshal had his dignity to consider. Policemen Lowell, Way and Green were active men, however, unhampered by fetters, and eager in the chase. At Mulberry Street they were gaining on the runner. At the very foot of Lock Street bridge they came up with him. In two minutes three powerful men, armed with the law and their own strong sinews, had overpowered the fugitive.

It was a struggle, they said afterwards. That coon fought like all possessed. You'd have thought he was plumb crazy, as Constable Peter Way said, telling of it in the back room of the Police Court after it was over. We couldn't hardly hold him. It took all three of us to get him down and make him stop fighting.

"They needn't blame us for roughing him up some," the Constable said to his wondering audience. "If he'd held still, we wouldn't have had to hurt him. But you couldn't kick any sense into him," Officer Way said plaintively. "He's more like an animal than a person, and that's the truth. If we'd ever tried to walk him back here to the police office, he'd have slipped away from us, sure. Like an eel he was, to hold on to. No, sir. The only thing we could do was to grab that truck-wagon and dump him into it, and then sit on him, all three of us, or we'd never have got him back here in this living world."

That was all there was to the recapture. Three vigorous policemen outran the Negro and returned him to custody, amid the furious yells of disappointed Abolitionists and assorted troublemakers now filling Clinton Square. And if the Nigger Lovers had had as much gumption as they brag about, they'd have tried to get their precious fugitive away from the police, right then and there.

"But they didn't dare to, you can bet your boots," Policeman Lowell told his friends, sitting around the unlighted stove in the back room, with the prisoner safely ironed beside them. "They gave us one look, and they saw we had Jerry there, all right enough. They saw that his shirt was torn off and he had a bloody nose and he was yelling fit to kill. But they didn't try to monkey with us," Lowell said, defying anyone to reproach him. "Those Nigger Lovers knew better. We drove right up here to the Raynor Block and hauled that nigger out of the wagon, right under their noses, and marched him into this building, and not one of 'em dared to peep. They aren't so brave. All they could do was to stand around and gawk."

"Abolitionists, hell," Policeman Lowell said, spitting expertly at the belly of the rusty stove. "They aren't so much. All gas and no guts," he said, and everybody laughed.

Men poured down the stairs from Sabine's office and out into the Square like logs piling down a river when the log jam has been broken above. Some of them streamed east after the running man and his pursuers. Some of them flowed out into the larger body of the crowd in the Square. A few lodged near the foot of the stairs, waiting for what would happen next. Marshal Allen and his colleagues, hot and flustered for the moment, paused on the pavement to explain to Mr. James Lear, who was very angry, how his property had been allowed to get away. The Negro would be brought back immediately, they assured Lear, mopping their red faces. There wasn't a chance in the world that he could get away, with half the policemen in Syracuse after him, and his hands shackled and all. Mr. Lear needn't worry.

Commissioner Sabine, wearing a look of strong disapproval, turned his back on his officers and requested Mr. Lear and the rest of his party, including the notable Patriots present, to meet with him at his residence in the Syracuse House as soon as the prisoner had been apprehended. It was necessary, he said sharply, to prevent a recurrence of this disgraceful performance, and he marched off without waiting for them.

Mahala Palfrey, standing at the edge of the crowd, waited for John Palfrey to turn his head and see her. There was no need to call the attention of his companions. She stood quiet in the shadow of her large friend and, when the conference seemed to be ended, spoke. "John," she said. "I want to talk to you."

John Palfrey turned as though he'd been shot. His face flushed darkly when he saw Mahala standing beside him. "What are you doing here?" he asked, and Mahala thought, I've never seen him angry before. Never angry at me. Now he is my enemy, and I am his.

She looked straight at him and said, "You did this. You've known about it all along. You didn't tell me because you knew I'd try to stop it. You thought it would be all over before I got back from the Fair. But I'll stop it now," she said, her voice like steel. "If you don't make them give that Negro up, I'll see that he's taken away from you. You won't keep him." She stared at her husband, her eyes level with his, her face white. "If you get him back this time, we'll take him away later. This is a wicked thing you're doing," she said deliberately. "You should be ashamed to your very soul."

Palfrey caught her wrist. "Be quiet, Mahala." She could feel his fingers hard against her flesh. "You've got no business to be here. Go back home instantly. It's disgraceful to come into this mob of men. I forbid you to stay here. You're out of your mind."

Mahala looked down at her wrist, turning her head to stare at it until it was freed. "You knew I'd come, as soon as I found out," she said, brushing his words aside.

For a moment John's face changed; there was naked pain in it, and tenderness, the thing he gave her in love, even remorse and regret. "Don't fight me." Unmindful of the crowd, not caring who might see him, he took her hands, gently this time, held them in both his own.

Slowly Mahala drew away from him. You're a stranger, she thought while his eyes pleaded with her. I can't look at your face. I know it—but I don't know you. I'll never know you and you'll never know me. But I knew you were my enemy, she thought, and let the knowledge pierce her as a soldier might deliberately fall upon his sword. I did this. I knew I was selling out to my enemy when I loved you. How could I do it? she asked herself, staring at him. Your face is my answer, she heard the words echoing in her mind. Your face, your body, your fierceness, the sound of your voice, the way you move. I sold my friends because you had blue eyes; because you touched me. I forgot Martin. I forgot Dal. I forgot who I was, myself. Now I remember who I am. I remember Martin. I remember Dal. I'll never forget them again. I belong to them, not to you. Forget me, John. Hate me. Hate me, and let me hate you. Hatred is easier than love.

Palfrey cried, "Mahala, wait—" but before he could finish speaking a sound rose from the mass of people around them; a roar of anger, of outrage, of defiance. Turning involuntarily to look, Palfrey and Mahala saw a truckman's cart clattering straight up the Square toward them, its old horse whipped to a lunging gallop, its driver standing, wielding his whip. In the bed of the wagon three large men in the uniform of the police were lying across the body of a dark-skinned man.

"Jerry!" the crowd shouted. "They've got him!" It would have surged forward, blindly and without direction, with only the instinct to prevent this capture, but the driver swerved his horse suddenly and avoided them. In another moment he had pulled to a halt on the west side of the Square before the grimy building that housed the police office. The three men in the back of the wagon leaped out, dragging the struggling figure of the Negro after them up the incline to the main doorway, and into the police court.

"They've got him," the crowd roared again. "They've got him!" It could do nothing now, except to move, as water slides when a dish is tilted, to the other side of the open Square. In front of the Raynor Building they massed, hundreds of them; angry men, whose yell was a threat and a promise.

Mahala turned back from this spectacle as though she had forgotten that John was there. "They've got him," she said, echoing the crowd.

On her husband's face was a look of irrepressible triumph. She glanced at him, saw that exultation in the instant before it vanished. Over her own face came an answering look; she wore, suddenly, the face of a stranger, an enemy. When she spoke, her voice was as hard as stone. "Good-by, John." She turned away from him.

Palfrey caught at her hand once more. "Where are you going?" The triumph had fled. There was anxiety in his voice. "I'll be back at the hotel in a little while, and we can talk it over then," he said coaxingly. "You go home and rest. You're exhausted by all this crowd."

Mahala said a single word, dropped like a rock at his feet. "No." She walked away from him across the Square toward the canal bridge.

The sitting room at Old Lib was empty, cool, its shades half drawn so that sunlight falling through the soft green of the curtain made the room look like a cave under water. Nothing was changed in the room. On the mantel was a pair of milk-glass vases filled with flowers, as they had always been. On the center table, an old workbox of her own stood under the unlighted lamp as though she might in a moment seat herself and begin to stitch again at her embroidery. Her chair stood beside the table, drawn up opposite her father's chair. Everything the same. Everything different.

I've lost this, Mahala thought, staring around her. I gave this away and took something else instead. This belonged to me. What I took didn't belong to me, and never could. I stole when I took it. I had no right to it, and I knew that when I stole. Underneath, I've known all the time. When I loved John I knew it; in his arms I knew it. Thief, she said to herself, staring around the quiet room; traitor, turncoat.

From outside the window, the crowd in the Square a quarter of a mile away made a deep undertone of sound that drifted on the still air like the roar of a waterfall, far distant. In the old tavern, someone walked along the uncarpeted floor with light, hurrying footsteps. Mahala paid no attention. I can never go back to John, she was thinking. That was the end of us. I never want to see John again. Anger was blowing through her mind like a high wind, tearing at the structure of her thoughts, sweeping old dreams, old feelings before it, as autumn leaves blow before an equinoctial gale. I knew we were enemies, from the first moment I saw him, the anger spoke in her mind. I said so, then. I should never have seen him after that. I should never have known him—except as an enemy. How could I have forgotten? How could I have fallen so terribly in love with him, when I knew he was my enemy? He knew what I believed, but it meant nothing to him. I was a woman, she thought hysterically. I had no right to think. John believed I would stop thinking when I was married and happy.

"Happy," she said aloud in the empty room, and heard the word echoing back to her. Loving when I should have been hating, seeing nothing, suspecting nothing, doing nothing. "Happy," she said once more, aloud, and began to laugh.

The latch moved under a hand, the door opened. Mahala turned slowly. The man in the open doorway was Moses North. He moved forward a step, looked at her sharply. "Mahala," he said, and in three steps he was beside her, his hands grasping her shoulders.

Under his strong touch, Mahala stood, shaken with sobbing, uncontrollable laughter. "Happy," she said, gasping. "Happy!"

Moses said violently, "Mahala—stop this. Stop it!"

She could not stop. That was immediately evident. Tortured, hysterical laughter pealed through the room. Her father, holding her with one hand, slapped her across the cheek. "Stop," he said.

The shock of his blow broke off the laughter between one breath and another. Resting weakly against North's arm, Mahala whispered, "You hit me." Her voice trembled as though the frantic sound would begin again. "You *should* hit me," she cried, clinging to him. "You *should* strike me—"

"Hush," her father said. "Hush." His great hand pressed her face gently against his shoulder, his arms encircled her like a fortress. Above her bowed head she could hear his voice, warm and comforting. "You've come home, girl," he said. "Back where you belong. It's going to be all right."

The wildness had gone now, and Mahala was weeping in her father's arms. "It's my fault," she said at last. "All this trouble. If I hadn't known John, you and Dal would never have been discovered. Your work is spoiled here. All your plans. And now this arrest—" a sob shook her—"John did that. I know he did. He had to show them that he was loyal, after they searched here that day." She looked up at her father's face. "He told me that they doubted him after that. But he said he was able to convince them. I should have known then," she said, anger rising in her once more. "I should have suspected that he would have to do something to make them believe in him. I've known he was working hard. And he stopped talking to me about it. But I never suspected. I was happy—"

Moses' arm tightened around her. "Steady, girl," he said, and waited until her trembling ceased. "You weren't to blame. A man has to do what he thinks right—and so does a woman. John thought he could have you and fight you, too. You thought for a while that it was right for you to marry John. I wondered about it, at the time, but I could see you'd have to find out for yourself. Well—you did find out. It didn't work. You and John were fire and water, and you couldn't mix. Now you've come back, and that's all right, too. It was a kind of experiment, and it did break things up some, but there's no reason why you can't begin to pick up the pieces."

Mahala drew a long breath. "That's what I came back to do, if you'll let me. But can you ever trust me again, after this?" Her face was filled with apprehension.

Old Moses laughed. "Talk sense, girl," he said, and bent over to kiss her forehead. "You're the best man I've ever found for the cause."

With tears still wet on her face, Mahala smiled for the first time. "I'll be a man," she said. "I'll go out with you. There must be something I can do. Tell me what you're planning."

Her father walked over and looked out the window. From beyond the Canal a steady roar was still coming from a thousand throats. Far away, in the Square, a black mass showed where the crowd was still gathered before the Raynor Building, waiting. Moses North frowned.

"I came back here to see about getting someone to drive a rig to pick Jerry up after we get him out," he said slowly. "Nothing was ready when he jumped out before, so they got him back. This next time we must get things fixed. I want every step planned ahead of time."

Suddenly Mahala was whole again, able to think and act. Her father saw with relief that she was wearing the expression he had seen on her face a hundred times in the heat of battle. "Have you got a carriage?" she asked.

Moses nodded. "Yes. Leavenworth's rig. It's a good fast horse, and the buggy's got side curtains. But I haven't figured out yet who'll drive it. It's got to be someone we can trust. I could do it myself, but I kind of hate to miss the shindy in the Square," he said, and grinned like a boy. "It ought to be pretty good."

Mahala had an answer. "I'll drive," she said. "I know exactly where to take him. The marshals will be sure to watch this place, and Dr. May's and Loguen's. We'd better hide him, at first, in one of the Negro's houses. There are a lot of them, and the marshals won't know where to start looking, if we get him away clean. After that, we can take our time about moving him to a safer place, when the hunt has died down a little."

Her father nodded, his eyes narrowed as he considered her plan. "I don't know but you're right," he said at last. "I'd thought of keeping him here in town for a spell, but I hadn't settled on the house. What Negro did you have in mind?"

"Sudie Watkins," Mahala answered immediately. "She's smart, and she's anxious to help. I've talked to her. She'd be safe, and no one would think of looking there. Jerry could stay in her place long enough to get the irons off and then we can disguise him and move him late at night."

Moses North made up his mind. "I think that's a fine plan. You'd better not be alone in the rig, though. Maybe you'd better not go to Sudie's house with them, at all. It would look more natural if we had another Negro driving. There's plenty that would do it. You could just stay with him to make sure he connected with us, after we've got Jerry. Then you could walk the rest of the way and meet him at Sudie's house."

Mahala was on her feet now, eager for action. "I'll go and get dressed. I'll be noticed less in man's clothes. Then we can find a driver and I'll stay with him and be ready when you want me."

Her father said, "Good, good," and strode to the door. Watching her face he thought with relief, She's over the worst of it. If she can work, she'll get through. I don't want her to see Dal or John until she's ready for it. Aloud he said, "We'd better get along. That crowd over yonder isn't going to wait all day."

He heard Mahala's light footsteps running up the stairs to her old room.

[283]

CHAPTER SIXTEEN

"Dr. May! Hi there, Dr. May!" The cry seemed to come from all sides, to rise spontaneously from every part of the crowd, as the old man made his way up the incline toward the entrance of the police office.

"Dr. May—what are they doing with him?"

"Dr. May—say the word, and we'll have him out here in two shakes of a lamb's tail."

"Dr. May . . . Dr. May . . ."

It was necessary to stop this embarrassing helpfulness at once. Dr. May halted, and tried to find the last speaker. "What will you do with him, when you have got him out?" he inquired of the crowd. "You've just seen what happens when you act without a plan. You got him out, and the police were able to put him right back again. Wait, I tell you—" He raised his voice to top the chorus of eager voices that replied to him. "Wait. You've got to hold on until we get our arrangements made. When we're ready, we'll give you the word, and then you can get him out. But if you act too soon, you'll lose everything."

The crowd murmured impatiently. It seemed foolish, they thought, to hang around and do nothing while Allen and all those out-of-town marshals fixed things up so's they'd never get him out.

Dr. May pleaded with them. "Be patient. I beg you to wait until we have made our plans. Stay here," he entreated them. "Stay here and block the entrance. If the officers should attempt to remove Jerry from this building, you must stop them and take him away, at all costs. But unless they do that, simply stay here and wait for the signal. I promise you that we're all working." He was smiling at them now. "We won't let them send this poor man back into slavery. But we must go at it leg over leg, as the little dog went to Dover."

This pleased them, and brought a laugh. Very well, they'd wait, they said, letting the old man pass through, watching him mount the platform outside the police office and enter one of the pair of double doors into the building. They'd wait, but whoever was making those plans had better get a move on. They'd better hurry up about it, or Hank Allen and those bullies he'd hired from Rochester and Auburn would spirit that nigger out and whisk him off to the penitentiary, and then it would take more than a few stout arms to get him free. It was all right to talk about plans, the hotheads among them said, picking up cobbles from the road, weighing them in their hands. Plans were all right, but the thing that had to happen was a few good busts with a rock. A few bricks in the window. A few smart kicks on the door. That would do more good than all of any minister's arrangements.

Next to the speaker, a man said in a soft southern voice, "Don't worry, son. You're going to get your chance to fight. All they're trying to figure out is where to take him, after they've got him out. Then you can tear the house down, if you want to."

The hothead, who was no more than a boy for all his size, shook a curly forelock out of his eyes, like a bull calf, and stared at the owner of the voice. "Damn me, but you sound like a Southerner, yourself. Are you Lear?" he bellowed in sudden excitement. "Look, fellows. I bet we got Mr. God-damned Lear right where we want him."

The man with the southern voice grinned at him. "Careful, son," he said with amusement. "You'll bust a blood vessel if you get too excited." He smiled at the ring of faces looking at him. "I'm from the South, all right," he said with meaning, "but it happens that I bring niggers *up*. I don't take 'em back. Jerry's a good man." He nodded his head toward the building. "I've known him before. I've traveled with him," he said, so that they understood. "And I don't care for the notion of making that journey all over again, just because a man like Jim Lear wants me to."

The crowd was listening to him now, holding its breath. He's one of those Underground Railroad folks. He is? I thought they was all from the North. How does it happen that a southern man joins the Railroad, to steal from his own folks?

"Hell," one man said, as though he knew all about it. "There's Underground Railroad lines all over the country, North *and* South. You can't tell by that."

A boy gazed with awe at this new hero. "How did you get Jerry up here?"

The Southerner shook his head. "Can't tell too much. The whole thing has to be a secret." The crowd nodded and agreed with him. "But I can tell you that it was quite a jaunt. The patrollers followed us onto a river boat coming up from Missouri, and I thought we were done for, because the captain was a strong proslavery man, and he'd have been glad to turn us over to the officers. But a woman on the boat helped us to get into the ship's skiff, that was tied to the stern of the boat, and when we got to the right place where I knew the way, she cut the rope and we floated in to shore, as neat as you please. After that it was just a matter of getting on the right line and coming east."

The crowd sighed with pleasure over this tale. That was something like it, they said, talking it over. If more folks had nerve enough to do a thing like that, the marshals wouldn't have a Chinaman's chance to put through this new law. We've got to show 'em right here in Syracuse, they said, doubling up their fists. They can't bamboozle us. They can't flummox us. We'll watch every move they make in that office. A dozen men were stationed at the back door to watch for a move in that direction. A flock of excited little boys volunteered to act as messengers between the two groups. Ira Cobb and the Reverend Mansfield walked boldly into the court itself, and somehow managed to stay there, to keep an eye on things.

The Abolitionists were making plans, but the army outside could make some plans too, they said to each other. When the time came, they'd get along faster if they figured out just exactly what to do, and laid it down so that everybody understood what was expected of them. Under the leadership of the southern man they planned their attack, stationed their forces. Now, they said, with satisfaction, if Fitch and Allen and Bemis want to try conclusions, let 'em come. We're ready for 'em.

In the office of the police court, the hearing was about to reconvene. The room was larger, there was more air, more space than in the Commissioner's office, but the crowd inside was still troublesome, and that in the street had reached alarming proportions. It was thought safer to seclude the prisoner in a small room back of the police court, where he could still be heard through the thin partition. He made such a commotion that after a while the Chief of Police let politics go hang, and appealed to Dr. May to quiet the frantic creature.

"You know how to talk to him," he said apologetically. "Mebbe you can sort of calm him down. We can't hear ourselves think, with all that bawling and yelling going on. And if those lawyers don't hump themselves," he said, shaking his head with disapproval, "the whole of Onondaga County'll congregate outside this block. I dunno *what* makes 'em so slow. If that crowd out there really gets its dander up, Mr. Lear'll think he's tapped hell with a two-inch auger, and no pitcher ready." He went grumbling back to his seat.

He was certainly right about the condition of the slave, Jerry. Whether it was the rough handling he had received during his recapture, or sheer terror that caused it, he was in a dreadful state, struggling against his bonds, throwing himself about as well as he could, shackled with handcuffs and leg irons, crying and screaming like a demented creature. Dr. May tried to soothe him, but still the cries rose, wild and hysterical.

"Let me go! Let me go! I ain' done nothin'. I ain' a slave no mo'. Let me up out of here . . ." Dr. May shook him firmly by the shoulder.

"Jerry! Listen to me. Try to be calm, so I can talk to you."

The Negro roared, "I ain' studyin' calm. I wants to git out of here." But something, perhaps, in the minister's tone did arrest the storm for a moment. The black eyes rolled, looked sensibly at the old man, seemed to realize who he was. "Is you Dr. May? Would *you* be calm, if you all had these irons on you? Let me up!" he cried again. "Take off these here spancels!" He drummed on the floor with his heels. "Take off these gammons. Let me fight! If I can't whip my way through this crowd, I'll go back and be a slave."

Patiently, Dr. May tried again and again. "You must listen to me, Jerry," he said for the twentieth time. "You must be quiet and hear what I'm telling you. I've come to help you." He leaned forward to whisper in the Negro's ear. "We're making plans to rescue you. You've got to be quiet and pay attention, so you'll be ready to jump up when we come for you."

There was a blessed silence in the little room. The Negro looked from the three officers standing near the door on the other side of the room back to Dr. May, beside him. "When y'all comin'?" he whispered.

"As soon as we can. But you've got to wait. Be ready." The old man rose from his knees beside the bound Negro. "I'm going now. We're going to arrange everything. But we'll be back, and if you're ready to come when we call for you, you'll be free."

Jerry said under his breath, "I is ready now, Dr. May, sir," and watched the slight figure of the old man disappear through the door into the courtroom.

Lear said savagely, "We're wasting time. The nigger's back in custody, and there's nothing to stop us from finishing up the hearing and letting me start for home." He looked around the group of men gathered in Sabine's apartment and said, "What's the point of talking about it here? There's nothing to say in private that can't be said before the Court. Let's go back to the police office and get this business over. I'm tired of all this lally-gagging."

Mr. Sabine was offended. "We have no desire to delay you longer than necessary. I was obliged to move the proceedings to a larger court, and in the confusion the prisoner was able to escape, temporarily. No time was lost in recovering him." He looked sharply at his guests. "No one can claim any negligence on our part. And we're waiting now," he said, growing rather warm about it, "because we hope the crowd in Clinton Square will get tired of waiting, and disperse. A crowd like that might be dangerous." He glared around the room. "They might take a notion to riot, and we'd have a hard time to stop 'em."

What Lear said to this was unprintable. Major Burnet stepped into the breach. "We understand that, Commissioner," he said diplomatically. "We don't want any violence in this affair. But it's possible that the longer we wait, the more exasperated the crowd will get. They've been pretty peaceable so far, but they're getting riled up. They know where Jerry is, and they might take a notion to rush the place and try to get him out." Through the open window, the roar of the hundreds in Clinton Square could be heard plainly.

John Palfrey said, "I've said before, Commissioner, that I don't think the police office is a safe place to hold him. If there's any chance of an attack by the mob, you ought to have the prisoner removed to the penitentiary. I don't like the way things are going." He looked hard at Mr. Sabine. "If anything should slip up now, it might be thought that you had antislavery sentiments, and were making it easy for the Abolitionists to deliver this fugitive."

Mr. Sabine reddened furiously. "No one has any right to say I'm not carrying out the obligations of my office," he said angrily. "I'm proceeding according to law. I'm giving the claimant every protection and every opportunity to prove his case. I've provided a guard for the prisoner. I can't legally hold a hearing without having the accused man present, and if I put him up in the penitentiary we couldn't hold the hearing. If the claimant wishes to postpone the hearing indefinitely, I'm willing to have the prisoner transferred to the jail. Not otherwise."

"I'm not going to wait," Lear said impatiently. "I'm not afraid of that gang out there. If they'd been going to riot, they'd have done it when he got away just now. They yelled some, but they didn't even try to prevent the policemen from bringing the nigger back. We're acting like a bunch of old women, scared out of our wits and afraid to do anything because a handful of hayseeds are standing around out there looking at us. If anyone was to pull a gun, that whole crowd would run like the devil was after them, before you could fire a shot." He turned his back on Mr. Sabine and spat deliberately into the elegant cuspidor provided by the Syracuse House. "Riot, hell," he said with profound contempt.

Palfrey was beginning to sizzle. "That simply shows that you don't know the temper of this town," he said to Lear, giving him back contempt for contempt. "Those men out there aren't just hayseeds. They're red-hot Abolitionists, and they've proved what they're capable of doing, not once but several times. We know them. They're smart as well as violent. And we're leaving it wide open for them to try something. If we don't take every possible precaution, we're fools."

Before Lear could answer, the Major interposed again. "Palfrey's right, of course," he said smoothly. "This town has a reputation for being radical. More than any other town around here. We've had proof of it. But maybe Mr. Lear's made a good suggestion. We've never had any demonstration with firearms. It might not be a bad idea to call out the military, just as a threat. If they saw soldiers with rifles and bayonets, they might think twice before they tried anything violent."

There was a general stir at this suggestion. The militia. That's never been done before; we might get into trouble over it. "Those young squirts," somebody said, laughing. "A bunch of boys dressed up for a parade. They wouldn't dare to fire a shot.

Part of 'em only just organized this summer. They don't know enough to point a gun."

Lear grinned. "I don't care what you do," he said carelessly. "Call out your tin soldiers, if you want to. All I say is, get a-going. I can't sit around on my tail for another month. I've waited long enough for you to get your fixings done. Now I aim to get this nigger and light out for home."

Sabine said with all the dignity he could summon, "I've called the hearing for five-thirty. If you want to do anything about the militia, you'll have to take care of it yourselves." He looked with meaning at Major Burnet. "That's outside my province, and I won't have anything to do with it. I don't hardly think it's legal," he went on in his fussy, disapproving way. "I'm under the impression that the militia can only be called out in the case of an actual riot. If you do call them, it's on your own responsibility."

The Major soothed him. "We understand that, sir. If we take any steps, we'll do it on our own hook. You needn't worry. We only want to make sure that nothing unfortunate occurs. We represent law and order in this town," he said impressively. "Our intention is not to injure any citizen of Syracuse, but only to prevent radicals and firebrands from obstructing justice." He looked very hard at Mr. Commissioner Sabine.

The Commissioner avoided his eye. "In that case, I needn't detain you any longer," he said, standing up briskly. "The hearing will reconvene in the police office at five-thirty o'clock. Good day to you, gentlemen."

The gentlemen filed out of Mr. Sabine's room and downstairs for a little refreshment at the bar of the Syracuse House. They had no more than gone when Mrs. Sabine opened the door to the bedroom and darted out to talk to her husband.

"I heard what they said," she cried, in a perfect twitter of excitement. "That Lear's a wicked man, and Moses Burnet and John Palfrey are about as bad. Calling out the soldiers!" she said, rushing over to the window to look at the crowd. "Shooting off their guns and killing innocent people, as like as not. You've got to stop them, Mr. Sabine. You've got to tell them they can't call the militia."

Her husband sighed wearily. "I can't prevent 'em," he said. "Come away from that window, Margaret. Someone will see you, and a lot of people know you favor the Abolitionists. It don't look well."

Mrs. Sabine said with spirit, "Well, they know *you* do, too. I guess I've got a right to look out of my own window if I want to."

"That's just the trouble," Sabine said, exasperated. "Folks know about both of us. Burnet said as much, just now. It puts me in a very awkward position, and I oughtn't to have let you persuade me not to resign. If you hadn't raised such a hullabaloo, I'd have resigned as soon as I knew about this arrest. I knew they'd make it hot for me. But no," he said, blaming her for everything, "nothing would do for you but that I should stay in. You thought I could help the Abolitionists if I was Commissioner. Well, now see what you've done," he said, accusing her. "See what a pickle I'm in. I can't lift a finger to help the slave, and Palfrey and Burnet suspect every move I make. It's a shame," he said, glaring at his wife. "It comes of letting women get mixed up in things they don't understand."

Mrs. Sabine was reduced to tears.

The militia was in a terrible chowder. An order, coming from Marshal Allen through William Gardiner, sheriff of the county, commanded all of the three units—the National Guard under Captain Prendergast, the Citizens' Corps under Lieutenant Chandler and the Washington Artillery under Captain Saul—to assemble at their respective armories, ready for duty. A lot of them were as green as grass, Prendergast said regretfully, watching them strutting around in their brand-new uniforms. Not three months' training, and God alone knew how they'd behave. He was glad to do whatever he could, of course. It was time somebody put the fear of God into those nigger-loving bastards. He was glad somebody had guts enough to do it. The other units had been longer organized and, presumably, were better equipped to face the foe. Lieutenant Chandler had the Citizens' Corps drawn up, looking as neat as you please in their uniforms, and Captain Saul's boys trundled their lone cannon out into City Hall Park and prepared to defy the universe.

But, at this point, some hitch occurred. A messenger ran posthaste to Prendergast with a message from his superior officer, Colonel Origen Vandenburg, ordering him not to move his troops out of the armory until the Colonel had consulted personally with the sheriff. Captain Prendergast was obliged to obey. Anyone could see that he hated to do it, the men said, standing around, leaning on their rifles, polishing up their bright-work. Prendergast hates the Nigger Lovers, and he knows the Colonel favors 'em. It was worth a dollar any day, the men said, grinning at their commander, to see a dust-up between those two.

When Mr. Wheaton appeared on the scene, steaming in like an engine on the upgrade, the fun really began. Wheaton said the sheriff had no authority to call out the militia. Captain Prendergast said he didn't care whether he had or not, he was going to do as the Colonel said. It was a slam-bang argument, and the guardsmen enjoyed it to the full. They really hated to see it finish up, as it did presently when another messenger brought the Captain another message from Vandenburg formally ordering him to disband his men at once. After that, there was nothing Prendergast could do except to call the whole thing off and tell his men to go home. There was a good deal of laughing about it, which didn't make Prendergast any happier, and the men disbanded, right enough; but it seemed a shame to go home without having any fun at all, so most of them went off in high spirits to join the crowd in the Square.

Lieutenant Chandler also was ordered to disband the Citizens' Corps, and did so. What happened to the third order no one knew. If Captain Saul got it, he did not obey it. In any case, the Washington Artillery were the only ones to have any fun, and to hear them tell it, they had put down insurrection singlehanded, although their only part in the battle was to fire their cannon once, after everything was over. Fortunately, they only fired a blank so that no one was injured, and the only effect this had was to distract the crowd's attention, which was a real help to the rioters.

Mr. Wheaton, hot with hurrying around from sheriff to captain to colonel, was justifiably pleased with the results of this action, and Colonel Vandenburg, who was an open sympathizer with the Abolitionists, said that the whole affair was a disgrace to the city. It was a boon to the newspapers, the next day, when they were able to publish a half dozen conflicting accounts of military actions which never took place, and to censure, severely, all of the officers involved. But it would never have done, as Mr. Wheaton said to his brother, to have shooting in the city of Syracuse. Further, as he did not say, an unarmed crowd will freely charge another unarmed crowd, but it will certainly hesitate, if not openly refuse, to attack against loaded weapons. The militia might not be much, but it did have guns. Major Burnet was probably responsible for calling them out, Mr. Wheaton thought. Major Burnet was smart. But this time he had not been smart enough. Mr. Wheaton was hot and tired by the time he got to Dr. Hoyt's office on South Warren Street, but he was full of satisfaction.

When Dr. May arrived, the meeting in Hoyt's office really got down to business.

"Plans," the old man said in his silvery voice, throwing back his head, straightening his bent shoulders. "We've got to plan our campaign and then go through with it, right on the dot. We mustn't fail again, the way we did this noon. There's no use delivering the man, Jerry, if we haven't arranged every detail of what we're going to do with him."

Lawyer Hillis didn't like to abandon the legal battle for one of mere force. "We oughtn't to be hasty. The District Attorney's done a lot of talking, but he hasn't proved that the man's legally a slave. I think we can beat them in this trial. We don't need to use force."

This was no way to persuade Gerrit Smith. That old war horse had sniffed the battle afar off. "Maybe we *could* win in the trial. But we don't want to win that way. That won't be anything but a moral effect. A moral effect," he said, leaning forward and shaking his white mane at the lawyer. "That wouldn't compare with a rescue. We must be bold," he said, his eyes kindling. "Bold and forcible. A forcible rescue will demonstrate the strength of public opinion against the Fugitive Slave Law." He looked around the circle, seeing eager faces in the candlelight, gathering up their spirits with his. "This act will live forever. Free men will remember it. It will honor the city of Syracuse, and be an example all over the country."

"I agree, I agree." It was strange to see Dr. May joining old Gerrit in a call for violence. The others, Moses North, Ord, Charles Wheaton, Loguen, were men of action, experienced, prepared, willing to fight. But Dr. May, so gentle, so saintly. He could not resist saying, even now, "I hope that we can accomplish this delivery without physical violence. I do not believe in fighting. I trust that if any are to be hurt, it may be some of us. But I agree with Mr. Smith. The effect of a forcible delivery will be very valuable. For this reason, I am opposed to purely legal means."

Somebody in the shadowy room said, "You can't always make an omelet without breaking eggs, reverend," and there was a ripple of laughter.

Mr. Smith agreed with him. "We trust that no one will be injured. We will endeavor to injure no one," he said to Dr. May, looking as innocent as a babe. "Every one of us will pledge ourselves to refrain from injuring our fellow men. But just the same," he said, forgetting to be pacific, forgetting to be calm, "we must strike with force. We must show the base minions of the law that the forces of freedom are invincible." He was beginning to orate, waving his arms. "We must show the slaveowners of the South and the doughfaces of the North that this infamous law is trampled underfoot by lovers of Liberty."

There was a little pause after this stirring speech. No one knew exactly how to go on from there until a husky voice said, from the darkness of the room, "All right, but what do you want us to do?"

"That's Cale Davis," Moses North whispered, looking easily over the heads of the crowd. "He'll be a good man for us. I wonder what made him plump for our side. I've always heard him raving around about what he'd do to the Abolitionists, if he could lay hands on 'em."

Ord said, "He's a friend of mine. We were having a drink together in your bar when the news came about taking Jerry. Cale agreed with me that it didn't seem fair to grab a defenseless man. We thought we'd better do something about it. It'll go all right. I've got other friends. I'll see that we have reinforcements when we need 'em."

He did not mention these friends as the plan for the attack went forward. Everything was to be orderly, disciplined, military. Mr. Smith, like a general, outlined the scheme, appointed his officers. Give the lawyers half an hour or so, to be sure that everyone was there in the courtroom. Then rush the building, force the door, remove the prisoner and take him away in a carriage, beyond pursuit. The men in the room nodded, agreed, wagged their heads. Was the crowd in the Square to be encouraged to assist? someone asked. Mr. Smith thought not. It would be impossible to explain the plan to them, or to make sure that they refrained so far as possible from out-and-out violence. Dr. May agreed. The crowd would be unreliable, rough, dangerous perhaps. It would be better if the actual delivery was managed by the group of men in this room. The crowd was simply to block the pursuit.

Cale Davis said, "We ain't enough to do it. This ain't goin' to be any tea party, getting into the police office and taking a prisoner away from 'em. We got to have more men."

Dr. May said gently, "We shall have the Right on our side. We shall be doubly armed."

Cale Davis was heard to mutter in the back row. "Old men," he was saying. "Too old to fight, and even if they was younger, they ain't had any experience. They're afraid they'll hurt someone. That ain't what *I'm* afraid of. *I'm* afraid they won't. Mr. Smith and Dr. May couldn't no more break into that police office than I could get into the U.S. Mint. It ain't practical."

Dal grinned at him. "Don't worry, son," he said to the huge man. "You and I can take care of that part of it. They can make the plans and we'll help carry 'em out."

Cale spit on his hands. "Let's get going," he agreed with enthusiasm. "If we wait too long, somebody else may take a notion and do the job before we get there. We ain't got all night."

The deliberations of such an august gathering could not be hurried, however. Every man of them had to stand before the appointed judges and identify himself, prove his *bona fides*, before he was allowed to take part in the affair.

"We can have no traitors," Gerrit Smith said eloquently. "Every man in this party must remember that he has pledged his life and his sacred honor to the cause of freedom. There can be no lukewarm spirits, no one halfhearted, no doubters. We are taking a great risk." He dropped his flowery manner so suddenly that every man in the room turned to look at his face. It was grave and his voice was quiet. "Some of us may be recognized and arrested. God knows what may come of this act. I can promise you," he said with great simplicity, "that if any are taken for their part in this rescue, I will defend them with all the power and money at my command. I want you to know that before you go." He stood up and shook the hand of the man standing before him.

"This list of names may be dangerous," he said. "We will destroy it now." He held the sheet of foolscap in the flame of the candle until its edge caught, the flame licked up the page. Then he threw it on the floor and trampled it to dust. "No one outside this group will ever know who has made this pledge," he said, looking at them with his fierce old eyes. "Every man of you will know. And I will know. Now go." His voice filled the darkened room. "Go forth, and God go with you. Release this man!" His voice rang over them. "I desire his release! I desire his release!"

As they trooped down the stairs into the street, they could still hear those words. "I desire his release!"

CHAPTER SEVENTEEN

Someone yelled, "They're coming back!"

The crowd turned, as well as it could, and craned to see the stately figure of Mr. Sabine, with books under his arm, stalking through the aisle that opened to admit him.

"There's Hank Allen and his bullies . . ."

"The sheriff . . ."

"Major Burnet . . . Palfrey . . . Noxon . . ."

"The rest's all lawyers," someone said with such disgust that the crowd laughed, jostling the dignified persons as they pushed their way through the multitude. Justice House, and after him, glaring at the crowd, Mr. Lawrence, the District Attorney, with Jones and Anderson who were only lawyers, the men in the crowd said. Marshal Allen got a good yell that sounded as though it might mean business. Coming immediately after him, Lear, the southern man, the claimant, drew hoots and catcalls, to which he paid no attention. He was not jostled, however, since he carried a pistol in plain sight at his belt, and everyone knew that a Southerner would shoot you as easy as breathing. The lawyers for the defense did not receive a much warmer welcome than those for the prosecution. The crowd was not fond of lawyers, on principle; they'd all of 'em skin you if they could, was the general opinion. Mr. Hillis said, "You men had better clear away from here. You're only making it worse for the Negro."

A large man with a square black beard said, "Run along, bub, and speak your piece. You don't cut any ice with us."

Mr. Hillis made no further efforts to influence the crowd.

The bare outer room of the police office was filling with shadows. From its windows which, on one side, looked down two full stories to the street, the city could be seen, dusky, sprawling, here and there an occasional lighted house, here and there a windowpane blazing with the last coppery reflections of the setting sun. Above treetops a few streets away, the eastern sky was a cool green. Wood smoke from leaf fires drifted in the open window, and mingled with the damp, indescribable smell of the Canal itself, as it flowed sluggishly past the north walls of the Raynor Building. Everywhere the city was calm, quiet, settling for the night—except in the Square before the police office. There the sound was rising, mounting imperceptibly, growing in pitch and in volume as the crowd talked to itself, talked to the officials who passed through it, talked to the gathering of persons inside the police office while they made ready to try the fugitive Jerry Henry, alleged fugitive slave.

Commissioner Sabine looked around the courtroom sharply and said to Officer Green, "Light those lamps. We can't carry on this trial in the dark."

Officer Green hesitated. "The marshals told me to leave them be. They said they didn't want the folks outside to see in here."

Mr. Sabine was annoyed. "I don't care what the marshals said. I'm not going to hold a hearing in the dark. Light those lamps."

Naked gaslights flared over the Judge's bench where Commissioner Sabine now sat; over the group of lawyers gathered around Mr. Lear and the District Attorney, conferring busily; over Mr. Hillis and his assistants, Morgan and Sheldon. It shone over the party of visiting marshals, Fitch from Rochester, Swift from Auburn, Bemis from Canandaigua, supporting Marshal Allen from Syracuse and Police Constables Way, Green and Lowell, all grouped near the door that led to the little back room where the prisoner lay. In the uneasy moments before the hearing recommenced, papers were rustled on the heaped tables, chairs scraped over the rough floor, men coughed, murmured to each other, turned to stare at the Commissioner, at the door behind which

Jerry had begun to moan and cry, at the open windows through which the crowd's voice, unabating, menacing, came to their ears.

Lear's soft accents rose, speaking easily, giving evidence once more of the ownership of the escaped slave. Again, as it had happened before, he was interrupted, cut in upon, heckled, first by one and then another: by Mr. Hillis, nagging away about the status of slavery in Missouri; by his underlings, quoting from lawbooks, citing instances, former decisions; by Mr. Sabine, allowing objections, overruling objections, rebuking the defense, complaining about the way the business was proceeding.

"This will take us all night, gentlemen, if you won't allow the claimant to finish his statement."

But it was not Mr. Hillis's interruptions that broke up the hearing. A stone, half a brick, a stick of wood, flew in at the open windows, clattering to the floor, striking against the Commissioner's desk, sailing straight through the upper sash and bringing in with them a shower of broken glass. The enemy had opened fire. Another stone flew in, missing Mr. Lear but hitting Mr. Lawrence a painful blow. By this time, the room was in an uproar.

"Stop those men from throwing stones," someone said foolishly.

"Shut the windows!"

"What good will that do? They'll only smash them all. I say, open them as wide as you can. It'll save any more broken glass."

"Turn out the lights. If they can't see—"

Mr. Sabine shouted. "Gentlemen, gentlemen. Please preserve order. The more you move around and make a fuss, the more they'll throw at you. If we move back farther in the room these missiles can't hurt us—"

As he spoke, busily dragging his chair down from the bench into safety, an immense stone shot past his ear, missing it by a miracle, as he told his wife afterwards.

"It might have killed you," Mrs. Sabine said, trembling to think of it.

"It *would* have killed me," Mr. Sabine agreed. "It was the most dangerous moment of my life."

Stone and bricks and every other sort of object were coming in a perfect storm now, and there was certainly no use in trying to hold a court under such conditions. Mr. Sabine said nothing more about moving back in the room. He grabbed up his armful of books and papers and hurried out the door, letting the crowd see clearly who he was. An egg missed him too narrowly for comfort, but nothing else happened, and he was permitted to dart across the street to the Syracuse House.

The rest of them gathered for a hasty consultation. Defense and prosecution alike were in a pickle. It was getting dark, and the men outside might not care what kind of lawyer they hit, as long as they hit someone. Lear and Marshal Allen would be taking their lives in their hands if they ventured out of the building. Everyone agreed to that. There was only one thing to do. Let someone talk to the crowd, hold their attention if possible, while the others got away or hid somewhere.

That seemed to be the best solution. Mr. Hillis, supported by the Reverend Samuel Ringgold Ward—as black as the ace of spades—walked out on the platform outside the front door of the building. Beyond this raised landing, the long slope of the canal bridge raised the front ranks of the crowd almost level with the speaker. Near the bridge itself, a street lamp shone down upon a mass of people jammed between the iron railings of the bridge, shone past them to the black and oily waters of the Canal itself. Lamps from the street corner by the Raynor Building shone over the heads of a thousand, two thousand, men and women, filling the whole depth of the Square, from sidewalk to canal. On the platform, Mr. Hillis was talking to this crowd, begging it to go away, to be quiet, to be peaceable.

"Jerry will be freed!" he bawled at them. "We'll get him off legally, if you'll leave us alone. You'll make trouble if you keep this up. We don't need a crowd to help us. We'll win our suit," he shouted despairingly, his voice cracking from the effort. "We'll get Jerry off, if you'll stop yelling and throwing stones. They'll come out here and arrest *you*—"

It was no use. His voice, hoarse and exhausted, faded into the deeper voice of the multitude. "No!" the crowd answered him. "Go on home," they said to him contemptuously. "You ain't getting him off. You've been at it all day, and he's still in jail, ain't he? Go roll your hoop," someone yelled in derision, and Mr. Hillis gave up. He got down the steps to the street as best he could, and made his way through the press with his head down, not a word to say to anyone. A troop of little boys followed him as far as Salina Street, yelling and skipping.

The Negro preacher, Mr. Ward, went down better with the mob. "This man's a nigger himself," they said. "He's been a slave. He knows how it feels to be chased." He was wise enough, also, not to advise his hearers. Instead, he began to tell them about slavery, and they stood still to listen.

"I've been sold in a coffle." His voice, as rich and mellow as a bassoon, flowed out to them. "I've been sold on the auction block, like an animal. I've been beaten by my master until I fainted, and the blood ran down my back in a stream. I've worked in the fields like a mule, from sunup to sundown, and I've gone home to my cabin to bed with no more than a lump of cornbread to stay my hunger. That's the way they treat slaves." He spread his long arms, a black figure crucified under the gaslight. "That's what Jerry ran away from. That's why he's here. That's why he's crying to you not to send him back. There may be a law," the richness of the oboe-voice said to them, "this may be a law—but it's not God's law. God won't let such a law be obeyed," he cried, and the multitude roared like a lion.

Suddenly, the din rose higher. "That's Allen," a voice shouted, and the crowd pivoted, struggling, pushing, pressing upon itself to see, to reach the place where the man pointed. "He sneaked out," the voice yelled hysterically. "He sneaked out behind Ward's back and ran down the steps. He's got a coat pulled around his ears. Stop him!" The voice was a shrill scream.

It was too dark to tell whether they had caught the man, but it was not too dark to see that no others slipped out behind the speaker. A volunteer from the crowd ran up the steps and planted himself before the closed doors.

"Keep 'em in there," rose in a single voice from the crowd. "Keep Lear for us. We'll come and get him."

Inside the building, James Lear said, "It's no use trying that. They've got the back door held, too. I'll have to hide in the building. Who lives upstairs?"

One of the policemen said, "It's a dentist or a doctor or something. He might keep you, if you pay him. I hear he'll do most anything for money," and he giggled while Lear ran up the stairs.

The lights were going again, the broken window shutters were closed as well as might be, and the handful of policemen and marshals huddled together near the doorway to the back room. Behind them, the voice of the prisoner, Jerry, moaned without ceasing.

Fitch, the senior officer now that Allen had gone, saw to his defenses and came back to sit before the jailroom door. "It's the best we can do," he reported. "We can give 'em a fight for it, if they want to come in."

Policeman Lowell said timidly, "Mr. Allen told us we was to take the prisoner to the penitentiary."

Fitch let out a howl of rage. "He did, did he? And how the blazing hell are we supposed to get him past that crowd, I want to know. What does Allen think he's doing, running away and telling *us* to put the prisoner in jail? *We're* to put him in the penitentiary, while Mr. God-damned Allen sneaks out on us in *my* overcoat—"

Constable Lowell shrank back into the shadows. "Maybe he didn't mean it that way," was all he could think of to say.

Marshal Fitch enlarged upon his theme.

"Davis—Cale Davis!" Ord's voice pierced the clamor. Davis was cutting a furrow toward him through the crowd. "The whole bunch is here—Loguen and Bates and Merrick and the others. It's time to start."

Davis said briefly, "I got the men. They're ready when you say the word."

Coming from the south, edging past the main mass of the crowd, a band of men was swinging into the Square from beyond the lower canal bridge. Beside the leader, Ord stopped.

"Are you armed? Have you got anything to strike with? I told you to bring clubs."

The leader said, "Some of 'em have got axes. We didn't wait long enough for everybody to get fixed."

Ord laughed. "Mr. Wheaton will be glad to provide you." He pointed to a heap of building material. A new building was going up, to take the place of the one recently burned. On the heap, odd lengths of wood and a pile of short iron rods were ready to their hands. The men, marching like a disorderly army, shouted and ran to the pile. In a minute, every man had a club, a cudgel, an iron pipe in his hand.

"Come on!" The yell might have come from a pack of Indians on the warpath.

Once more, Ord stopped them. "Wait a minute. We've got to get the doors down, and Cobb said there was a partition inside." His eye ran over the heap of lumber. "We need a battering ram."

"I got one." A Negro towered beside him, holding a long four-by-four timber on his shoulder as though it was a straw. "This'll do us, Mr. Ord."

Ord said, "That'll do us," and the party turned like one man and made tracks across the Square.

Under flickering yellow street lights, the crowd had broken its formation. It was no longer a solid and threatening mass before the building at the end of the Square. Now it was a thousand men, running at the building from every direction. Men battered at the windows, at the doors. Men climbed over the platform, swarmed in through the broken sashes of the windows. On the platform before the front door, a little army of men with faces black as soot marched up the steps carrying a stick of timber fifteen feet long.

A voice called furiously, "Jo! Jo! Get out of the way with that ax. You can't get the door with that. This'll take it."

The timber drew back, guided by a dozen hands, plunged forward against the heavy panels of the door. Under the street lights, black faces showed streaks where sweat ran down, leaving tracks of white; above black hands, white wrists strained with the weight of the ram. Someone screamed, "They're white men! They ain't niggers! I saw yellow hair!" Inside the police office, light went out.

The ram smashed again, again, cracking the panel this time. An iron bolt screeched as it tore loose from sound wood. The panel split in a dozen places.

"It's giving! It's busted! Hit again! Once more, now—" The ram went all the way through as the doors buckled, and attackers streamed through the narrow space, fighting each other for a place in the ranks.

Inside the police court, pale light showed in the squares of the broken windows, but no policemen appeared in the gloom, and a voice that sounded like Cobb's yelled from behind a partition, "We're in here, boys. Bust down the wall. It ain't thick."

Ord commanded, "The ram again. Right against the wall."

The wall was only a flimsy thing of matchboarding. There was going to be no trouble here. With the first blow, Jerry's scream told them they were at the right place. Marshal Fitch's voice drowned him out.

"You try to come in here and someone's going to get shot. I've got a gun."

The ram drove home as nearly as possible where his voice had been. "A gun, have you?" The wooden beam pounded again. "We'll gun you, you dirty bastard—"

There was a hole there now, big enough to stick a head through. No head appeared, but in the gloom a short steel barrel poked through the blackness of the opening, and light from the window gleamed on metal. There was a little flash of fire and the room boomed and echoed with the shot.

Ord's voice cried, "Let him have it, boys," as coolly as though nothing had happened. The ram went home once more.

The partition had been intended for no such defense as this. It went over suddenly, as a screen topples, cracking and tearing from its moorings, falling upon the men in the room beyond, so that a chorus of shouts and curses arose.

"We'll come out—we'll come out!"

"Don't hit any more—"

"Get off me, God damn you—"

Feet trampled, more wood broke, there was a scrambling and pushing as the prisoner's guards crawled out of the wreck. "We'll give up. You can have him. He's right in there, if you can find him under all this muss you've made."

Ord's voice said, "Where's that gun? Hand it over before we let you out." His tone was vicious.

A voice said pitifully, "Fitch dropped it right on my feet when the wall went over. He'll have to find it for you—"

Before it could finish, footsteps ran past them toward the open window on the north. A man's figure made a frantic silhouette against the evening light.

"It's Fitch—Fitch! He's getting away—"

Ord moved, but not fast enough. The figure slid over the sill and dropped out of sight.

Someone said, "Goddy! He's dropped clear to the heel-path. He'll be killed, sure."

If Fitch was gone, there was nothing to be done about it. Ord, still in command, said sharply, "Get the prisoner out. Hurry up. He may be hurt under that wreckage. Be careful."

The poor creature was beyond speech when eager hands found him, picked him up, dragged and carried him into the outer room. Heavily shackled, he could hardly stand; could not walk three steps without falling. Cale Davis said, "We'll have to carry him," and picked the man up in his arms. "I've got him. We'll have to get him out of this muss. He acts like he was going to die."

Outside, the crowd had turned into a battle royal. Men were fighting everywhere; generally, in groups, or separately, as they found opponents. If it was impossible for the prisoner to walk in the shattered room inside, it was twenty times as difficult for him to walk through that furiously struggling mob outside. At the door, the huge figure of Moses North stepped forward holding out his arms.

"I'll take him," he said, lifting the burden from Davis and moving out through the mass of rioters. Over his shoulder to Ord he said, "I'm sorry I missed the fun, Dal. I was kind of delayed."

Ord's voice sounded queer. He asked, "What happened to you? I was counting on you to help inside."

Moses asked, "Are you hurt? Your voice don't sound right."

"It's nothing," Ord said impatiently. "What were you doing?"

Moses said regretfully, "Well, that's it. I sent someone to get the carriage, and one of the constables went after me. It didn't amount to anything," he said, striding along with his burden as though he had been carrying a child. "I didn't have too much trouble with that policeman. The only difficulty might be that he knew who I was. I hadn't got round to blacking my face, and this fellow knew me. He won't cause us any trouble now, but he may raise considerable of a dust later, if he remembers. He swore he was going to have me indicted for attacking an officer." He had to laugh as he remembered it.

Dal asked quickly, "Did you get the rig? Will it be ready to pick us up?"

Moses said, "Sure, sure. You can count on it, for sure. A colored boy named Devil Thompson'll drive. He knows all the Negroes in town, and he had some place he wanted to take Jerry when we get him." He turned to look again at Ord. "Sure you ain't hurt, Dal? You don't walk like you felt good."

Ord waited until his breath came back, then said, "I'll last long enough. Don't worry. One of the marshals winged me, but it's not serious."

At the corner of the Square a tangle of men were fighting like tigers. One went down heavily and lay in the gutter without another motion. As Moses and Dal drew near, a second man swung wildly—you could see the haymaker starting from his shoelaces and see it miss—then lost his balance altogether, so that he rolled forward ludicrously in the dust of the street. The remaining man stood waiting for him to get up and, as the victor moved under the street light, North saw John Palfrey's face like a mask of fury. Palfrey's coat was gone, his shirt was ripped away from one shoulder and hung in ribbons below his arm. Blood was trickling from one corner of his mouth. As he turned under the light he saw his father-in-law and Dallas Ord coming toward him, carrying the shackled Negro.

Moses North stopped and stood holding the colored man lightly in his arms, gazing over the body of the slave at John Palfrey. He said, "Well, John," and waited for Palfrey to speak.

Palfrey cried, "Damn you! You can't do this—" and would have sprung forward to seize the Negro but the crowd was too quick for him. A dozen hands closed on his arms, pinioned him as he stood.

"It's Palfrey—Burnet's man—"

"Grab the nigger chaser—"

Palfrey ceased to struggle. "All right. You've got him. But we'll get you. By God," he said, looking straight at North and Dallas Ord. "You'll regret this."

Ord said wearily, "Come on, Moses. We can't wait to talk," and the two men moved on across the Square, while the crowd yelled and cheered behind them.

The crowd—the part of it that could bear to stop fighting—was beginning to stream after the hero of the occasion, running after Moses North and the man he carried, pouring after him out of Clinton Square into Salina Street, past the Syracuse House, swarming around the rescuers, cheering like crazy people, shouting encouragement to them, commending them, getting in their way, forestalling them wherever they went, making any final escape impossible. No curses or entreaties would separate them from the rescued man and his saviors. On they came, gathering forces as they went along. At the depot they made such a crowd that North could not get through with his load. At Dr. Clary's office in Warren Street they hovered and hung. There was no way to get rid of them or discourage them.

"It's no use," North said, stopping in his tracks. "We might as well put him in the carriage here as anywhere. These idiots'll follow us around all night." He lifted his head and shouted, and a buggy drawn by a tall bay horse slued up to the curb and stopped. A bony Negro was driving, and a slim boy jumped down and helped the shackled man in beside him.

"Drive where I told you," the boy said to the driver. "Do exactly what I said. We'll meet you later."

A cannon boomed behind them in the direction of Hanover Square, and this noise, so strange and violent in the night, shook the crowd loose from the carriage, like a charge of dynamite dislodging an ice jam.

"What's that?"

"They're shooting—"

"They've called the militia out!"

Men began to run up the street toward the sound. The driver in the buggy lashed his horse and had it running before anyone could stop him. Voices all around were shouting, "Fire! Fire!"

On the sidewalk Mahala, transformed once more into the slim boy Dallas Ord had seen first by lantern-light in a Kentucky jail, cried, "I'm sorry I was late, father. I couldn't get away from the crowd." Then her voice died in a gasp. "Dal," she whispered, and the breath whistled between her teeth. "I didn't know you were here." Insensibly she moved toward him, but the look on her face was as though she had seen a ghost.

Ord did not answer her. "If I could rest for a moment—" he said to Moses North, never meeting Mahala's eyes. "If I could find a doctor—" His left hand was gripping his own right shoulder. He turned his back on Mahala, his body swaying.

North cried, "God Almighty!" and caught him as he slid to the pavement. "He's been shot."

Instantly Mahala was beside the fallen man, her arms reaching to hold him. "He's bleeding—he's dying. Father, we've got to get him home."

Ord's eyelids fluttered. Once more he looked past Mahala to Moses North. He said with great difficulty. "No. Help me up to Clary's office. You stay with me. Send Mahala after Jerry. He mustn't be left alone."

"Father can go," Mahala said fiercely. "I'm going to stay with you. I'm going to take care of you." She was trying to hold him now, as Ord moved away from her clasping arms. "Father can see about Jerry. I'm the one to stay with you."

Painfully Ord lifted himself, struggled to his knees. "No," he said, and that was all.

"Let me—let me—" Mahala's voice broke. "Dal," she cried in agony. "Let me stay. I'm the one—"

Ord said again, "No. I want Moses." He would have fallen if the big man's arms had not caught him.

Moses North ended the thing. "I'll take him. I can carry him. It's right upstairs here." He lifted Ord, took a step toward the doorway nearby, then turned back to his daughter. "It's all right, Haley," he said to her, and his face was filled with pity. "I'll see that he's fixed up."

For a full minute after they had gone, Mahala stood looking after them at the empty doorway. Around her on the pavement, the crowd swirled and eddied like a torrent around an obstructing stone in its course. She saw no one, nothing; all her being was centered in one thought. Dal—he wouldn't let me touch him. He didn't want me. For the first time, he refused me. I've always been the one. I've always helped him. I've always taken care of him. When he was in jail, I was the one he wanted; the one he sent for. When he was sick I tended him, and he called for me when he was delirious. Now he refuses me. He won't have me. He may die—away from me, away from me. When he left me before, I knew that he still loved me. Now, he hates me. Now, he's gone. He's gone forever. He sent me away to help Jerry.

For a moment her thoughts seemed to pause, to hesitate. Jerry, her brain repeated, Jerry. That's all that matters to Dal now. I must go to Jerry. That's the one thing I can do. Faithful to that, she thought dully. I can still be faithful to that.

Turning, she began to walk across the street, going east, slipping along in the shadows, running across vacant lots, through back yards, turning and twisting between outbuildings, until she came to a small house on a back street. Here she paused to draw breath before she rapped on the rough door.

CHAPTER EIGHTEEN

THERE HAD BEEN a single light in the little old house on Irving Street, but it went out just as Devil pulled his bay horse to a stop before the rickety gate. Slumped on the seat beside him, Jerry Henry seemed practically unconscious, except for the way he moaned from time to time. Devil didn't like those moans, or the lifeless way the body of the man slid against him in the buggy. Feels like he was dead, and moans like he was dead. And now the light has to go out. Maybe the women in there are just scared. He twisted the reins down behind the whip socket and jumped from the carriage. The house was as black as a pocket.

No one answered his knock for a minute. Then a voice said, quivering, "Who that?"

Just scared, Devil thought, and beat on the rough door panels again. "It's me. Let me in, Sudie."

The door opened a narrow crack, and Sudie's voice said, "I's got a flatiron right here in my han'. You better not come before I sees who you is."

Devil said, "Open up and look, then. Be quick."

There was rustling behind the flimsy door, and the scratch of a locofoco match being struck. In the wavering light of a candle, Sudie peered at Devil through a crack of opening, then pulled the door wide. "What you want? We's going on down to see the ruckus. Can't stay here talkin'."

Devil said, "Ain' no more ruckus. I got Jerry out in the buggy. Mis' Haley says for you to let us come in here, quick."

Sudie said in amazement, "Sweet Jedus," and backed away from the door. "Where he at?"

Devil said nervously, "I got him in the buggy, but there's folks after us, and I got to keep going. Mis' Haley says for me to drive around and fool the folks, after I gits rid of Jerry. We's got to git him in here right quick."

Sudie called, "Git out here, Fanny. Us got a load to tote." Her sister looked as though she could carry the man alone, but Sudie had another idea. "If Jerry's hurt, we got to take him easy. We'll make a queen's chair."

Their black hands locked together, wrist against wrist, making a seat as children do in play. Devil lifted the limp figure out of the buggy and placed him carefully between the two girls.

"Kin you carry him?"

Sudie said, "Git on your way, black boy," and they moved up the path and through the open door of the cabin. Devil was down the road at a gallop by the time they had closed the front door. Sudie listened for a moment, heard another rig following, and hurried back to her charge. "Us got to git those irons off." She knelt and examined the locks. "Can you talk, Jerry? Does you know how to loosen these here goggles offen your legs?"

The injured man moaned, opened his eyes. "Water," he said weakly. "I's powerful sick." Blood was streaming down his face from a deep cut over one eye, and the rags of his shirt were plastered against his ribs in great rusty blotches. Sudie commanded once more. "Git the whisky, Fan," she said. "He got to be fixed up first, before us kin git the irons off."

Raw, cheap spirits down the man's throat put some life into him, but Sudie had other uses for it, too. Carefully she washed the wound on his forehead with whisky, peeled away the tattered shirt and dabbed spirits on a dozen cuts and bruises on his back and sides. Jerry was stronger now and able to tell a little of what happened.

"When the door opened and Mr. Dal come in with those men to git me, a stone come in, too. That marshal put me right in front of him, so's they wouldn't git him first. Then he jumped away and run for the window. But I got a stone before Mr. Dal could grab me."

Fanny, hunkered down beside his chair, wept for him, for all of them. "Good Lawd Jedus, we's all goin' to git killed."

Sudie said, "Hush yo' mouth, Fan. I got to hear what Jerry says. How come you got hurt on yo' back?"

Jerry winced under the burning whisky. "That's when I runned off the first time. Those po-licemen was mighty mean to me." His moans joined with Fan's wailing. "I's goin' to die, sure. I's powerful sick, all over me. I's goin' to die."

A rap on the door stopped his moaning, but nearly killed them all with fright. No one moved. No one dared to say a loud word. From outside a voice called softly, "Let me in, Sudie. It's Miss Haley."

Sudie had the door open in a moment. "Praise God, Mis' Haley. I sure was scared to death when you come. We's got Jerry, but he sick and us don' know how to git the shackles offen his legs and arms."

Mahala, a pale, hard-eyed boy in her brother's clothes, took command. "We can't move him until we get the irons off. Someone would recognize him this way. We'll have to break the locks. Have you got something to pound with?"

Sudie produced her flatirons. "Could we pound one of 'em onto the other, the lock might snap."

It was a painful business because the connecting chain was so short, but ten minutes of battering broke the lock of the leg irons. The handcuffs were not amenable to flatirons, and Sudie had nothing else. After a half hour of desperate effort, Mahala straightened from her hopeless attack.

"This won't do it. We'll never get him out of them this way. We'll have to have a hammer and a chisel, and probably a file. Isn't there a blacksmith near here?"

Sudie said wearily, "Mr. Lily over on the corner. Might be he'd come and help us. He good to niggers."

Mahala knew the name. "He's an Abolitionist. I've seen him at meetings. You run and get him as fast as you can. Tell him to bring his tools. And be careful," she said, fixing Sudie with a look she wouldn't forget. "If you let anyone know who it is you've got here, you'll probably have the policemen here to arrest all of us. Don't breathe Jerry's name. Don't even let Mr. Lily know where he's going or who's here."

Sudie trembled. "I ain't tell nothin', Mis' Haley. I's too scared. I'll just git Mr. Lily and come back in a hurry."

Mr. Lily, when he arrived, was nearly as frightened as the Negro girl. Indeed, his hands trembled so much when he attacked the handcuffs that it looked as though he was going to hack poor Jerry's hands off, as well as the fetters. The cuffs were solid steel loops that fitted into a heavier crosspiece and locked there immovably. Between the cuffs, two links of chain bound them close together. Peter Lily's chisel bit through a chain-link with one stroke, but the cuffs, lacking a key to unlock them, would not stir. They fitted too tightly around the black wrists to allow a chisel stroke, and in Mr. Lily's hands the file made slow progress. Jerry was alarmingly exhausted now, as the fumbling hands worked over him.

"You've got to hurry." Mahala was supporting the poor creature, trying to force whisky between his gray lips. "He can't stand much more of this. You've got to get those cuffs off."

Get them off, get them off; her mind was grinding it out like a machine. Dal sent me to do this. It's all I can do for him. All I'll ever be able to do for him, now. He'll let me work for him because he cares more about this work than about himself. And I *will* work. "Get those cuffs off," she said again to the faltering man. "Do you want this Negro to die in your hands?"

Light footsteps outside the house, knuckles rapping on the door panels, very nearly unmanned Mr. Lily. "I've got one of 'em off—" he was saying when he heard the sound. "God Almighty. They're after us!" And he dropped his tools altogether.

Mahala said savagely, "That's my father. Get on with your work."

He'll know about Dal, she thought, her heart pounding until it seemed to shake her. He'll know how Dal is. I'll see it in his face. If it's bad, his face will look as he did that morning when Martin died. Old and sad and fierce. But if it's good . . . she didn't dare to think. As the old door creaked open her eyes flew to her father's face. Calm, confident, benign. Dal's alive, alive; relief drowned her. He isn't going to die. That's all I care about. Nothing else matters. If he never speaks to me again, or looks at me, I don't care, as long as he's alive and safe. I can stand anything, as long as I know he's safe.

Moses North's bulk seemed to fill the smoky little room. "Aren't you through with that yet?" His voice spurred the blacksmith to frantic efforts. "We've got to get a move on. Thompson's still racing around with a troop of policemen after him, and we've got to get this man moved before they begin to search somewhere else."

Mahala caught her father's arm. "Where's Dal? Is he all right?"

Old Moses said, "Clary fixed him up as well as he could. The bullet went high, through his shoulder, but he's bled some. I couldn't make him go home," he said apologetically, looking at his daughter's white face. "He wouldn't go. He's at Cale Davis's house, and we're going to take Jerry there and meet him."

I'll see him, she thought, and a fever of impatience filled her mind. He won't look at me. He turned his eyes away when he saw me, but I'll be able to see him.

"Get that cuff off," her voice rasped like the file. "What kind of blacksmith are you?" She was raging at the man. "You've taken time enough to saw your way out of jail. This is a life-and-death matter."

Fanny was kneeling on the floor, moaning and praying at the top of her lungs. She was clearly useless in this emergency. Mahala turned to Sudie. "Run and fetch me some women's clothes. Anything that's big enough to cover Jerry. A Mother Hubbard and a big shawl. Borrow them from somebody, and get them quick. As soon as the cuffs are broken, we'll dress him and get him out of here. He's got to have a doctor and good nursing. Hurry." The Negro girl was out of the room like a cat with singed whiskers. Mahala turned on Peter Lily. "I'll give you five minutes more." The file dug into steel.

Jerry was a queer-looking figure as he crept out of the house, bunchy, shapeless, walking feebly between Moses North and his daughter. The yard behind the cabin was a black wilderness where they stumbled over rubbish, slipped in muddy holes, toward the high back fence. Sudie was ahead of them, brave as a little lion, tugging an old box against the fence railings, holding it steady while they climbed over. She would have gone farther if they had let her.

Moses North sent her back to her house. "They might come looking for you. It's better to have 'em find you here. We know the way after this. We'll go by Amos Benedict's to Hoyt's house, and then it's easy to get around back to Cale Davis's. You're a good girl, Sudie," he said to her kindly. "Folks'll remember that you did this for Jerry. You're a good girl."

Down an alley, across back yards, skirting a barn, an outhouse, clothes poles, tool sheds. There was one place where it was necessary to pass the pool of light from a street lamp. Once a party of searchers crossed the road just beyond them, while they crouched in the shadow and waited. Jerry's strength was waning with every step, and toward the last Moses North was practically carrying him. Jason Hoyt's barn on East Genesee Street was safe enough for a resting place. After that, another back yard to cross and they were behind Cale Davis's house, waiting in the shadow while Mahala ran up the back steps and gave the signal raps on the door. A light went out inside, a voice whispered, and dark figures slid out of the house to help the fugitive.

"We've done it." Moses North looked at the men in the room. Jason Hoyt and his brother the doctor, Caleb Davis and his brother James, Dr. May, Jarmain Loguen, Dr. Clary, Dallas Ord.

Grave men made a circle around the grotesque figure in its bunchy calico dress. "He's got away," Moses North said, holding the shapeless body in his arms. "But he won't live to tell about it if the doctor don't fix him up. He's bad off."

In the yellow lamplight, Ord's face was pale but the look of deathly weakness, of faintness, of final yielding to oblivion like a man drowning in dark water, was no longer there. Against the pallor of his skin his eyes were perfectly black, his lips were set in a hard line. When Mahala and her father came into the room he looked up to nod once, briefly, then turned to speak to the man next him. Mahala found a chair in a shadowy corner. She must watch him. If he should faint again— Her hands clenched in her lap. Even then, she might not touch him. The memory came back, searing her mind like a hot iron. He had said, "No. I want Moses." No, she thought, struggling with the pain. No. He wants father. Not me. Not me.

Dr. Clary was a good man for sickness, even if the other doctors had thrown him out of the Medical Society because he was a homeopath. A little drop of this in a barrel of that. Maybe it sounded silly, but it seemed to work all right, and lots of people swore by Dr. Clary.

"You can trust him," Dr. May said peacefully, gathering his flock in the sitting room, while Clary worked his watery miracles in the room upstairs. "Jerry's been roughly handled. He's got some wounds. But I believe the rest of it's only exhaustion. And fear," the old man said, looking at them. "Fear can kill a man. We have delivered him from fear."

"He won't be out of danger as long as he stays in the city." Dallas Ord rested his bandaged shoulder stiffly against the chair back. "Canada's the only safe place for him now. We've got to move him as soon as possible."

Jason Hoyt asked, "Tonight?" They were all of them willing enough, but command of the affair was in the hands of the professionals.

"No." Ord shifted again minutely. He said with great formality, "I only make the suggestion, of course, gentlemen. I have had some experience. I brought this man up from the South, two years ago. I know what he's capable of. He's a good man—intelligent. But he's easily rattled. He stampedes, the way he did today. We can't count on him to help much in escaping. It's got to be carefully planned, and someone's got to go with him practically to the border, or he'll give himself away."

Mahala couldn't resist saying, "You can't go with him, Dal. You ought to be in bed, yourself. You're as white as a sheet."

Ord did not look at her. He said, "I'll be all right in another day. And I'm better fitted for it than anyone else."

Moses North was calm. "There's no need to worry about tomorrow. I'd vote against trying to move him so soon, anyhow. The marshals and their friends will be expecting us to get him through right away. They'll be waiting for us on every road. We've fooled them so far, but if we move too quick, we'll be playing right into their hands."

Loguen said hotly, "The forces of the Lord cannot be confounded. Only with their eyes shall they behold and see the ways of the wicked."

Moses grinned. "Well, I don't want to presume, but I'd be willing to make a small bet that the Lord don't want you should move that man for two-three days. I've always heard He believed in the wisdom of the serpent."

Dr. May smiled at him. "What about the devil quoting Scripture, Moses?" he asked in his charming way.

Ord broke in impatiently. "The thing can be done very simply. But we must wait until the hunt has died down. Three days, four days, at least. That will give Jerry time to recover, in the first place. As soon as the excitement's faded, it'll be easy to drive him out of town, and there are a dozen stations that could take care of him."

Moses North said, "Sure, sure. I'll take him myself," but a stir at the front door interrupted his words. Gerrit Smith's valuable person was unwrapped from a greatcoat. Mr. Wheaton and Dr. Pease crowded into the little room after him. And with new arrivals, it was necessary to say everything over again. Mahala watched Ord's drawn face with terrible anxiety.

The plan of waiting, Mr. Smith said, was a good one. Today was Wednesday. Not before Saturday or Sunday, in his opinion, would it be safe to move. But Moses North could not go with the fugitive, he said, shaking his head.

North rebelled at this. "I'm just the man, Mr. Smith. I know the ropes. I know most of the stationkeepers on the route. I could take him through as easy as winking."

Gerrit Smith said heavily, "The trouble is that you are about to be arrested. I have talked with Mr. Sabine and some of the officials. That's why I'm late." He looked around the gathering. "They sent for me to tell me what they are going to do. They have the names of more than a dozen of our people. They're issuing warrants for arrest against the ringleaders of the rescue. They know who these men are. I have arranged to post bail for them."

Dallas Ord said bitterly, "The forces of the Lord can never be confounded." He turned to Gerrit Smith. "How many of us are known?"

"Not you." But the words were asking a further question.

Mahala forgot caution, forgot that she had no right to speak for Dal. She stood up suddenly in her corner and began to plead with them. "He can't do it. He's injured. He was shot. He *can't* make such a journey now." She was pleading with them. "*I* can do it. I've done such things before. I'm perfectly able." She turned away from the doubting faces of the men, to appeal to her father. "Tell them that I can do it," she begged him. "I got Dal out of jail. I've done a hundred things as risky as this."

Cale Davis settled his square, butcher's body and said one thing. "You're a woman." So far as he was concerned, there was nothing more to be said.

"We don't doubt your courage," Dr. May told her. "We know how much you have done for the cause. But in this case, we feel that a man must be responsible. This is important to all of us. We have all risked a great deal to get this man free. Now, we must not fail in the final act."

It was Wheaton who delivered the final blow. He said to Moses North, "Your daughter is the wife of John Palfrey, a well-known proslavery man. Burnet's right bower. I don't distrust her, myself, but some of our people would wonder at it, if she was allowed to conduct Jerry's escape. It's out of the question."

Mahala did not know whether Ord had looked at her while she spoke. She had been fighting too desperately to notice anything or anyone. Perhaps he had been angry that she dared to interfere. It was impossible to tell now. He rose with an effort and turned to Gerrit Smith. "I can settle it," he said sharply. "I suggest one of your own men, but one who would not be thought of as an Abolitionist. Caleb Davis would do admirably. Let him, with perhaps another, drive the Negro out of the city, not before Sunday. I'll go along in another carriage, and be ready to—distract their minds if they follow." The threat was unmistakable under his quiet words.

Dr. May said quickly, "We want no further violence, if it can be avoided."

Ord smiled wearily. "There will be no violence—if it can be avoided."

Gerrit Smith made the decision. "That's a good plan. If you're agreed—" he gathered their eyes around the room "—we'll ratify this plan. Caleb Davis will harbor the man Jerry until such time as we may safely remove him from the city. Unless for some reason otherwise decided, on Sunday Caleb Davis will make arrangements to drive Jerry to the next available station. The details—" he hesitated slightly "—will be left in the hands of Mr. Ord."

There was a general murmur of agreement. It was a relief to have something settled, and after all, Ord knew the ropes. Gerrit Smith was winding things up. "If anything happens to make this plan inadvisable, we will meet again and discuss an alternative.

Meanwhile, we will stand together in this hour." His eyes kindled, his lion's head lifted. "We will stand steadfast together, come what may. We are in the right!" he cried, the fire rising in him. "We are in the right! The Lord will make His face to shine upon us!"

Just the same, Mahala thought, walking between Dal and her father along the disreputable street that led to the Old Lib. Everything the same, to look at. Old Lib itself, with its ramshackle veranda and its row of ancient spindle-back chairs lined up along the rail; with old Wilgus and Mr. Bobbin tilting their chairs back in the pool of light that flowed from the barroom window, waiting for something to happen. Something to happen, she thought, looking at the two old derelicts. Everything has happened while they have been sitting there. The world has turned upside down; it has split open under my feet. But these two foolish old men know nothing about it. Here they have sat for twenty years, seeing horses and men pass on the street beyond them, seeing boats and men pass on the water below them, but no precipice has opened at their feet, between one step and another. Today they have seen a thousand men fighting in the public square, but nothing happened. The fight is over, the men have gone back to their homes, and these two old men have seen nothing very strange.

I am walking up the steps to my home, beside my father and Dallas Ord. I am walking down the passage to my room, as though there had been no break, as though I was the same person who used to live here and talk with them. But I know that something has happened. I know that I've committed a crime, and I know that I'll pay for it. I tried to change my colors. I tried to be what I was not, and because I tried, my father will be arrested. Dal is shot and perhaps will die. He has put me from him and will not know me again. That is my punishment.

With her hand on the latch of the door, an instinct like an alarm bell warned her not to enter. She began to say, "It's too late to talk. I'm tired—"

Before she could finish, Dallas Ord had pushed past her into the green room. The lamp was lighted on the center table, and beside it stood John Palfrey with a face like death. He said, "I thought you'd be here by this time," and he looked, not at his wife, but at Ord.

John, Mahala thought, and a kind of paralysis settled upon her mind. John—I'd forgotten John. Long ago, long ago—how long it seems—I left John in hatred and anger. At that moment I knew I had to leave him. I knew I never should have married him. I knew I'd been wrong. But I was so angry that I wasn't even sorry for John. I was only sorry for what I'd done. I only thought how to atone. That's all I thought of—until I saw Dal. And since then I've only thought of Dal. I forgot John. I never wondered if he'd come after me. I never even wondered if he was angry or hurt. He was forgotten, like a dream after I'd waked up. Now he must go, he must go away, she thought in terrible agitation. I've hurt him bitterly before. Now I must hurt him once more so that he'll go away. I want him to forget me. I want him to forget that I ever lived.

Ord walked farther into the room and stood easily, facing John. "That's right," he said in his soft voice. "I'm here. What do you want with me?" The question was light as a feather. It could have been a challenge or the most careless courtesy.

Palfrey still looked only at Ord. "You know what I want." He took a step forward. Suddenly his face changed. He said sharply, "You're wounded," and the tension in his body relaxed, as though he had no further need for it.

Ord laughed. "That needn't trouble you, Mr. Palfrey. If there's any matter you want to discuss with me, this slight scratch needn't interfere. We might step outside—"

Life came back into Mahala's frozen veins as Ord spoke.

"Stop this." Before they could move she was between the two men. "John has nothing to say to Dallas Ord. Whatever he has to say is to me." Her eyes flew to Palfrey's face. "This is between us," she said slowly. "There isn't anything for me to say except to tell you I'm sorry. It's my fault that all this happened. I should never have known you. I shouldn't have married you. I told you that a hundred times. I knew I had no right to marry you.

"I was a traitor," she said deliberately, and for a moment she turned and looked full at Ord. "Dal knew I was a traitor, but he would never say so. You didn't know it, and so you wouldn't believe me. But I knew it." Her voice was heavy with loathing. "It was treachery. Treachery caused all this."

Her father said, "Wait a minute, Haley. That's pretty grand talk. There wasn't any treachery about it. We're on different sides in an argument, that's all. We don't happen to feel the way John does about a certain political matter. Today the matter came up for decision, and you found you had to fight on the side you believed in, that's all. John must understand that."

Palfrey said violently, "She wouldn't have had to fight on that side if you and Ord hadn't been on it. This isn't just politics."

Before Mahala or Ord could speak, Moses North answered him. "You're right about that," he said thoughtfully. "It's more than just politics. It's people. It's what kind of people you are. And that's something you can't help. If you're a sound, conservative businessman or politician or whatever, you see it one way. You see how good things are the way they are. And if you're a crazy, go-to-hell idealist you see that things are wrong, and you've got to change 'em if it kills you. Mahala didn't have to fight on my side because I was on it," he said with his slow smile. "She had to fight on it because she was the same kind of critter I am. She says she's a traitor because she tried to move over to the other side of the fence, and it didn't work. She had to come back."

Palfrey said brutally, "She wouldn't have had to come back if it had been just you. It was Ord she came back to." As he raised his hand they could see that it was trembling with anger.

Ord spoke at last. "How do you know that? Did Mahala say so?" His eyes glittered as though a fever had come upon him.

"She didn't have to say anything." Palfrey brushed Ord's words aside scornfully. "Do you think I don't know? She thinks she belongs to you. That's why she feels like a traitor. If you're in trouble, she thinks she's got to help you. This slave business doesn't matter." He looked at Mahala. "I won't let you go," he said to her. "I won't let you get into trouble. These men are going to be arrested." His words fell like the strokes of a hammer.

"If they are arrested, I should be arrested too." Mahala stood before him, her eyes only a little below his, her head thrown back so that she could look directly into his eyes. Her face was haggard; hollows seemed carved under the cheekbones and around the eye sockets; only her mouth had any color, and her eyes were too large in her white face. Facing John Palfrey, she said, "You think they're outlaws. Very well—" her eyes blazed at him "—then I am an outlaw, too. I came back here because I belonged here."

"Don't talk that way." Palfrey's hand closed on her wrist, drawing her toward him. "This arrest is no business of yours now. You're my wife. You've left these people. Whatever you thought and did before has nothing to do with this thing today. You're my wife," he said again, his face as bleak as winter. "You've forgotten that, Mahala. You're married to me, and you've promised to obey me. Whatever you felt before, you've got to take my side now, and leave these men alone."

Mahala drew her hand from his and took one step backward, away from him. Whatever I say or do will hurt him, she thought, her mind as heavy as lead. The more cruel I can be now, the sooner he'll hate me and forget me.

"Put your shackles on me, then." She held out her hands. "You take sides with the slaveowners; you're a slaveowner, too. If I went back as your wife, I'd go as a slave. Do you want to take me?"

Palfrey cried furiously, "You've got no right to say that. You married me because you loved me. You came of your own will.

Now you want to leave me because Ord and your father are in trouble. They got into trouble because they were breaking the law. We arrested that Negro to show such people that the law is stronger than they are. And we'll prove it yet," he said, turning his eyes upon the two men in the room. "This isn't over." The words were a threat.

Both men stiffened as he spoke, but before they could answer, Mahala spoke for them. "You'll never prove it," she said with passion. "You arrested a helpless man today. Beat him. His blood's on your hand. Yours," she said, looking at John Palfrey's clenched fists. "Dallas Ord's blood is on your hands. If I went back with you, my blood would be on your hands, too. I'd die before I'd take your side."

Palfrey said in a harsh voice, "Do you mean that?" His face was colorless, his eyes were like ice.

With one motion, Mahala stripped the gold ring from her finger and held it toward him. "I was a traitor once. I'll never desert again."

The ring dropped unheeded on the floor between them. John Palfrey said between his teeth, "By God, you've made your choice," and without another word he turned and walked to the door and out of the room.

In that room, silence rang deafeningly, as though a gun had exploded. Standing alone, her hands clenched against her breasts, Mahala made a sound like a moan. "I've killed him," she said, and stared blindly at the closed door. "I've killed him. I had to kill him. And I've killed myself."

Her father touched her arm. "You couldn't change this, Mahala," he said with profound tenderness. "John couldn't change it. It had to happen. But you've got courage. You'll come through it. We'll all come through it, you and Dal and I. We've got to come through, because we've got work to do."

Mahala looked at him, unable to speak, unable to move, and saw Dallas Ord turn slowly away from the window and walk to the door. Once his step faltered but he caught himself up and went on. The door closed behind him.

Moses North touched his daughter's arm. "I've got to go and help him," he said gently. "He's a sick man."

Motionless, Mahala watched him go.

CHAPTER NINETEEN

The police wagon rolled down the street away from Old Lib. Mahala stood at the window, her hands clenched, her face white with anger.

"They've taken him," she said. "They'll keep him in jail forever, if they can."

Ord's voice was kinder than she'd heard it. "Don't worry about your father, Mahala. He'll be all right. And Mr. Smith will see that he gets out. He promised to give bail for all the men arrested."

Mahala turned furiously. "But what are we going to do tonight? They took father today because they suspected we'd move soon. Everything's planned. We can't change. It's almost time to leave now."

Ord said easily, "I can handle it. Davis knows what he has to do. We'll get along."

"You can't drive with that bad arm. And besides, it would spoil everything if only one man went in the carriage. You want Burnet's watchers to think you're Jerry, trying to escape in disguise. But Jerry couldn't go alone. Someone's got to drive you, or it won't fool them. And if we don't distract their attention, they'll follow Davis as sure as fate, and get Jerry away from him."

Ord said, "I'll get a driver. One of the other men will drive for me."

"Who?" Mahala asked scornfully. "None of them were very anxious to go when we talked it over. Father was the only one to volunteer. They know they might get in trouble if they're caught, and after all these arrests, nobody wants to take a chance." She looked at Ord's frowning face. "You know that's true." Grimly she smiled. "Father and I are the only ones left who like to take chances. And now father's gone, you'll have to take me."

Ord hesitated. "I'll find someone," he said, but his voice was uncertain.

Mahala faced him. "You've got about ten minutes to do it in. It's after seven, and we've timed it for Davis to leave at seven-thirty. We ought to be at his house, ready to move ten minutes before that. I'm going," she said passionately. "I *will* go. You're so weak that you oughtn't even to ride that far, let alone drive two horses. I'm going, I tell you. You can't stop me. I know how you feel about me, but that doesn't matter now. We've got to do this thing."

Ord's expression was unreadable. He said, "All right, Mahala. You'll drive. We'd better start."

Mahala moved swiftly. "Give me five minutes to get into Martin's clothes. They'll have to think I'm a man." Then she was gone.

It was just like Cale Davis, everyone said indulgently, to start off after his beef when decent folks went to church. Cale was a card, a regular character. A regular Vermonter, someone else said, craning around the doorway of Palmer's Tammany Hall tobacco shop to watch Cale talking with some of the bigwigs on the Syracuse House veranda.

They weren't going to church themselves, the loungers admitted; still, they weren't working, either, and never did work Sunday nights. But you could count on Cale to pull up his old butcher's wagon, as big as life, where everybody could see it, and stomp into the shop for a segar and a package of fine-cut for his journey. He did it every Sunday night the Lord sent; you could set your watch by him. Folks talked, said he was a heathen, but they bought their meat of him just the same, and everybody had a good word for him when they met. He was an old soldier, they said with some pride; fought in the war of '12 against the British, when he was just a boy. Tough-bitted, a Hunker Democrat from 'way back, and independent as a hog on ice. He didn't care what he said to anyone; he spoke his mind, to Dr. May or anyone else. He was a sound man, voted the right way and hated the Nigger Lovers fit to kill.

He was coming along now, swinging through the door with his stocky figure, swaggering up to the counter and clinking his money on the board. "A bag of fine-cut and a couple stogies." That was what he always said.

Palmer dug up the merchandise and said, "Here they be, Cale. You risking your immortal soul again this Sabbath?"

Cale said, "I'm taking my chance," and ripped open the chewing tobacco. "Prob'ly won't be able to, long. These moral reformers in our midst," he said comically. "They'll make it against the law for a man to spit sideways, pretty soon."

Everybody knew how he felt about the Abolitionists. "You'd better tell that to Dr. May," someone said, provoking a general laugh.

Davis was too busy stuffing his cheek with tobacco to reply to this sally. Another man said, "Seems to me I saw you in that muss in the Square last week. Which side was you fighting on? I always calculated you was a strong Democrat."

Cale said, "Show me the man that says I ain't," and turned toward the door. "I got to mizzle, or I'll be late."

They watched him swing into his wagon, take up the reins and turn his team back toward the Square. "He's a funny cuss," one of the men said. "I saw him a-Wednesday, right enough, fighting like a good one. He's a bad man in a fight."

"That's a nice pair of horses he's got," Palmer said with envy. "He must have swapped his old pair. They're light for a wagon, but I'll bet they can cover the ground. Cale's always a great one for a horse."

The new team spanked along up North Salina Street so that the old butcher's cart rattled and bounded over the cobbles. Jason Hoyt said, "You'd better go easy, Cale. Jerry ain't too good yet.

We don't want to have him turn sick on us before he gets to Mexico."

Cale pulled the team in. "They're a nice pair," he said. Then he spoke softly. "You all right, Jerry? Riding comfortable?"

From beneath a heap of sacking in the back of the wagon, a voice said cautiously, "I's all right, Mr. Cale. It bounces me some, but I ain't sick."

Davis said, "It'll ride easier when we get on the plank road. We can make time then."

"I hope everything goes all right," Hoyt said nervously. "It seems kind of risky to do it this way."

Cale said, "Hell, we're safe enough. Ord's a smart duck. If anyone gets chased, it'll be him. He's got it all laid out, hog-tight and horse-high." He grinned to think of it. "He's one of those reckless cusses. He'd be real pleased if some Patriots got ambitious and chased him a piece. I'd liked to have gone with him."

Jason Hoyt looked apprehensive. "It's better this way." He peered cautiously into the streets as they trotted past. "I don't see anyone looking at us."

Caleb Davis leaned out over the wheel to spit. "You *won't* see anybody, neither. We're safe as a church."

As he spoke, the church bells began to toll; near by, far away, east and west and south, one after another, pealing sweetly in the fall dusk, calling the faithful to evening service.

"We're just about right," Davis said, listening to the clear strokes of the bells. "We're just about on time. They'll be starting now. Giddap," he called to his team, and heard their hooves strike smartly against the wooden planking of the Cicero Road. "Giddap along, boys," he said with pleasure, snapping the whiplash above them. "We got to make time."

The team fairly flew.

It was nearly dark in the street now. Stars had bloomed softly in a pale sky, but beneath the trees there was shadow. A carriage and pair were hitched to the iron post by the horse block. The street was quiet, no passers-by, but farther down the road another light buggy was standing.

In her darkened doorway Mrs. Davis whispered, "Now be careful," and swung the front door wide to allow the little procession to start. Two men went on either side of a bent and tottering man who walked between them. They moved slowly, to accommodate their steps to the dragging gait of the invalid. Slowly and carefully they guided him to the carriage and helped him inside. Another man climbed in front and picked up the reins. In a moment the carriage was moving rapidly down the street toward the canal bridge.

The bridge rumbled under their wheels, and Mahala thought, Maybe they won't follow. Maybe John's given up. Don't come, don't come, she begged him in her mind. Let this go. Let us get away out of your sight. Let me disappear altogether and forget me.

The bridge thundered again hollowly behind them, and through the little window in the back of the carriage another buggy was visible, moving the same way, riding after, giving chase. Ord said, "They're coming. Get ready to run for it."

The plank road began at Wolf Street, in the northern part of the city, cutting slightly north by east in its path to Brewerton at the west end of Oneida Lake. For the first four miles the Plank Road Company, which was the first in the country, and a smart, up-to-date outfit, everyone said, had put in a double track. A half dozen upstate winters had broken the planks of the road here and there, the bed had heaved some in places, but take it all in all, it was the best place for a race you might wish to see.

Ord touched the driver's shoulder. "Let's see their paces, Haley," he said softly. "Mr. Woodruff's proud of his horseflesh. Let's see it run."

Mahala said, "Hold on, then. You'll see it," and her whip touched the pair urgently. The horses' trot lengthened, broke for a moment into a gallop, steadied to a long swinging gait, their feet beating like a drum upon the wood. Behind them now another team was running, so that the hoofbeats seemed to have an echo coming after, now gaining, now falling back.

Mahala, sitting forward, the reins straining in her hands, felt the wind in her hair, felt the blood rising in her face. "Beat them," she said, and the words seemed to blow out of her mouth as she spoke. "Beat them. Don't let them catch us."

Ord looked back at their pursuers. "We're holding them." He touched her shoulder once more. "I'd like to show that we're better than that. Stir them up a little more," he said, and Mahala knew he was smiling in the darkness.

This time it was a flat gallop, ta-ta-*ta,* ta-ta-*ta,* over the hollow timbers, so that the light carriage swayed like a boat in rough water, and Ord caught Mahala with his free arm to hold her against the rocking of the carriage. "It's all right," he said in her ear. "Don't be afraid. This will be all right."

Mahala cried, "I'm not afraid."

Ord's voice came through the darkness. "This is the best way. This will be the end of it."

Behind them, two horses with a lighter carriage were actually drawing up, however hard Mahala used the whip. The other team was close behind them now, so that the hoofbeats of the four horses sounded together in a thundering roar on the planks of the road.

Suddenly, something was wrong. In the gray dusk the shape of the road seemed to change, to narrow sharply. Too late Mahala remembered that the double track ended somewhere beyond the city, became a track wide enough for only one team. She cried out once, and then saved her breath. The break in the road was just ahead of them now, and she was using every atom of her strength to saw on the reins.

Ord was shouting. "Pull up! Let them pass! We can't make it on the single track—" Even as he spoke, the horses plunged wildly, the carriage lurched off the raised planks and careened forward in the mud. One wheel cut downwards into the ditch, and in a moment the carriage canted over sidewise while the horses struggled and fought against their bits. Beside them on the single, left-hand track of plank road, the quick hoofbeats of the other horses rattled, slowed, stopped.

Ord's arm crippled him. He could not brace himself, he could not hold Mahala as the carriage lurched. Together they were thrown forward helplessly while the horses lunged and the light body of the carriage pitched from side to side. Someone was in the road beyond them, shouting and running.

"Get their heads! Grab their heads!"

Dal's arm was trying to hold Mahala, and at the last she heard his voice crying, "Look out—we're going over—" Then thinking and seeing ceased in an explosion of violence. A pain in her head and after that nothing at all, until arms were lifting her, and the cool air of the night touched her face.

John Palfrey's voice said, just above her, "She's coming around."

Mahala opened her eyes to behold John's face bending over her. She struggled to sit up. "Dal—Dal—"

Palfrey cried, "Mahala, are you hurt?"

Words were as heavy as lead. She managed to say, "I'm not hurt."

Another voice was raised. Someone in the road shouting at the horses. Hooves plunged wildly against soft earth, then upon wood, and wheels rolled after them. The angry voice cried, "Where's the other man that was in this rig? We saw him get in. What have you done with him?"

None of this mattered.

Mahala struggled against John Palfrey. "Dal—Dal! Where is he?" One terrible fear was commanding her. Frantically she broke away from Palfrey's arms and got to her feet, reeling, dizzy, searching through the darkness for Dallas Ord. "Where is he—"

Palfrey was beside her instantly, a guiding hand on her arm. "He's all right. Just knocked out. Don't try to walk—"

Before he could finish speaking, Mahala had seen the unmoving shape and was down on her knees beside it on the grass of the road's verge. Her hands found Ord's face, her arms were gathering him up. Pure panic filled her with the touch of his cool brow.

"Oh, God, you've killed him," she cried in a voice John Palfrey had never heard. "You've killed him. He isn't breathing—" She was making blind and despairing efforts to rouse the unconscious man, hearing nothing that was said, seeing nothing, knowing nothing except the terror in her mind.

Palfrey was down beside her now, trying to calm her, trying to loosen her hold of Ord's body. "It's all right, Mahala. He isn't dead. He's breathing. If you'll let him lie still a minute he'll come around. You're the one that's hurt. You're cut. There's blood on your face. You've got to let me take you to a doctor." Then, as she paid no heed to his words, he said bitterly, "He let you do this, and you might have been killed. But you don't care. You don't care about anything but him."

Against her cheek she felt the gentle exhalation of a breath, and her heart seemed to turn over in her breast with joy. "Dal—he's breathing—he's alive—" There was nothing in the world but that.

Beyond her Palfrey's voice was saying, "—I knew you were in love with him. I might have known you'd run away with him."

For the first time she lifted her head to answer. "I loved him. I've always loved him." In the darkness her face was a white blur. "I told you that, long ago. But we weren't running away. We were doing our work. That's all Dal wants from me now," she said with awful bitterness. "I thought I'd got over loving him. I thought I was in love with you. But it wasn't true. It wasn't right. Nothing I did was right—until I came back to Dal, where I belonged."

Palfrey's voice was hard. "He knew he could take you away from me. That's why he came back."

"No." Mahala was quieter now. Sadness was filling her mind, pity and compassion for all of them. "No. He didn't come back for me. He doesn't want me now. He doesn't love me. I've hurt him and I've hurt you. I've lost you both. But I'll never leave Dal again. I'll work for him all my life."

In her arms, Dallas Ord stirred and she forgot everything else.

"He's moving. Help me to lift him into the carriage. I'll take him home."

Palfrey said sharply, "You can't drive. You oughtn't to be looking after anyone. I'm going to take you to a doctor. Deacon can drive Ord back." She could feel his hand urgently upon her arm. "He'll come to, in a minute. You're the one that's got to be driven home."

Mahala spoke slowly. "No." It was as final as doomsday. "Never with you again, John." His head bent and she saw his hands clench suddenly. "It isn't your fault. But I can never go back. Forget me, John," she said in a whisper.

Palfrey said, "Mahala—" and then Dallas Ord spoke for the first time.

He only said her name, "Mahala." Then, as she bent toward him, he moved strongly, gathered himself, and in another moment he was on his feet, helping her to rise. He said to Palfrey, "I'll see Mahala home."

Mahala couldn't believe it. "Dal—are you sure? Are you strong enough—"

Ord's hand touched her, reassured her. He spoke to Palfrey. "We needn't trouble you. If the horses and carriage are all right—"

Palfrey said stiffly, "Nothing's broken. Deacon got them back into the road for you." He turned toward the highway where the dim shape of his companion was standing at the horses' heads.

"We may as well go back." For one last moment he spoke to Ord. "I suppose that while this was going on, our man got away. It was a neat trick. I ought to have known."

Ord said gravely, "Thank you. It seemed necessary, at the time. I'm sorry to have been inconvenient. I must have alarmed Mahala."

John Palfrey didn't answer. He spoke a word to Perley Deacon and the two men entered their carriage. Hoofbeats rang on the road once more.

In the darkness, Mahala stood listening, waiting. She could feel Ord's hand on her arm, and it seemed to her that everything that was living in her body was centered in that touch, longing for it to remain, dreading the moment when it should be withdrawn from her again. He touched me because I was afraid, but after this he'll never touch me again. I shall be cold for the rest of my life, she thought, holding her breath as though, by not stirring, not breathing, she could prolong this moment.

The beat of hooves grew fainter in the distance. From the woodland beside the road, from pools in the fields, the latest singing creatures of the year, crickets and katydids, were lifting their chorus. One of the horses stamped and his harness jingled softly. On her arm, Dallas Ord's hand tightened, drew her toward him. His whispering voice said no more than her name.

"Oh, Mahala—" This kiss and his last kiss were one, with no interval between them, just as she and Dallas Ord were one person, indivisible, indissoluble, joined, inseparable. Sighing at last, she stood, her forehead resting against his cheek, not speaking, but understanding from the touch of his hand, from the beating of his heart and the uneven breath he drew against her breast, all that he might have said to her.

In the road, the horses stamped again, impatient to be home. At last Ord moved. Even then he did not let her go; his arm around her shoulders drew her toward the carriage. His voice, burdened with tenderness and love, sounded as she had heard it years ago on that river bank after their first kiss. "A friend with friends, Mahala," he said.

It was late that night when Amidon Palfrey tiptoed into his wife's room for a last word. Emma was not asleep, and before he had finished fumbling with matches and lamp, she was sitting up in her billowy feather bed, sharp with questions. Amidon said, "Mother, I wanted to tell you I've seen John and he says he wants to move back here to live, now that Mahala's gone. He told me to ask you if it was all right. I said not to be foolish. We'd always want him here. But he told me to ask you."

Mrs. Palfrey fished under her pillow for a handkerchief. "Good

Mercy, where else would he go, I'd like to know." Her easy tears began to fall. "Oh, Amidon, why did he ever marry that wicked girl? I told you it would lead to trouble. I told you it wasn't right. But no one would listen to me."

Her husband sat down wearily. "It won't do any good to cry over spilt milk," he said, rubbing his eyes. "I told you at the time that I didn't know how it would work, but John wanted it, and I was going to stand by him. And I told you that Mahala was a good girl that you needn't be ashamed of."

Mrs. Palfrey sat up like a ramrod among her pillows. "And who says she's a good girl now, I'd like to know?" she inquired. "Running off and leaving her husband before she's been married two months! If that's a good girl, I don't know what is! Running out and getting into a mob of rioters! Helping a lot of good-for-nothing Abolitionists break the laws of the country, and making a great show of herself in men's clothes! Breaking her husband's heart," she cried, sobbing as she thought of it. "If that's a good girl—"

Amidon Palfrey sighed. "I want you to know how John feels, or it won't be comfortable for him when he comes back here. He talked to me about it tonight." The old man paused and gathered his forces. "He said it wasn't Mahala's fault. He said she had refused to marry him for a long time because she felt they didn't think alike, and should never try to live together."

"*Think* alike!" Emma Palfrey exclaimed. "Who ever heard of such a thing! What does it matter what she *thought*? If she'd been a good wife, she'd have let John do the thinking, and minded her own business making a home for him."

Old Amidon waited for a moment while his wife's sobbing sounded in the quiet room. Then he said, "John's going to divorce her."

"Oh—" Poor Mrs. Palfrey couldn't bear it. "That's a disgrace. We'll never be able to hold our heads up after this. I knew she would lead us to sorrow. I *knew* it was wrong. But nobody would listen to me. Women taking up with causes and thinking and running around like men! I knew it would come to a bad end."

Amidon Palfrey said, "It isn't only women, mother. We're going to have a war, John says. The South against the North. The proslavery folks against the antislavery folks. It'll be a horrible thing."

His wife moaned. "Do you mean that John will go off down south and fight against his own people?"

Frowning, her husband worked it out. "No. I don't think so. I don't think many northern men'd actually fight against their own folks. It was like this before the other big war we had—the Revolution. Folks quarreled amongst themselves until they had to fight somebody from outside, and then they pitched in together and fought the British until they settled it. Maybe a war here would end the slavery business and let us quiet down again."

Mrs. Palfrey wiped her eyes and glared at him like a little old gray fury. "Well, I wish they'd hurry up and do it, then, and get it over," she said, with a comical vindictiveness. "If they've got to have a bloody war to make folks decent again, I hope they get about it and stop this nonsense." She shook her finger at her husband, scolding him, scolding all men for their foolishness. "It'll be a lesson to them," she said, as though she was the mother of the whole country, and every man in America was her wayward son. "It'll be a good strong lesson to them."

In a farmhouse in the town of Mexico, New York, a Quaker opened his door and stepped into the night. A butcher's cart drew up to the barn and men were getting out. "Ames," a voice called softly. "Ames."

"In here," came the answer, and figures moved, as still as shadows, toward the house.

A woman in a Quaker bonnet had made all ready. There was food for the travelers, fresh lint bandages for the wounded man; later, a bed in an attic room. Daylight never saw him. If any had come searching, the farmer would have made them welcome, shown them the place with honest pride, for it was a fine farm; shown them cows in the big barns, hay in the loft, oats in the bins, cheeses in the dairy. They would have been offered buttermilk to drink, or a hot meal if they cared to stay. Any day that week they might have searched and welcome, but they would not have found the man in his hidden room.

Later, in the night once more, Mr. Ames hitched up his horses and drove a load over to his friend and neighbor, Deacon Beebe, and after this, the smuggled man, the contraband, slipped into a great barn. Cows moved and stamped in the pungent dusk; there was a dog that ran beside the stranger to a room hollowed out of a hayloft snug and comfortable, where he lay by day, hearing the noises of the cattle, hearing heavy boots stamping on the barn floor, hearing wheels rattle as a buggy came back from Oswego after a day's business.

At noon and at night, the hay would rustle, the little door would push open and plump Mrs. Beebe would come into the tiny room with a basket on her arm. She would lift the napkin and bring out food: cooked chicken, biscuits and butter, a pie, a jar of new milk. She would talk to the black man, telling him not to worry, not to be afraid. The Deacon would fix it, she told him comfortably. Deacon was a good man at making plans. And then her son, Windsor, knew how to go at things. He was looking around. It would all be fixed up in a little while. She would dress the wounds on the man's head and on his wrists and ankles. Yes, a fresh bandage would be a good thing, but the cuts were doing very well. They'd be healed in no time at all.

At four o'clock of an October morning, Windsor Beebe hitched up his nag to go to Oswego for a load of wheat. The Beebes owned a mill, and no one looked twice at Beebe's wagon, piled with empty bags for the mill. No one saw the shape of a man lying beneath the sacking. In the dark of an autumn morning, no one saw him get out at a house on the plank road, two miles out of town, just east of the river.

They all knew the Clarke farm; Lombardy poplars on either

side of the gate could be seen for miles, and there was a well with a well sweep in the old-fashioned way; there was a family burying ground surrounded by a stone wall, and the fine barns and granaries and stables made you look with envy as you drove into Oswego to market.

The Clarkes were prosperous farmers, and no mistake, highly esteemed, as well, and who would suspect them of harboring a runaway slave that the papers were talking about, and the marshals and police officers were looking for all over New York State? The Clarkes wouldn't get mixed up in such a business, neighbors would say if you had suggested it; not them, not steady folks, church members, well-to-do people. Mr. Clarke could go about the city, go to the docks or the shipyards or anywhere he liked, talking to men, making careful inquiries, and no one thought anything about it.

Well, there were a-plenty of darkies around town, too, come from God knows where, but everybody was used to seeing them, and if old Mr. Clarke should be seen walking along a street, tap-tapping with his cane on the flagstones of the sidewalk, who would bother to notice that a bent old Negro man was walking along a hundred feet behind him? No one looked; no one noticed. On went old Mr. Clarke, northward on Tenth to Bridge Street, past a great conglomeration of lumber yards and warehouses, down across the river to Water Street, and along to the place where a sloop was tied up against a wharf.

No one noticed that the Negro followed along, followed along, stopping when the iron ferrule of the cane stopped tapping, going on again when he heard the tap of the cane until he came to the very shadow of the boat. No one looked; no one saw him slip on board the boat; no one heard what the captain of the boat said to him. No one saw him hide away, where no one would ever see him until the boat was out in the middle of the lake, and Canada just beyond the blue water.